INTERNATIONAL POLITICAL RISK MANAGEMENT

Needs of the Present, Challenges for the Future

INTERNATIONAL POLITICAL RISK MANAGEMENT

Needs of the Present, Challenges for the Future

Theodore H. Moran, Gerald T. West, and Keith Martin, Editors

THE WORLD BANK
Washington, D.C.

1818 H Street, NW
Washington, DC 20433
Telephone: 202-473-1000
Internet: www.worldbank.org
E-mail: feedback@worldbank.org

1 2 3 4 10 09 08 07

ISBN: 978-0-8213-7001-8 eISBN: 978-0-8213-7002-5
DOI: 10.1596/978-0-8213-7001-8

Library of Congress Cataloging-in-Publication data

Needs of the present, challenges for the future / Theodore H. Moran, Gerald T. West, and Keith Martin, editors.
p. cm. -- (International political risk management; v. 4)
Includes bibliographical references and index.
"Based on a symposium held November 5, 2006, under the joint auspices of the Multilateral Investment Guarantee Agency (MIGA) of the World Bank Group and the Karl F. Landegger Program in International Business Diplomacy at the School of Foreign Service, Geogetown University"--Preface.
ISBN 978-0-8213-7001-8
1. Insurance, Investment guaranty. 2. Risk (Insurance) 3. Risk management--Political aspects. I. Moran, Theodore H., 1943- II. West, Gerald T. 1944- III. Martin, Geral Keith. IV. MIGA-Georgetown University Symposium on International Political Risk Management (2006 : Georgetown University)
HG4538.5.N44 2007
368--dc22

2007034298

Cover design: Serif Design Group, Inc.

CONTENTS

Tables

PREFACE

International Political Risk Management: Needs of the Present, Challenges of the Future is based on a symposium held November 5, 2006, under the joint auspices of the Multilateral Investment Guarantee Agency (MIGA) of the World Bank Group and the Karl F. Landegger Program in International Business Diplomacy at the School of Foreign Service, Georgetown University. This volume is the fourth in a series based on the biennial symposia. The 2006 event brought together 220 senior practitioners from all sides of the political risk insurance industry—insurers, brokers, investors, lenders, academics, and representatives of the legal community.

As with its predecessors, this symposium elicited lively debate of the 15 papers presented, both from the commentators and the audience. Based on the comments and on their own further reflections, the authors revised their papers—in many cases substantially—for incorporation in this volume. For our part, the editors have sought to add value to the presentations in two ways. First, each part of the book contains an overview that synthesizes the main points made by the authors. Second, at the end of each section, readers will find an overview of the main points raised by the audience, as well as the responses and elaborations of the speakers. In this way, we hope to capture some of the richness of debate that has historically characterized these symposia.

The main subjects discussed—providing coverage based on bilateral investment treaties (BITs), unifying terrorism and traditional political violence insurance, incorporating recent experiences in the power sector in risk management plans, and improving protection against regulatory takings—are at the core of investors' concerns in the current marketplace. Despite the upsurge in foreign direct investment (FDI) going into a fairly limited number of emerging markets, and notwithstanding the lack of major regional macroeconomic crises over the past five years, investors remain worried. First, events in Bolivia, Ecuador, and República Bolivariana de Venezuela have highlighted the resurgence of classic expropriation worries many thought had disappeared. Furthermore, regulatory takings at the national and subsovereign levels in various infrastructure subsectors, such as water and power, have caused numerous traditional investors in those areas to abandon or limit their exposure to developing countries. The dual threats of terrorism and civil conflict also continue to hang over many investors in a variety of regions.

What connects these threats is the common perception among lenders and investors that traditional political risk insurance may not be able to provide adequate protection against the risks investors are now facing. Our authors address these issues head-on, describing in detail both the problems, e.g., in power projects, as well as possible ways forward. Potential solutions described in this volume include coverage based on BITs; expanded political violence coverage that takes into account terrorism-related issues, such as temporary business interruption; improved breach of contract coverage; and enhanced public–private partnerships within the PRI industry. One suggestion—increased transparency from the insurance industry regarding the number and nature of claims—also addresses the issue, albeit from the standpoint of trying to change the perception of the market through improved client access to information. Several authors point out that we are now in a "buyers' market," which is causing many insurers, both public and private, to be more flexible in their policy wording and pricing than they have ever been.

Yet, the authors themselves—and many of the commentators and audience participants—point out that the cyclicality of the market is likely to continue and warn against excessive expectations. In particular, certain coverages investors have long wanted, such as devaluation protection, are unlikely to be provided, even in this soft market. In the words of several authors, PRI providers are facing an unprecedented situation of a relatively high supply of PRI and reinsurance capacity, putting downward pressure on premia, as well as historically low spreads on developing-country and emerging market loans, which are squeezing the bottom line of project financings, in particular, even further. This leaves little room, they argue, for pricing to risk, and may be a medium-term threat to the health of the PRI industry. In sum, what becomes clear from this discussion is that there is more agreement on the problems and threats to the PRI industry than on the solutions to those problems. All of the authors, commentators, and participants in this book do, however, share a dedication—as we hope will the readers—to sustaining and strengthening this market, which provides a valuable service in promoting FDI in developing countries and emerging markets.

This is a goal also shared by the two institutions that, for the past 10 years, have been sponsoring the symposia and the books resulting from them. MIGA's mission—to promote sustainable FDI in its developing member countries—and the political risk guarantees that it provides are inextricably tied to the broader health of the PRI industry. Its sponsorship of the symposium itself is an expression of how broadly MIGA interprets that mandate and seeks to build cooperation across the marketplace.

For its part, the Karl F. Landegger Program in International Business Diplomacy at the School of Foreign Service at Georgetown University is a leader in research and teaching at the nexus of international risk analysis and management, public policy, business–government relations, and the role of multinational corporations in development. The program has direct, hands-on teaching and research programs on political risk management techniques for practitioners from the business, lender, insurance, and government communities.

The shared objective of these two institutions, as expressed through the symposium and the publication of this volume, is to enhance the exchange of views on risk mitigation techniques, with a broader objective of improving the economic growth of developing countries and the global fight against poverty. We hope that readers find that this book does contribute to achieving that goal and that they are stimulated by the vigorous debate reflected in these pages.

The editors wish to express our gratitude for the support this symposium and volume received from Lola Brown and Kathleen Klingenberg at Georgetown University.

Keith Martin
Editor

ABBREVIATIONS

AAA	American Arbitration Association
AAD	Arbitral award default (coverage)
ABA	Azurix Buenos Aires (Azurix's Argentine subsidiary)
ACP	Africa, Caribbean, and Pacific
ADB	Asian Development Bank
AGOA	African Growth and Opportunity Act (United States)
AGOSBA	Administración General de Obras Sanitarias (Argentina)
AICPA	American Institute of Certified Public Accountants
AIG	American International Group
ASA	American Society of Appraisers
BIT	Bilateral Investment Treaty
BOT	Build-operate-transfer
BPS	Basis points
CAFTA	Central America-Dominican Republic-United States Free Trade Agreement
CATV	Cable television
CEN	Confiscation, Expropriation, and Nationalization Coverage
CERA	Cambridge Energy Research Association
CI	Currency Inconvertibility Coverage
COFACE	Compagnie Française Pour L'Assurance Du Commerce Extérieur (France)
CSR	Corporate social responsibility
CUP	Cooperative Underwriting Program (MIGA)
DEG	Deutsche Investitions und Entwicklungs Gesellschaft (Germany)
DFI	Development Finance Institution
DPC	Dabhol Power Company (India)

DR-CAFTA	Dominican Republic-Central America Free Trade Agreement
ECA	Export Credit Agency
ECGD	Export Credits Guarantee Department (United Kingdom)
EDC	Electricidad de Caracas (República Bolivariana de Venezuela)
EDC	Export Development Canada
EFIC	Export Finance and Insurance Corporation (Australia)
EMBI	Emerging Market Bond Index
FCIA	Foreign Credit Insurance Association (United States)
FDI	Foreign Direct Investment
FIPA	Foreign Investment Protection and Promotion Agreement (Canada)
FMO	Financierings-Maatschappij voor Ontwikkelingslanden, N.V.(Netherlands)
FRCP	Federal Rules of Civil Procedure
GATS	(WTO) General Agreement on Trade in Services
GATT	General Agreement on Tariffs and Trade
GOA	Government of Argentina
GOE	Government of the Arab Republic of Egypt
GOI	Government of India
GOJ	Government of Jamaica
GOM	Government of Maharashtra (India)
IBA	International Bar Association
ICC	International Court of Arbitration
ICSID	International Center for the Settlement of Investment Disputes
IFC	International Finance Corporation
IMF	International Monetary Fund
INTESA	Informática, Negocios y Tecnología, S.A. (Argentina)
IPP	Independent Power Project
IPTL	Independent Power Tanzania, Ltd.
JNH	Jamaica Nutrition Holdings
JOSCO	Joseph Companies
JSPI	Jamaica Soya Product Industries
LCIA	London Court of International Arbitration
LG&E	Louisville Gas and Electric (United States)
MDB	Multilateral Development Bank
MERC	Maharashtra State Electricity Regulatory Commission
MIGA	Multilateral Investment Guarantee Agency
MOD	Memoranda of Determinations
MSC	Marine Shipping Corporation
MSEB	Maharashtra State Electricity Board (India)

NAFTA	North American Free Trade Agreement
NGO	Nongovernmental organization
OECD	Organisation for Economic Co-operation and Development
ONDD	Office National du Ducroire/Nationale Delcrederedienst (Belgium)
OPIC	Overseas Private Investment Corporation (United States)
ORAB	Organismo Regulador de Aguas Bonaerenses (Argentina)
PDVSA	Petróleos de Venezuela, S.A.
PPA	Power Purchase Agreement
PPP	Public–Private Partnership
PPI	U.S. Producer Price Index
PRI	Political risk insurance
PV	Political violence coverage
RNCO	Russell Novak & Company
SACE	Istituto per i Servizi Assicurativi del Commercio Estero (Italy)
SEC	U.S. Securities and Exchange Commission
SSA	Sub-Saharan Africa
TGS	Transportadora de Gas del Sur (Argentina)
TRIPS	Agreement on Trade-Related Aspects of Intellectual Property Rights
UNCITRAL	United Nations Commission on International Trade Law
UNCTAD	United Nations Commission on Trade and Development
USAID	United States Agency for International Development
WMD	Weapons of mass destruction
WTO	World Trade Organization

INTRODUCTION

Yukiko Omura
Executive Vice President
Multilateral Investment Guarantee Agency

It is a great pleasure to introduce this latest volume in the *International Political Risk Management* series. The papers and commentary that follow represent the breadth and depth of discourse undertaken by some 220 participants at the 2006 Symposium on International Political Risk Management, hosted by MIGA and Georgetown University on November 5, 2006.

The theme of this symposium, "Meeting the Needs of the Present, Anticipating the Challenges of the Future," is indeed timely. As many of the speakers and participants noted over the course of the day's events, today's demands are in a constant state of flux, making the task of anticipating the challenges of the future a daunting proposition. In this context, then, the collective challenge of the political risk insurance (PRI) industry must be to stay close to our clients, to listen attentively to their needs in order to remain nimble and relevant.

External Environment

The external environment in which we operate has been changing rapidly over the last several years. In the aftermath of their rapid decline in 2001, FDI and private capital flows have quickly rebounded and reached record levels in 2006. This upward trend and the increased availability of foreign capital supply for emerging market assets have been reflected in declining interest rates charged by creditors, which have reached record lows. In April 2006, the JP Morgan Emerging Market Bond Index (EMBI) stripped spread monthly average reached just 190 basis points (bps), and was below 180 bps at month-end.

However, much of the capital flows have gone to a limited number of countries. Not all developing countries have been winners—and particularly not those perceived to be risky and where capital availability is limited. Traditional investors continue to exercise extreme caution when it comes to investing in less developed countries, troubled by lower-than-expected earnings and disputed concessions, especially in the infrastructure sector. Investors choose instead to invest in more stable and developed emerging markets.

At the same time, the emergence of a new and growing force—so-called "South-South" investors—is making notable inroads on the investment landscape. Investment from developing countries now accounts for one-third of all FDI going to developing countries, which is good news because it typically reaches very poor and remote areas and tends to deliver products better tailored to the needs of low-income consumers.

Nontraditional donors (including China, India, and some Arab nations) are increasingly active in financing and constructing infrastructure projects in Sub-Saharan Africa (SSA). China has moved from being a net aid recipient to a net aid donor and has rapidly expanded its assistance for SSA infrastructure projects. While India has not been as active in the continent as China, recent activity suggests that it is beginning to play a more significant role. It is also becoming clear that Arab donors such as the Kuwait Fund for Arab Economic Development and the Saudi Fund, as well as other donors like the Islamic Development Bank and the OPEC Fund, have begun playing a significant role in providing low-interest loans aimed at facilitating the development of SSA's infrastructure.

Much of China's recent involvement has been aimed at financing SSA's infrastructure through deals typically tied to implementation by Chinese (mostly state-owned) firms. The financing for these infrastructure projects has come in large part in the form of loans from China's Export-Import Bank and other state-owned institutions. These loans are almost always backed by natural resources that are of direct commercial interest to China, with infrastructure projects being included as part of a package either to facilitate natural resource development directly, or to provide broader assistance to the host country. The energy sector has received the most financing, with the construction and financing of hydroelectric power stations in Benin, Cameroon, Republic of Congo, Ethiopia, Gabon, Mozambique, Nigeria, Sudan, Togo, and Zambia.

New Models for Financing

A so-called "new" model for financing is emerging whereby risks are shared more evenly between the government and the private sector under public–private partnerships (PPPs). This is certainly an area where the World Bank Group is playing an active role. The key, of course, is the risk-sharing aspect of the formula. PPPs mean different things to different people—and for them to work, there has to be a genuine partnership and genuine risk sharing. A good deal is one where the risks are apportioned to the parties most capable of managing them efficiently and cost effectively. This allows a good investment to go ahead even in a country perceived to be risky.

The renewed emphasis on these partnerships is due to the fact that private investors are no longer willing to take risks exclusively on their own. The perceived failures of privatizations in the 1990s and the negative experience in the power and water sectors in many markets have forced numerous investors to reconsider their strategies with respect to emerging markets. PPP structures are perceived as less risky, with earlier and more secure returns (such as leasing contracts and operation and management contracts). From a government's perspective, PPP structures are often needed because of budgetary restrictions, cost savings, lack of state personnel and expertise, and the need for high-quality service and speedy implementation.

Nevertheless, just because there's the will, doesn't mean there's always a way. A country's investment climate, particularly the regulatory framework, is often a stumbling block to bringing in new business. Laws often need to be changed or even adopted, such as those related to devolution of competences to regions and municipalities, concessions, foreign investment, intellectual property, bankruptcy, taxes, and so on.

Even if PPP structures can be put together, lenders and investors need to consider project risks, both commercial and noncommercial. Before moving ahead with an investment, companies must be sure that the project is first and foremost financially viable—that is, able to provide essential services at an affordable price and on a profitable basis. And to support the country's development, the investment needs to be economically viable as well. This requires a framework of sound sector strategies, good policy planning, and willingness to uphold contracts, even in adversity. Too often, risk mitigation solutions are viewed as an alternative to proper project structuring. Indeed, poor project economics enhance pressures to renege on commitments (such as "take or pay" contracts and commitments to raise rates). Likewise, poor project design and poor public policy affect project outcome, good documentation cannot offset weak demand, and poor projects may exacerbate direct or indirect public contingent liabilities. As a result, financial engineering and risk mitigation need to go hand-in-hand with strong project fundamentals.

New Demands on PRI Providers

With these changes in the external environment come new demands placed on PRI providers. As was noted in Amsterdam at the 2006 Berne Union[1] Annual Meetings, the market is (as should be expected) asking for different types, or expanded forms, of cover, such as more specific coverage of regulatory risk; expansion of the breach of contract coverage to something beyond nonenforcement of arbitration awards; local currency coverage; longer tenors (e.g., 22 years for some capital market transactions); and coverage of projects at the subsovereign level, given the growing trend to decentralize government control of services such as water delivery from national to local authorities.

Many of the papers in this volume examine these issues in greater detail. In Part One, several authors consider BIT-based arbitral award coverage, and whether or not war and terrorism coverage needs to be restructured. Part Two examines private power projects in emerging markets, the lessons learned, and the promising new models for financing and risk management. And in Part Three, there is a review of the current consensus on the international law of regulatory takings and whether or not new approaches are needed, and which regulatory risks can and should be insurable. Part Four ties these threads together and explores the likely impact they will have on the market in the coming five years.

Cooperation

While opportunities currently abound in emerging markets, many projects will require cooperation among private and public providers of political insurance, and other players (such as monoline insurers) are also increasingly keen to collaborate. In the case of MIGA, we will continue to focus on our niche areas, complementing the activities of private and public insurers. This is why our strategy is focused on post-conflict countries, frontier markets, "South-South" investments, and infrastructure—meaning that much of our activity will continue to focus on Africa. As we continue to develop our partnerships, we must all realize that the more we work together, the more effective we will all be.

Current market spreads are tight, and there is excess liquidity, resulting in tremendous pressure on the pricing of our coverage. In this type of environment, it is important to take a serious look at our pricing and the underlying assumptions that go into that pricing. However, we know that the market is cyclical and that the soft market will eventually turn into a tighter one. On our side, we will continue to price to risk. It is tempting for some to slash prices and undercut others, but such a proposition is not sustainable over the medium term and results in greater confusion in the marketplace.

Finally, in relation to the theme of building cooperation across the industry, I am delighted to note that MIGA recently launched an online industry resource called the PRI Center (www.pri-center.com). This site is designed to provide a neutral, web-based, information source on PRI (on names of insurance providers, current thinking on specific issues, country risk analysis, and so on) for all of us in the industry, as well as for potential buyers of PRI. In developing the PRI Center, we conferred with many of our industry partners, including many private and public insurers as well as the Berne Union.

Conclusion

To meet the needs of the present and anticipate the challenges of the future, we must adapt quickly to the changing business environment to best serve our clients and our shareholders. We must constantly challenge ourselves by broadening the investor base to which we market; by developing new and innovative structures to finance good projects; and by strengthening cooperation with partners and clients to best manage risks and share information.

Note

1. The International Union of Credit and Investment Insurers, better known as the Berne Union, is the international organization of export credit agencies and investment insurers, both public and private. Most major investment insurers, except the Lloyd's-based ones, are members of the Berne Union.

Part One

NEW PERSPECTIVES ON POLITICAL RISK INSURANCE PRODUCTS

OVERVIEW

Theodore H. Moran and Gerald T. West
Editors

In Part One, two veteran participants of the international political risk insurance industry offer their perspectives on two very different political risk insurance coverage opportunities—one that may be developed in the future, the other of which is already at hand. In the first paper, "*A BIT of Insurance*," Kenneth Hansen, a partner at Chadbourne & Parke LLP, notes that the willingness of the political risk insurance marketplace to provide coverage against host government failure to pay arbitral awards might be improved by covering not only arbitral awards based on project contracts with host government instrumentalities, but also awards arising under bilateral investment treaties (BITs). Hansen logically links the market's current willingness to cover arbitral awards to the phenomenal rise in the number of BITs, and asks why insurance coverage cannot be extended to cover a BIT arbitration award.

Hansen notes that BITs typically seek to specify certain standards of treatment for the foreign investor, to improve the clarity of investors' rights, and to provide for an arbitral forum to allow an investor to pursue recovery against a host government that fails to live up to its treaty commitments, and that has, as a consequence, harmed an investor. But winning an arbitral award under a BIT does not necessarily resolve the matter, because the investor's problem then becomes one of enforcement of the award. This is where political risk insurance could be helpful, and Hansen marshals a number of reasons to support his argument that such coverage would be of benefit to both insurers and investors.

Hansen implicitly argues that the sheer number of BITs that have been concluded between countries assures that there will be a rising number of such arbitrations and that there has already been ample demonstration of the difficulties of enforcing awards. While Hansen conservatively estimates that there are more than 2,000 extant BITs, UNCTAD estimates[1] that, as of 2004, there were 2,392; presumably even more BITs exist today. Thus, his argument concerning the potential demand for such coverage has strong substantiation.

However, in conclusion, Hansen acknowledges that insurers have apparently not offered such coverage—perhaps, he suggests, because they have simply not been asked. He reports that informal queries to six public sector insurers revealed that they were willing to consider such coverage, but that no one had requested it. Three private sector insurers also replied that they would be willing to consider such coverage.

The chairman of the panel suggested that, given the large number of insurers, brokers, and investors in the audience of about 200 persons, one could empirically test the Hansen contention that investors have not sought such coverage and insurers have not offered it. In response to an open query, a show of hands indicated that no insurer present acknowledged that he had been approached for such coverage, nor did any investor acknowledge seeking such coverage.

In his paper, "*The Convergence of the Terrorism Insurance and Political Risk Insurance Markets for Emerging Market Risks: Why It Is Necessary and How It Will Come About,*" Charles Berry, Chairman of BPL, addresses a complex set of issues relating to terrorism and political violence insurance covering physical loss or damage to property in emerging markets from both demand and supply perspectives.

Berry begins by contrasting the stagnant fortunes of the traditional political risk insurance market since the events of September 11, 2001, and the dramatic growth and success of the stand-alone terrorism insurance market in the same period. He estimates that the premium flow to the latter is now between two and three times the premium flow to the former. Moreover, the profitability of this terrorism coverage has been excellent. Berry argues that this separation of the two markets (for terrorism coverage and for political risk insurance), may be convenient for some insurers, but that it fails to deliver the coverage needed by clients with assets in emerging markets. For a variety of reasons, Berry asserts that these two markets can, and should be, merged.

Before building his argument for the necessity of a merger of these two markets, Berry reviews the historical origins of the current separation of these two markets and the mindsets that perpetuate it. Using a hypothetical example of a foreign investment project in Russia attacked and damaged by Chechen insurgents, Berry considers the likelihood that four different insurance policies might pay the $50 million of property damage and the $75 million of business interruption loss: a conventional "all-risk" property insurance policy, a stand-alone terrorism policy, standard equity political risk insurance, and standard lenders form political risk insurance. The shortcomings revealed by this comparison, Berry argues, reflect serious neglect by the entire insurance industry—underwriters, brokers, insurance advisors, and even insurance buyers.

To alter the current situation and the predominant mindset in the market, Berry develops four sets of arguments:

1. In emerging markets, terrorism cannot be separated from war risks and political risks.
2. Insurance buyers have never had, nor will they ever have, effective terrorism insurance for emerging market assets within their general property insurance policies.
3. The terrorism insurance market's standard wording does not provide effective terrorism insurance for emerging market assets.
4. Only specialist political risk insurance (PRI) insurers can provide effective terrorism insurance for assets in emerging markets.

When these wording changes occur, the terrorism and political risk markets will have effectively merged into the realm of a specialist political risk insurance underwriter.

Berry argues that the merger process has already started and cites several cases involving BPL, which have resulted in both better coverage and considerable savings to the insureds. As more buyers become aware of the shortcomings of the current market and the wording of policies, demand for better coverage will increase.

Obviously, some traditional political risk investment insurers need to rethink their own policy wordings and the direction in which they wish their war risk coverage to evolve. In so doing, such insurers need to squarely address one of the industry's taboos—the writing of land-based war risks. In this respect, Berry describes the multiple effects and long shadows cast by the 1937 War Risks Agreement. He argues that the political risk insurance market today is much better equipped to manage the aggregations associated with land-based assets than in the past. Moreover, the key principles for underwriting war or terrorism risks are well established in the PRI market, which has successfully operated for more than 30 years, often in close cooperation with government insurers.

Berry concludes by noting that buyers are clearly interested in terrorism and political violence coverage, but that the market has thus far not supplied the right coverage to deal with the risk and that only PRI policies can fill the void. He views this as an opportunity for the industry: not to abandon their more traditional PRI coverages, but to offer an additional reason for using the political risk insurance market.

Two equally experienced commentators, David Neckar of Willis and Edie Quintrell of Overseas Private Investment Corporation (OPIC), offer reactions to the Hansen and Berry papers and provide their own perspectives on potential new political risk insurance products.

David Neckar argues that while the BIT coverage Hansen proposes is theoretically attractive, in practice it will be difficult to sell because of the long period before an investor can secure compensation. Likewise with respect to the Berry proposal, the reality of who makes corporate decisions (the risk manager vs. the credit manager or chief financial officer) with regard to terrorism coverage will likely be a significant obstacle. Neckar argues that, for the PRI industry to rejuvenate itself, it needs to focus on where it can add real value to its clients.

For her part, Ms. Quintrell notes that there are overall signs of good health in the PRI industry, based on Berne Union statistics—though, she notes, much of the activity is now from a select number of providers, and much of it is for nonhonoring coverage. With respect to coverage against political violence, she notes that OPIC has had difficulty supplying stand-alone terrorism coverage with alacrity. However, OPIC's coverage of political violence has broadly met investors' needs, as evidenced by the fact that it has paid 46 claims since 1971. With respect to Hansen's BIT proposal, Quintrell raises a number of practical problems and questions whether there is significant latent demand for such coverage, which would need to be tested by the market.

Note

1. UNCTAD (United Nations Conference on Trade and Development), World Investment Directory Online. New York and Geneva: United Nations. Available at http://www.UNCTAD.org.

A BIT OF INSURANCE

Kenneth W. Hansen
Chadbourne & Parke LLP

It can be hard to take host government promises seriously, particularly in the arena of private investment in the development and operation of public infrastructure. This paper suggests how a partial solution currently available in the political risk insurance market—coverage against host government failure to pay arbitral awards—might be improved by covering not only arbitral awards that are based on project contracts with host government instrumentalities, but also awards arising under bilateral investment treaties.

The Problem—Taking Government Promises Seriously

Why is taking sovereign undertakings seriously so difficult? The first problem is that they are sovereign. Governments have broad immunities under international law—and are likely to have broad immunities under their own domestic law. This permits them broad discretion to do what they choose, with little regard and less responsibility, for the damage they may cause.

Secondly, they are powerful. Even to the extent they are subject to legal limits on their flexibility of action, they are likely to have tools at their disposal—such as declaring fines on, or confiscating the passports of, foreign nationals present on their territory—that can intimidate adversaries into abandoning pursuit of their theoretical rights.

Thirdly, they change. Whether as a consequence of elections, coups d'état, or job rotation within the civil service, the officials from whom performance is ultimately sought may well not represent the views of the officials who approved a governmental undertaking. Successor government managers, especially following a political succession, may be motivated at least to criticize or begrudge, and perhaps to repudiate, their predecessors' commitments.

Fourthly, the conventional recourse for losses as a consequence of a breached contract—a lawsuit leading to a judgment for damages—will probably not work. Even if the government agency is not immune from suit, its influence in local courts will probably exceed that of the investor. If a suit succeeds in yielding a judgment against a host government, that judgment, or even an arbitral award, may face a host of impediments to collection. State-owned property may be immune to seizure and sale. Not-so-independent judges and police may be hesitant to take the steps that might lead, if one were dealing with a private sector defendant, to satisfaction of the court's judgment or the arbitral award.

Recent history shows this concern to be more than just theoretical. Investors in Indonesia, Thailand, and Pakistan in 1997–98, in India in 1996 and again in 2001, in Argentina in 2001, and Bolivia in 2006 have all found themselves in difficulties as a direct consequence of governments repudiating undertakings upon which the investors had relied. So, there are ample grounds for an investor doubting whether its ostensible rights against a government have practical value.

Finding a Forum

What can an investor do if a government breaches a contract on which an investment depends? As noted above, a traditional suit for damages may not work well. The search for a fair-minded forum that will assert jurisdiction, hear the dispute, and have the authority to issue an enforceable award often leads to an agreement to refer disputes to binding, offshore arbitration.

Arbitration rights matter in several ways. An effective arbitration clause will, of course, provide a vehicle for obtaining an award for damages. More interesting, at least in the limited sense of being more relevant to political risk insurance, are two other aspects of arbitration rights.

First, attempts to pursue arbitration rights may trigger retaliatory actions by the host government. Those actions may contribute useful color to a creeping expropriation claim where the claimant's case may depend on showing government acts aimed at taking, or otherwise impairing the value of, a foreign investment. Consider, for instance, Overseas Private Investment Corporation's expropriation coverage of the Bank of America's loans to Enron's Dabhol Power Project in India. OPIC did not explicitly insure either the payment of an arbitral award or compliance with the arbitral process. The expropriation coverage did, however, insure against any violation of international law by the host government that constituted a "substantial factor" in the inability of the project company to make payments on the insured loan. OPIC concluded that the injunctions against the project company pursuing arbitration rights that were sought by Indian government instrumentalities and issued by Indian courts constituted a "denial of justice" in violation of international law that contributed substantially to the loan defaults—thus satisfying a critical requirement of the bank's expropriation claim under its OPIC coverage. Second, political risk coverage is likely to be available to insure payment of an arbitral award issued against a host government counterparty.

Insuring the Outcome

When an investor sues the counterparty agency, there are three possible outcomes—the investor can win, lose, or settle. For purposes of this paper, the problem arises if the investor wins. The investor may have an award, but what good is it? Perhaps the government will respect it, but that cannot be assumed or, in many jurisdictions, even expected. Argentina has declared that it will not pay any International Center for the Settlement of Investment Disputes (ICSID) awards. Indonesia's state oil company, Pertamina, continues to elude enforcement, years after having lost arbitrations (related to cancelled power projects), though both sides continue to make huge investments in lawyers as the attempted enforcement process continues.

Winning an award is no guarantee of seeing any compensation. Arbitral panels do not have police. Even if you manage to win a judgment against the government, the process of finding assets not immune from seizure against which to satisfy that judgment may well require more time and expense than the judgment is worth. Depending on how clever the host government is at protecting its offshore assets, the only enforcement solution may be to work through those very domestic courts whose favoritism toward the government (of which they are a part) prompted the insistence of an arbitration clause in the first place.

This is where political risk insurance can be helpful. One coverage that has become widely available over the last 10 or so years is so-called disputes coverage—in which the insurer agrees to pay an arbitral award if the defendant or respondent government does not. The insured investor still bears the risk that it cannot prove its case. But if it does prove its case, wins an award, and the government fails to pay that award within the time period provided in the policy, then—after the investor has taken certain required steps to attempt to enforce it—the insurer will pay the award in exchange for subrogation to the investor's claim against the government.

This is an excellent solution, subject to a few caveats. One is cost. A price will need to be paid for this policy, a price that will vary widely depending on the specific circumstance of the investment. (It would not be surprising, however, to see an annual premium of 0.5–1 percent of the amount insured.) Second, this solution requires the arbitration to go forward and reach the final stage of issuance of an award. Governments have been known to attempt to interfere with investors pursuing their arbitration rights. Third, and most important for this paper, this all assumes that the investors have a right to take the relevant governmental authority to arbitration.

Arbitration rights may arise in any of three ways: consensus, contracts, and treaties—especially BITs. Mutual agreement at the time a dispute arises is always possible, but obviously an investor cannot depend upon it. As a practical matter, arbitration rights need to precede the dispute. That leaves contracts and BITs.

Many international investments lack any contract negotiated with a government agency. Although such contracts are more likely to be present in the case of infrastructure investments, the government agency that undermines the value of an investment may not be among the agencies that signed contracts with the project company or its investors. For example, an investor with disputes coverage might conclude a concession contract with a local government and an offtake agreement with a state-owned corporation, but run into problems when customs officials refuse to permit the importation of a critical raw material. Unless the government entities with which the investor contracted had guaranteed the performance of other agencies, the investor could find itself with no arbitration rights against the offending agency and thus no basis for a claim under its political risk insurance policy.

Insuring BITs

Enter BITs. BITs provide investors with arbitration rights against a host government with which they have no privity of contract. Foreign investors are third party beneficiaries of BITs.

The first bilateral investment treaty was concluded in 1948 between Germany and Turkey. Twenty years ago there were only a handful of such treaties. They proliferated in the 1990s and today there are roughly 2,000. For the 140 largest countries in the world to have such treaties with each other would require 9,730 treaties. Although there are not yet as many BITs as that, most countries that an investor is likely to target will probably have at least a few.

A BIT will typically provide both (1) increased clarity of investor's rights and (2) an arbitral forum to pursue recovery against a host government that has failed to live up to its promises made in the treaty and that has, as a consequence, harmed an investor from the country with which the treaty was concluded. Thus, BITs can do for foreign investors what project contracts do—they can provide both performance obligations for a host government and, if those obligations are breached, a forum for determining the damages due to an aggrieved investor.

BIT arbitrations face, however, the same limitations as arbitrations based on project documents—winning is no guarantee that the offending government will pay. One might hope that a government that cared enough about attracting foreign investment to conclude a BIT would be concerned to be seen as taking its obligations seriously. On the other hand, that might not be the case. For example, Argentina has already declared that it has no intention of paying any awards that should come out of the many pending ICSID proceedings.

Why not use the same solution for BIT arbitration rights as for arbitration rights based on project documents—that is, why not simply purchase political risk insurance of a BIT arbitration award? The problem is practical. No commercial or public sector political risk insurer provider offers such coverage. I spoke to several leading brokers. None had heard of such a policy being sought—or granted. Although it is difficult to be sure, since PRI is such a secretive business, I suspect that no such policy has ever been issued. There is, however, precedent.

A client had Multilateral Investment Guarantee Agency (MIGA) coverage of an investment that was damaged by "pesification" in Argentina. The client was considering filing a claim with MIGA. The definition of expropriation under the MIGA contract did not fit squarely with the circumstances that the client had experienced as a consequence of pesification, though we thought that with some creative lawyering, we could build a plausible case—certainly one that, if MIGA were to turn down the claim and we were to take that denial to arbitration, might find sympathy from the arbitrators. It was also clear, however, that the rights promised U.S. investors under the U.S.-Argentina BIT were broader than the rights insured by the MIGA contract. We thought our chances of winning an arbitration against Argentina under the BIT were better than in an arbitration against MIGA under their political risk guarantee contract. We suspected that MIGA, on the other hand, if it were to pay a claim, would prefer to seek reimbursement from Argentina if the claim were based on the solid foundation of an ICSID award rather than an ad hoc arbitration between MIGA and its client (where Argentina would not have been a party or have had an opportunity to defend its actions).

So, we negotiated what was, in effect, a swap of the disputes coverage under the investor's MIGA contract for MIGA insurance of any BIT award that the investor might achieve. That is, it became the investor's challenge to prove compensable damages in a BIT arbitration against Argentina. If, however, it were to succeed in doing so, and Argentina were to refuse to pay—as it has declared it would do—then MIGA would pay the award and seek collection against Argentina.

Hence, if there is precedent, and if it makes sense, why have insurers not offered such coverage? It may be largely because they have not been asked. I also approached senior lawyers in a half-dozen public agencies that provide political risk insurance or guarantees. Each one said that, to his knowledge, no one has asked for such coverage. They also thought, however, that if such a request were to be presented, they saw no reason why it should not be seriously considered by their institutions. I have also spoken with underwriters at three commercial political risk insurers and with two major brokers. Each has said the same thing: this is novel—but it looks doable. One Lloyd's-focused broker with whom I spoke was quite confident Lloyd's syndicates would be prepared to offer such coverage.

It seems that the next step is for investors to ask for it.

THE CONVERGENCE OF THE TERRORISM INSURANCE AND POLITICAL RISK INSURANCE MARKETS FOR EMERGING MARKET RISK: WHY IT IS NECESSARY AND HOW IT WILL COME ABOUT

Charles Berry
BPL Global

Introduction

This paper addresses terrorism and political violence insurance covering physical loss or damage to property in emerging markets. Surprisingly in the current environment, this is an area of neglect in the insurance industry.

The paper begins by contrasting the fortunes of the investment insurance market since the events of September 11, 2001 (namely, a decline in demand for traditional equity and lenders' PRI), with the simultaneous dramatic growth and success of the stand-alone terrorism insurance market. The paper notes this separation of the PRI market and the terrorism insurance market, a separation that suits the insurance industry's conventional approach, but fails to give clients with assets in emerging markets the cover they need.

In calling for an end to this separation and a merger between the terrorism insurance market and the PRI market, the paper advances a four-point argument concerning terrorism and political violence insurance for emerging market assets. Central to this argument is the view that in emerging markets, the separation of terrorism risk from war risks (as understood by the insurance industry) and political risk is a practical impossibility. Once this point is understood, the implications for traditional property insurers, for the stand-alone terrorism insurance market, and the PRI market become clear. Understand emerging market terrorism, and the door is opened to a transformation in insurance industry thinking, one in which terrorism insurance in emerging markets is seen as a specialist PRI product.

The merger is already underway, and the transformation is beginning. However, the paper argues that the process needs to be driven forward by both clients and the PRI underwriters. Specifically, clients need to be more demanding and refuse to accept terrorism insurance that contains an exclusion of conventional war risks for their emerging market assets.

On the supply side, PRI insurers need to shift focus. In doing so, they need to confront their own prejudices, and those wider taboos in the insurance industry, that have hindered the writing of property damage covers for political violence and war risks. In this regard, the PRI market can take comfort in its own underwriting principles, and in the recent experience of the terrorism insurance market. By writing terrorism and political violence in a property insurance form (rather than just in an equity or lenders' form) the PRI market will experience a revival in its fortunes. It will then be providing a new policy that is both simple and highly relevant. From this platform, the PRI insurers can then tackle exotic "beyond the fence" terrorism risk, contingent business interruption, threat, and abandonment, etc. However, that is for later. This paper is about ensuring that the basics are right. This is necessary, as currently the insurance industry is fundamentally wrong in its approach to straightforward, property-based terrorism and political violence covers in emerging markets.

Only the PRI market can put this right.

Stagnation of Traditional Investment Insurance

The political risk investment insurance market is not in good health. Demand for traditional equity and lenders' policies, covering expropriation, breach of contract, political violence, and currency inconvertibility, is weak.

Lloyd's premium income figures for the risk code for confiscation and related perils (PR) dramatically illustrate this decline in demand (see figure 1).[1]

The figures show a slump in investment insurance business between 2001 and 2002, followed by a gentler, but continuing decline. I would accept that part of this decline is due to Lloyd's losing market share on traditional investment insurance business over this period. However, there is plenty of evidence that the rest of the investment insurance market has been having a torrid time as well.

FIGURE 1 Lloyd's Premium Income for Investment Insurance by Year of Account (Risk Code PR)

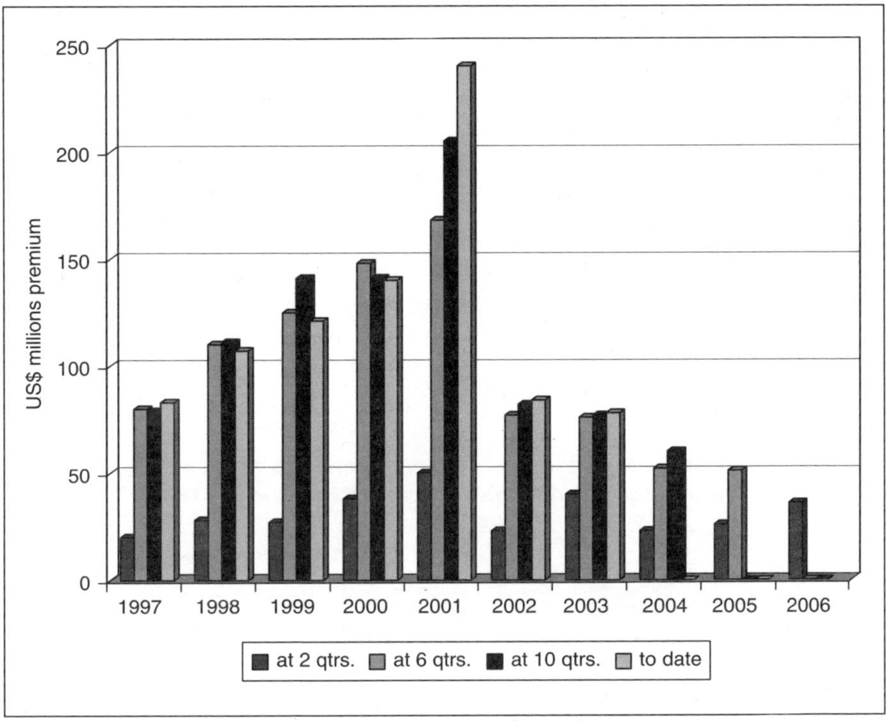

Source: Author.

OPIC's political risk insurance premiums have certainly been on the decline. We suspect the same applies to other national agencies. MIGA's premiums and exposure have at best plateaued. Non-Lloyd's private sector insurers have also been sending out distress signals about their investment insurance business.

Additionally, in absolute terms, the investment insurance market remains small. Hard figures are difficult to come by, but industry veterans agree that if one added the investment insurance premiums of the public and private sector insurers together, one would be hard pressed to reach US$500 million per annum, small in insurance market terms. Political risk investment insurance is not a hot ticket.

Nevertheless, many of the underwriters employed by Lloyd's syndicates to write confiscation, contract frustration, and related political risks, have been very busy. They have turned their attention to the neglected area of the investment insurance market, political violence. Specifically, they have been writing terrorism insurance.

Growth of Stand-Alone Terrorism Insurance

The stand-alone terrorism insurance market has grown dramatically since the events of September 11, fueled by the decision of the general insurers and reinsurers to exclude terrorism from their general insurance policies. Figure 2 shows Lloyd's premium income for stand-alone terrorism and political violence risks in recent years.

The terrorism insurance market clearly took off in the last quarter of 2001, following the events of September 11, and since then has continued to grow in absolute premium terms, despite premium rates probably now being less than half of their 2002 levels. Today, Lloyd's alone is writing US$500 million per annum of terrorism insurance premiums, a higher premium income figure than that of the investment insurance business globally.

FIGURE 2 Ten-Year Overview of Lloyd's Premium Income for Stand-Alone Political Violence (Risk Codes TO WL TE TU 6T)

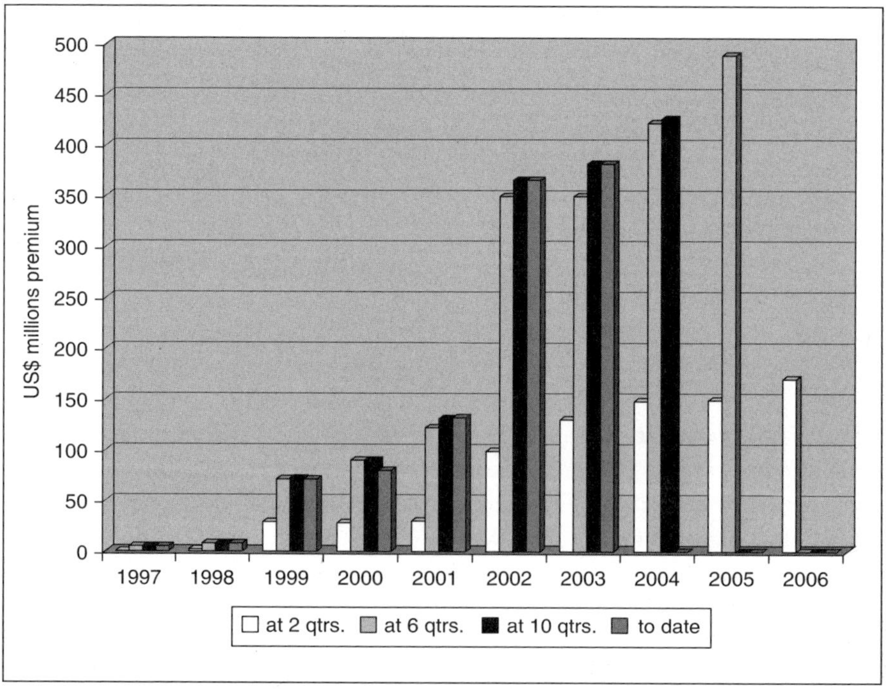

Source: Author.

FIGURE 3 Incurred of Loss Ratios for Lloyd's Political Violence Risk Codes by Year of Account

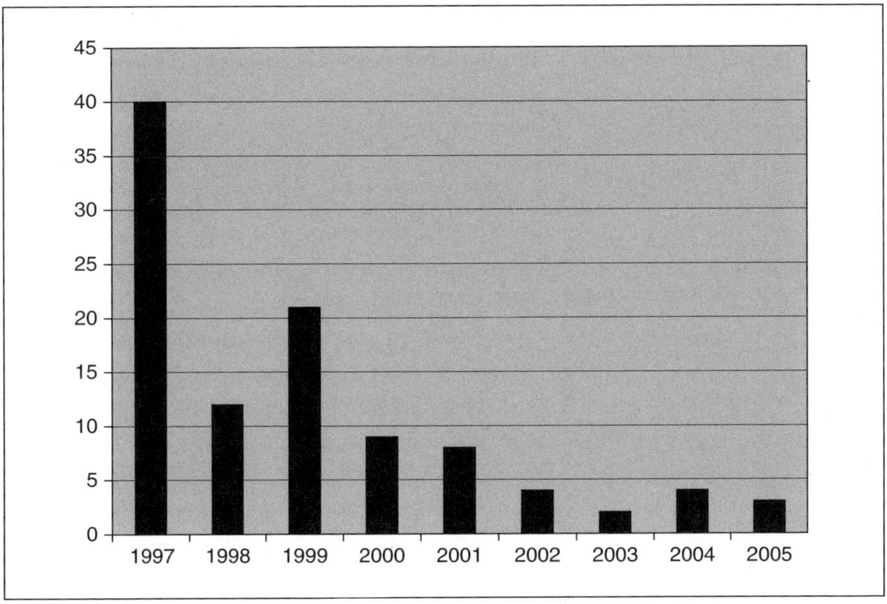

Source: Author.

The main Lloyd's practitioners estimate that Lloyd's market share is between one-third and one-half of the total market. This means that the total stand-alone terrorism insurance market is now generating US$1.0 to 1.5 billion of premiums per annum.

The stand-alone terrorism insurance market has also been very profitable. Since the growth spurt in 2002, loss ratios in Lloyd's have been below 5 percent (see figure 3). Nor is this a class of business with a long tail. Losses are reported immediately, with generous reserves (fully reflected in the loss ratios in figure 3) established within days or weeks of claims notification.

Indeed, the class has been so profitable that the underwriters in the market are eager to find any opportunity to pay claims to prove the efficacy of their product. The product they sell covers terrorism in a conventional property form. The T3 wording and its variants cover physical loss or damage to tangible property caused by terrorism, whereas the business interruption extension (T3a) covers loss of profits while damaged property is repaired and replaced. T3/T3a is used by both Lloyd's and non-Lloyd's terrorism insurers.[2]

The Separation of Terrorism Insurance and PRI: Does It Make Sense?

The terrorism insurance market exists in its own separate silo in the insurance industry, sandwiched between the general property insurance market on the one hand and the PRI market on the other. This makes sense when contemplating terrorism insurance in North America or Western Europe. Indeed, the terrorism insurance underwriters originally designed their T3/T3a wording with these countries in mind, and still write the majority of their business in the developed world.

However, property in emerging markets is becoming an increasing part of the terrorism insurance business. Terrorism insurance is sold to the large emerging market projects that are of interest to the PRI market. Additionally, multinational companies buy terrorism insurance in global programs that include large amounts of property located in countries where PRI insurers have significant appetite for risk. Can the separation of terrorism and political risk insurance be sustained in this context?

Let us take as an example a typical project in the power or oil and gas sector in Russia. Let us assume that instead of a Moscow theater or the Beslan school, Chechen insurgents attacked and seized the project. Let us assume that after a violent end to the siege, involving a battle between the terrorists and Russian security forces, the project is left damaged. The property damage is reparable, with an estimated bill of US$50 million plus US$75 million of business interruption loss, incurred while specialist replacement equipment is manufactured, shipped, and installed. Let us also assume that the project has bought all four of the insurances involving elements of political violence cover that the insurance market now normally offers a project of this nature:

- The conventional property insurance, covering "all risks" of property damage, for a property damage limit of US$300 million, with business interruption insurance of US$100 million for a 12-month indemnity period
- Stand-alone terrorism insurance for the same limit on the normal market wording
- Equity form PRI, taken out by the foreign sponsor who owns 40 percent of the project—this has a limit of US$40 million, representing 40 percent of the project's US$100 million equity
- Lenders form PRI, taken out by the project financiers providing US$400 million of cover for the lenders' share of the US$500 million project

Who will pay the US$125 million of property insurance losses the project has suffered? The answer is that despite the project's insurance program having been blessed by the lenders' insurance advisors (as the program is indeed in line with insurance industry best practice), and despite the project sponsors and lenders having bought US$440 million of specialist PRI that includes political violence coverage, only US$20 million of the US$125 million claim will be collected from this array of policies with any ease. The position on each policy is as follows:

- The conventional "all risks" policy covers riot and civil commotion, but will exclude war risks and, since the events of September 11, terrorism, so the loss is excluded.
- The stand-alone terrorism insurance covers terrorism, but excludes the political risk market perils of "insurrection, rebellion, civil war and war." The terrorism insurers would be entitled to argue that the Chechnian conflict amounted to a rebellion or civil war, and decline cover, pointing the client in the direction of the PRI market's policies, which specifically cover these "war risks."
- The equity PRI insurers should indeed provide some comfort. However, they only cover property damage, not business interruption consequent on property damage, and they will only cover their policyholder's share of the loss. They would therefore only be liable for 40 percent of the US$50 million property damage claim, namely US$20 million.
- The lenders' PRI insurers will resist the claim. They would acknowledge that the political violence fell within their causes of loss. However, their indemnity is not geared to paying for the cost of repairing or replacing damaged property, or for business interruption losses while the repairs are carried out. Rather their policy is geared to covering default on scheduled payments. However, no default should occur; there is no reason that the project cannot be repairable, and once repaired, its very profitable continuing operations are more than ample to service the debt.

The lenders' PRI insurers' position is fair; they are not intending to offer property insurance. However, given the absence of the right type of property insurance, the lenders' PRI insurers are the most likely target for a claim. They will not be happy, not because there is a claim, but because it is not the type of claim in which they would expect to become embroiled.

In summary, among the array of insurers who surround a project of this nature, none of them, with the limited exception of the foreign sponsors' equity PRI insurers, is responsible for paying a simple property insurance claim due to the type of political violence that is commonplace in emerging markets. This is a product of blatant neglect by the insurance industry, and a situation where no one involved emerges with much credit, be they insurers, brokers, insurance advisors, or for that matter, insurance buyers.

The neglect is based on the insurance industry's desire to treat terrorism and PRI as separate subjects. The industry views terrorism as belonging to the property insurance market, and writes terrorism insurance following property insurance conventions. The PRI market likewise is generally reluctant to write coverage on property insurance forms, even for political risk perils. This mindset is ingrained in the industry and is responsible for the current neglect. Industry mindsets are usually difficult to alter. To aid this process, we have developed a four-point philosophy about terrorism insurance in emerging markets that argues:

1. In emerging markets, terrorism cannot be separated from war risks and political risk.
2. Insurance buyers have never had, nor ever will have, effective terrorism insurance for emerging market assets within their general property insurance policy.
3. The T3/T3a terrorism cover and its variants do not provide effective terrorism insurance for emerging market risks.
4. Only specialist PRI insurers can provide effective terrorism and political violence cover for assets in emerging markets.

Some may already share this philosophy; many do not. For the latter, the following addresses each of the points in greater detail.

1. Emerging Market Terrorism Cannot be Separated from War Risks and Political Risk

Emerging markets are different. When it comes to terrorism, this difference can clearly be seen in comparing the terrorist group that perpetrated the London bombings on July 7, 2005 ("7/7"), and Hizbullah that conducted the recent war in Lebanon. The difference can be understood by looking at the level of support enjoyed by these two types of terrorist organizations.

The 7/7 bombers acted covertly. Not even their close family members were aware of their planned attack. Secrecy was essential, as they knew even friends and family would have handed them over to the security forces. The London attacks were condemned almost universally, even among the Muslim community in the United Kingdom. Only a small group of fellow travelers have voiced any support. These people are so outside the mainstream of political life in the United Kingdom that advertising their views immediately made them of interest to the police.

Hizbullah's situation is completely different. As a recent demonstration showed, when hundreds of thousands thronged the streets of Beirut to hear Sheikh Hassan Nasrallah celebrate "victory" over Israel, Hizbullah enjoyed huge support both locally and internationally. This political support enables its militia to engage with and at least frustrate the most powerful conventional military force in the region, the Israeli Defense Forces.

The 7/7 bombers were on the bottom rung of a terrorism ladder. Terrorism can escalate, stepping up the rungs of a ladder from insurrection, to rebellion, to civil war and war, and ultimately to successful revolution. In stable, mature western democracies terrorism will remain a problem, but it is hard to imagine terrorist organizations ascending this ladder. But terrorist organizations in emerging markets can and do step up the ladder, and many, like Hizbullah, are high on its rungs. The engine that takes terrorist organizations up this ladder is political support from within their community, from outside, or a combination of the two.

Throughout emerging markets, one can see different terrorist organizations on different rungs of this ladder. Take insurrection. Since the toppling of Saddam, Iraq has had up to four separate insurgency movements operating inside its borders. But Iraq is not alone: the term "insurgent" is used almost synonymously with "terrorist" when referring to emerging markets, and many governments in the developing world have areas of their country in a constant state of insurrection.

Rebellion is the next step up the ladder. The Movement for the Emancipation of the Niger Delta (MEND) terrorists are staging a classical rebellion in the Delta, with clear local support and identified political aims. There have been countless other recent or ongoing rebellions in emerging markets, from those in the Democratic Republic of Congo (DRC), Uganda, and elsewhere in Africa, to those in Thailand, the Philippines, and Indonesia. Many of these rebellions are separatist movements, seeking independence for a religious, tribal, or ethnic group trapped in the boundaries of what are often artificial nation-states. As the power of nation-states declines, many emerging market governments are finding it increasingly difficult to hold their states together. These states were often created by European powers, and the population groups within their boundaries may have little in common. Balkanization may not be limited to the Balkans.

Further up the terrorist ladder is civil war. I have mentioned Chechnya, but Sri Lanka too has drifted between rebellion, civil war, and war in the language of the popular press. While the rungs on the ladder each have their separate names, Sri Lanka and Chechnya remind us how difficult it is to be precise about which rung a terrorist organization occupies at a particular moment. Indeed, the media are contemplating a two-rung jump for Iraq, from insurgency to civil war.

Finally, when a terrorist organization gathers sufficient political support, like Hizbullah, it can conduct a sustained, open war against conventional forces. Hizbullah is not alone; few media commentators doubt that the current conflict in Afghanistan is war. Military historians recognize this type of warfare and contrast conventional war (between the official forces of rival nation states) to asymmetric war or low-intensity war, namely war involving subnational groups and guerrilla or militia forces. They note that conventional wars have been in decline since the end of World War II, obvious exceptions being the Korean War, the Iran-Iraq War, the Falklands War, and a few others. In contrast, low-intensity war has been on the rise, beginning with the conflicts that marked the withdrawal of European powers from Empire: Malaya, Kenya, and many more for the British; Indo-China and Algeria for the French; Congo for the Belgians; Angola and Mozambique for the Portuguese. A low-intensity war was then fought by the Soviet Union in Afghanistan. The Balkans was a low-intensity war, with a conventional ending when NATO forces confronted Serbia. All, or nearly all, conflicts in recent years in Africa, such as those in Angola, the DRC, Uganda, and Somalia, have been low-intensity wars involving unofficial forces. The "War on Terrorism" is simply an umbrella name for a number of conflicts between conventional forces and many different terrorist groups on different rungs of the terrorism ladder.

The military historians make two points about low-intensity warfare: first, the conventional forces hardly ever win; second, this type of war is contagious, with success in one theater encouraging rebels and insurgents in another. Conventional forces, aware of their record, have learned that the key factor for success in these types of conflict is the hearts and minds of the local population, the water in which the terrorist fish swim. (I will leave the reader to make his or her own judgment on whether the U.S.-led "War on Terrorism" is succeeding in winning the hearts and minds of local populations around the globe.)

If the "War on Terrorism" goes badly, we will probably see a terrorist organization achieve the top rung on the terrorist ladder: revolution. Revolution implies a successful rebellion. It means terrorist organizations achieving their often-stated goal of political power. This is at least a risk and if it occurs, it may occur in areas of countries rather than involve a whole state. Ironically, the more authoritarian the local regime, the more likely it is to keep the lid on the pressure cooker. Equally, if authoritarian emerging market regimes begin to reform and move toward democracy, the risk of revolution will increase. This is the lesson learned as long ago as the French Revolution, recycled today as the "J curve." Of course, terrorist organizations may also achieve power by election, as Hamas has demonstrated.

My interest here, though, is the risk of a government being installed by revolution or by force of armed revolt. Such governments tend to be expropriating governments, in the time-honored tradition of the victor taking the possessions of the vanquished. This certainly happened following the last proper revolution the world saw in the Islamic Republic of Iran in 1979. True, the expropriations were not accompanied by the legal niceties that PRI underwriters and their legal advisors like to see. But property was taken nevertheless. If this happens, some terrorist organizations will have attained their ultimate aim—deep down, many terrorist organizations and their supporters do not want to destroy the West's assets in emerging markets: they want to possess them.

Of course, sitting as we do in a mature, stable, western democracy, it is quite impossible to think of any terrorist organization here gathering sufficient political support to ascend the rungs of the terrorism ladder. But emerging markets are different. By definition, emerging market countries have weak, immature, and unstable political, social, and economic systems. Many also have large, disaffected, young, and poor populations, who feel that the only outlet for their frustration is to support, directly or indirectly, the activities of those who have taken up arms against the established order. It is this local support, together with assistance from outside the country, that propels the terrorists up their ladder.

In summary, I have not forgotten Hugo Chavez, Evo Morales, and Vladimir Putin. Opposition to globalization and western culture takes many forms. However, global terrorism, particularly radical Islamic terrorism, is central to the political risk faced by international business in emerging markets. Global terrorism cannot be separated from war risks as terrorists on different rungs of the ladder are engaged in insurrection, rebellion, civil war, and low-intensity war—all war risks in insurance terms, as we will see. Additionally, global terrorism represents political risk. This is because it is political support, whether from within or without their theater of operations, that propels terrorist organizations up the terrorism ladder. This support, if sufficiently strong, may propel terrorist organizations into government, either by the ballot box (as we have seen with Hamas), or by the Kalashnikov, in the form of violent revolution.

We can now proceed to the more prosaic question of how the geopolitical risk of global terrorism is addressed by the insurance industry in their policies.

2. *Insurance Buyers Have Never Had, Nor Ever Will Have, Effective Terrorism Insurance for Emerging Market Assets within Their General Property Insurance Policies*

Insurance buyers were not focused on terrorism insurance before the events of September 11. Their property policies often covered "all risks" of property damage, except for specifically excluded risks. As terrorism was not excluded, buyers could assume it was covered. Terrorism insurance only became an issue when terrorism exclusions were added to property policies after the events of September 11. Naturally, insurance buyers focus on this new exclusion. If they could remove the terrorism exclusion, surely they will once again have cover for terrorism.

For their assets in North America and Europe, where terrorists occupy only the bottom rung of the ladder, they may well be right. But in emerging markets they are wrong. The reason is to be found in the war exclusion.

Since the 1937 War Risks Agreement (of which more later), general insurance policies have contained a broad exclusion of war risks. The wording of a typical war risks exclusion is contained in box 1. The exact wording of this exclusion has evolved over the years, but the themes remain the same.

Box 1: General Property Insurance Market War Exclusion

Notwithstanding anything to the contrary contained herein, this Policy does not cover loss or damage directly or indirectly occasioned by, happening through or in consequence of war, invasion, acts of foreign enemies, hostilities (whether war be declared or not), civil war, rebellion, revolution, insurrection, military or usurped power or confiscation or nationalisation or requisition or destruction of or damage to property by or under the order of any government or public or local authority.

Source: Michael D. Miller. *Marine War Risks.* Lloyd's of London Press, 1990.

It is immediately clear that the war exclusion actually excludes far more than conventional war. Even if "war" were interpreted to only mean war between nation-states, other types of subnational conflict, including civil war, revolution, insurrection, and rebellion, are specifically excluded.

The legal definition of rebellion is contained in box 2. It makes clear that when an organized group takes up arms against the state with the intention to overthrow it, the war exclusion applies. Any separatist groups with the aim of achieving power over a region of a country are "rebels." Many, if not most, terrorist organizations in emerging markets fit the definition of "rebellion" very well.

The war exclusion also excludes confiscation, as the two often walk hand in hand. In effect, therefore, when talking about physical property, the perils the property insurers refer to as "war risk" are the same perils the investment insurance market call "political risk."[3]

The war risks exclusion is unlikely to exclude terrorism in the developed world. It would be difficult to say that the London 7/7 bombers were involved in an insurrection in the United Kingdom. But emerging markets are different. Where

Box 2: Legal Definition of "Rebellion"

Organized, armed and forcible resistance to the government of the country by its subjects (even though assisted from without). An essential aim is the intention to supplant or overthrow the government, even though in all the circumstances that aim may appear unlikely or impossible of achievement. Rebellion includes territorial separatists whose aim is to deprive rulers of authority over part of their territory.

Source: Michael D. Miller. *Marine War Risks.* Lloyd's of London Press, 1990.

Box 3: T3 Act of Terrorism or Sabotage

Definition

An Act of Terrorism means an act or series of acts, including the use of force or violence, of any person or group(s) of persons, whether acting alone or on behalf of or in connection with any organisation(s), committed for political, religious or ideological purposes including the intention to influence any government and/or to put the public in fear for such purposes. An act of sabotage means a subversive act or series of such acts committed for political, religious or ideological purposes including the intention to influence any government and/or to put the public in fear for such purposes.

Source: T3 Act of Terrorism or Sabotage.

terrorist organizations in emerging markets gather sufficient political support, they start ascending the terrorism ladder. When their activities amount to insurrection or rebellion, the war risks exclusion comes into play.

The war risks exclusion is a fixture in property insurance. No one in the industry believes it should be removed, and it is the war risks exclusion that excludes the activities of terrorist organizations that begin to ascend the emerging market terrorism ladder.

3. The Terrorism Insurance Market's Standard T3/T3a Wording Does Not Provide Effective Terrorism Insurance for Emerging Market Assets

The definition of "Act of Terrorism or Sabotage" in the T3 wording is shown in box 3. Note the reference to "influencing" government, not "overthrowing" government. Nevertheless, the issue with the T3 wording in the context of emerging market terrorism is that it contains a full war risks exclusion. The exclusion in box 4

Box 4: T3 War Risks Exclusion

This Policy does not insure against loss or damage occasioned directly or indirectly by war, invasion or warlike operations (whether war be declared or not), hostile acts of sovereign or government entities, civil war, rebellion, revolution, insurrection, martial law, usurpation of power, or civil commotion assuming the proportions of or amounting to an uprising.

Source: T3 War Risks Exclusion.

is Exclusion No. 2 of the T3 wording. Other political risks like confiscation, riot, and civil commotion are excluded elsewhere.

As we have seen, the activities of many terrorist organizations in emerging markets are better described by the words in the war risks exclusion than by the definition of "Act of Terrorism." Additionally, T3 contains a reverse "Onus of Proof" clause: the underwriters can require the policyholder to prove that the war risks exclusion does not apply. Of course, following the normal rules of construction, if, as is likely, a loss fits both the definition of "Act of Terrorism" and falls within the war risks exclusion, the exclusion will overrule the cause of loss: exclusions trump the insured peril. That said, the T3/T3a wording is not completely useless. The wording was designed for the developed world, and is arguably adequate in the context of New York, London, or Brussels. It works for the lowest rung of the terrorism ladder.

Even in the context of terrorism outside of North America and Western Europe, the T3 wording still provides some cover. Indeed, the wording has paid claims for losses in emerging markets, as its supporters are keen to point out. However, these claims payments testify to the integrity and commercial judgment of the underwriters; they want to pay these claims. The wording has not been put to a legal test.

However, I have taken the T3 wording to a Queen's Counsel (QC) in the United Kingdom who specializes in insurance law in this area. His verdict was that in the context of emerging market terrorism, the T3 wording is a "dog's breakfast"—a mess, in other words. In his view, the war risks exclusion removes much of the cover promised by the cause of loss. The QC stressed the practical difficulty to be found in any policy that covers some types of political violence while excluding others. In other words, the terrorism ladder is easy to understand, but deciding which rung a terrorist organization occupies on this ladder at a particular place and time, is very difficult. No doubt, this disinterested advice was given by the QC in the confident knowledge that many in our industry would continue to ignore it.

Many insurance buyers may assess the terrorist threat in a particular emerging market today as relatively low, but buy cover recognizing that the security situation may deteriorate. The situation deteriorates when local support for the terrorists rises, and the terrorists ascend the ladder. As this happens, the chance of having a terrorism loss rises, while the chance of the T3 wording responding declines. In other words, with the T3 wording, the more one needs terrorism and political violence cover, the less likely one is to actually have it.

Many in the property insurance world are so convinced in their own minds that "terrorism" and "war" are separate risks, that they believe that if an act constitutes terrorism, then by definition it cannot be war. They have convinced themselves that the "war exclusion" as they call it, only excludes conventional war and the actions of conventional military forces. In effect, they believe that if the damage is caused by a terrorist organization, cover applies, but if it is caused by conventional forces it is excluded.

This is fantasy in the context of the T3 wording. If the terrorists are involved in insurrection, rebellion, civil war, or war, their actions are excluded by T3. However, let us indulge the T3 supporters for a moment and pretend they are right. They are saying in effect that if in a conflict like Lebanon, a property is hit by a Hizbullah rocket, it is covered, whereas if it is hit by an Israeli artillery shell or bomb, it is not. Even on this interpretation, T3 does not work for emerging markets. The typical military engagement in the 21st century will continue to be one between conventional forces and "terrorists." Even on the erroneous interpretation of T3 put forward by its supporters, if a property is damaged in such an exchange, the ability to claim will depend on being able to show which side of the conflict fired the missile that caused the damage. In emerging markets today, T3 is not a viable grant of cover.

Buyers should take heed. So should insurers and brokers, given current demand for contract certainty. When used in the context of emerging markets, the T3 wording has a glaring internal inconsistency that needs ironing out. In the meantime, either the capital providers and reinsurers are covering a risk they had not bargained for, or the policyholders do not have the cover they have paid for.

I suspect the risk here is with policyholders. I believe insurance policies usually deliver on their promise. T3 promises to exclude losses caused by insurrection, rebellion, civil war, and war. The wording is inconsistent with the apparent intent of the insurers who imply they are covering terrorist activity on all rungs of the terrorist ladder. My view is that if terrorism insurance wordings for emerging market assets do not start to say what is meant, policyholders will find out that the policies mean what they say.

4. Only Specialist PRI Insurers Can Provide Effective Terrorism Insurance for Assets in Emerging Markets

By now it will be clear that the solution for emerging market terrorism wordings is to take the terrorism insurance market's property form (geared to property damage and business interruption), but to remove or severely restrict the war risks exclusion, and to take the words from the exclusion and place them in the causes of loss.

Exactly which words one needs to place where will depend not on a judgment as to which rung on the ladder the terrorists operating in the country sit today, but rather on how high up the ladder they might ascend, should they gather further political support. This in turn will depend on a judgment of the stability of the country's political and social framework internally, and the terrorists' political alignments externally.

By definition, where these wording improvements occur, the terrorism insurance and PRI markets will have merged. By venturing into the territory covered by the war risks exclusion, one has by definition become a specialist PRI underwriter.

The Merger of the Terrorism Insurance and PRI Market Has Already Begun

The idea of moving emerging market terrorism business from the T3 terrorism insurance market to the PRI market is not wishful thinking. We have done it. Furthermore, we know it can be done economically.

In September 2003, we launched our Global Political Violence Insurance wording. This provides property insurance for political violence that includes not only terrorism, but also such risks as insurrection, rebellion, civil war, and war. Later that year we moved an Asian energy project's US$100 million of terrorism cover from the T3 market to the PRI market. Instead of excluding insurrection, rebellion, civil war, war, and confiscation, the renewed terrorism policy covered all these risks. Additionally, the premium went down. Since then we have done the same for projects elsewhere in Asia, the Middle East, and Latin America. We have also taken global T3 terrorism policies and replaced them with programs on the Global Political Violence Insurance wording, a PRI product. We do not get the opportunity to do this unless the client also saves money.

So the transition is already underway. We have begun the merger between the terrorism insurance and PRI market. As the merger continues the drivers should be from both the demand and the supply sides.

Insurance Buyers Need to Drive Demand

On the demand side, more insurance buyers should simply look again at the nature of emerging market terrorism and the wordings of their policies. They will then demand that the war risk perils be removed from the exclusions and become insured perils. They will find that their terrorism insurance can only be supplied by PRI insurers.

London Market Insurers Are Best Placed to Drive the Supply

On the supply side, there are two groups of PRI insurers. The first group is those who currently write both PRI and terrorism insurance in the same area of their account. These insurers are mainly Lloyd's syndicates or insurers with a background in the London market and war risks. For them, the transition will be easy:

as and when more policyholders demand a better terrorism insurance cover, they are equipped to meet that demand.

This group of insurers may want to be more proactive. They may want to take on board our second point, that the general property insurers will still not be covering emerging market terrorism insurance effectively, even if they remove the terrorism exclusion from general policies. This is starting to happen, and where it does, the T3 market loses business. Indeed, the major threat to the niche occupied by the T3 underwriters is from the softening general property insurance market. This drift of business back to the property insurers can in part be stemmed if the T3 insurers start promoting a wider product for emerging markets. Obviously though, if they begin to focus clients' minds on the war risks exclusion in their property insurance policies, they will have to remove the war risks exclusion from their own terrorism policies.

Traditional Private PRI Insurers Need to Change Their View on Providing PRI in a Property Insurance Form

The second group of insurers consists of those currently writing conventional equity and lenders' form PRI, who have not yet fully entered the terrorism insurance market. These insurers are mainly based in the United States, but there are still some Lloyd's PRI insurers of the same mindset. If these insurers also have a pitch in the terrorist insurance market elsewhere within their large organizations, it is far removed from the PRI department. This group of insurers, key capacity providers to the PRI market, need to have a longer rethink.

Traditional investment insurers have never made a good job of writing political violence insurance. Most buyers of political violence insurance are looking first and foremost for property insurance; they expect coverage for property damage (PD) to tangible assets and for conventional business interruption (BI) consequent on such physical damage. This is exactly what T3 delivers: it is the right policy form, albeit with the wrong perils and exclusions. Investment insurers have not traditionally offered property forms, but rather have sold political violence cover in lenders' or equity forms. As we have seen, neither provides effective property insurance.

For the private insurers, the reason for this neglect can be found in the 1937 War Risks Agreement entered into by most London and international insurers that banned insurance of war risks for land-based assets. Nearly 70 years later this agreement is still in force and casts a very long shadow over the PRI market.

Although some insurers established after the War Risks Agreement, such as PanFinancial, began offering war on land insurance in the 1980s, it was not until the mid-1990s, 25 years after the private insurance market began writing political risk insurance, that exemptions were granted to permit specialist PRI insurers to write full political violence cover for land-based assets, including war, civil war, and related war risks. Though the regulatory shackles have been lifted, many of the myths and taboos of the 1937 Agreement prevent private insurers from taking a clear and rational approach to writing political violence insurance.

But it is not just regulation that has caused the neglect; insurers, both private and public, have shunned political violence insurance as a matter of choice. Much of the conventional wisdom about underwriting PRI on investments originated in Washington. Central to the philosophy of OPIC and MIGA, is their "umbrella"—that they can influence governments and prevent losses. Secondly, when the "umbrella" fails, paid losses should be recoverable over time. Though OPIC has a program offering terrorism insurance, the doctrine of prevention and recovery has generally steered government agencies away from focusing on property damage-related political violence policies. Many in the private market, particularly those close to Washington, have followed this philosophy. They need to rethink.

While rethinking, the insurers need to consider the current malaise affecting the investment insurance business. They need to respond to the current demand for war risks cover (in its widest sense) in a property insurance form. Without a change of direction, the investment insurers' business is soon going to consist only of a form of host government bonding, with private insurers standing surety for host governments in an effort to shield major infrastructure investors, in particular, against the obsolescing bargain. This is a product that, despite years of effort, is proving very difficult to construct in a manner that works for both insurers and policyholders at the same time. BITs may or may not help.

A Broad Change of Direction for the Investment Insurance Market

Indeed, when the investment insurance community focuses on an emerging market project, I sometimes wonder whether the insurers, the sponsors, the lenders, and the advisors are not focused on the wrong government and the wrong risk. The obsolescing bargain risk associated with the current host government is, of course, a real risk. But the current government would not be promoting the project unless they wanted it to succeed. So as long as the current administration is still in place, even if they seek to renegotiate the terms, a compromise is normally available. This alone often can make conventional PRI insurance a complication.

Meanwhile, what about terrorist organizations in the host country whose aim is to replace the government? If the political tide swept them up the terrorism ladder into power, it is likely the foreign sponsors, lenders, and advisors would have no leverage with the new government. This, of course, is a remote risk in most emerging markets. However, the risk of terrorist attack on infrastructure projects is not; in fact, it is bound to happen somewhere at some time in the future. Depending on the severity of the attack and the level of turbulence in the country at the time, the project will either be rebuilt or abandoned. Either outcome needs the insurance market. Yet most emerging market projects either have no cover for this risk, or only the very limited T3 cover. This is the area where the PRI market really can make a difference.

Confronting Insurance Industry Prejudice and Taboos

PRI insurers have begun to grasp the nettle. But in treating terrorism as a war risk and seeking to write it in a property form, insurers have to face the insurance industry's number one taboo, the class of business that hardly dares speak its name: war risks on land.

Though the 1937 War Risks Agreement was put in place 70 years ago, its effect is still felt throughout the insurance industry, as the war risks exclusion that it generated has been hardwired into the DNA of the industry through the reinsurance market. For a long time, minds have been closed on the subject. Indeed, it is this mindset that has erected the wall that separates the two silos: terrorism insurers on one side, writing property insurance, but not daring to look the war risks exclusion in the face; and PRI insurers on the other, writing war risks, but not on a property form. The time has come to take a fresh look at the 1937 Agreement.

Of course, the basic principle behind the Agreement stands. To quote Lloyd's own comment on the Agreement, that principle was "the need to ensure that war risks are only written in a carefully controlled manner." That remains an absolute requirement.

In 1937, a system of controls for marine war risks was devised, since marine insurance was, at that stage, still the main business of the market. Those controls have remained the basis of the Marine War Risks market (and the Aviation War Risks market) to this day. However, they felt at the time they lacked the systems and, indeed the authority, to produce a satisfactory framework for controlling the aggregations associated with land-based assets; hence the ban. However, times change. Not least, the nature of war has changed. In 1937, the most likely form of warfare facing the world was conventional war on an industrial scale. That today remains possible, but less likely, and the type of low intensity war currently in vogue is inherently a better environment for writing a book of war risk business, not least as the terrorists' ability to strike anywhere in the world reduces the problem of adverse selection.

However, the main change relevant today is the insurance market's progress in developing sound underwriting systems for classes of business capable of producing catastrophic losses. Additionally, unlike 1937, we now have a specialist private PRI market with a 30-year track record that has successfully devised systems for controlling aggregates, including aggregates for the "war risk" with arguably the highest aggregation exposure, confiscation.

Reinforcing Sound PRI Market Underwriting Principles

Therefore, in embracing war risks more firmly, PRI insurers need only reinforce the principles that have guided the market for 30 years. These include:

1. The Private Insurance Sector Cannot Deal with the Totality of War Risks and Political Risks

War risks, like political risks generally, can produce megacatastrophes. By a megacatastrophe, I mean one that exceeds the capability of the insurance market to absorb, given the capital deployed in the industry.

It does not follow that where the potential for a megacatastrophe exists, the class be banned altogether. The natural world has the potential for megacatastrophe too. AM Best, the insurance rating agency, says it is "only a matter of time" before a hurricane event generates insurance property losses of US$100 billion, and that that would make up to 40 insurers vulnerable to failure. But what about the US$200 billion hurricane, or the US$300 billion earthquake, or the US$400 billion tsunami? These types of exposures are within the range of the possible, but do not stop the industry from writing property insurance. Rather they control aggregates using modern technology. For this reason, the supply of catastrophe insurance from the conventional insurance industry can and does dry up.

2. Only Specialist Insurers Should Write Political Risks and War Risks

There is no argument to be made for allowing general insurers to write war risks and political risks in their general property account. These classes should only be written by specialist insurers.

There is, of course, an exception to this; general insurers can write insurance for classes with a megacatastrophe potential where they are underpinned by a government backstop. In the developed world, such backstops were already in place for terrorism risk in the United Kingdom and Spain. Post-9/11, similar government schemes were created for terrorism insurance in such places as the United States, France, and Germany, the more successful ones in the form of a government reinsurance safety net.

In the developed world, there remains a threat of a terrorism megacatastrophe should terrorists obtain and deploy weapons of mass destruction (WMD), a very remote but nevertheless, possible event, we are told. For this reason if no other, I believe these government safety nets should stay in place. Having terrorism covered in general policies that benefit from a government safety net is a good model for the developed world. If this model continues, the main opportunities for specialist terrorism and war risk underwriters will continue to drift away from the developed world to emerging markets, the countries where PRI insurers focus their attention and have their expertise and capacity.

3. *Extreme War Risks Excluded*

PRI policies normally contain exclusions of war among the five permanent members of the UN Security Council and exclusions relating to WMD. That should continue. In this regard, the PRI insurers build in greater safety limits to their books of business when it comes to the potential for megacatastrophes. The insurers exposed to megacatastrophes from natural perils do not have equivalent exclusions for extreme natural events.

4. *Strict Monitoring of Aggregates*

Terrorism insurers monitor aggregates very closely by postal address. As long as risk is well spread within a country or even within a city, the city or country aggregate is less important. That is appropriate for developed countries where terrorist activity is likely to remain only on the lowest rung of the terrorism ladder, where the threat is of covert, isolated attacks by terrorist organizations with little or no political support from the local population.

In emerging markets, where terrorist organizations can and do climb the ladder, powered by political support, aggregations at the city, district, and country level are far more important. PRI insurers have these country aggregation systems in place.

5. *Limited Supply of War Risk Insurance*

Monitoring of aggregates will limit the supply of war risk insurance. This will have two effects. First, even with an active war risks insurance market, most war risk losses will still be uninsured. Even with an active terrorism insurance market, most terrorism property losses since the events of September 11 have been uninsured.[4] Likewise, when Bolivia expropriated the oil industry in 2006, a loss of about US$4 billion, none of that loss was apparently covered by expropriation insurance, despite 30 years of effort by the PRI market to sell expropriation insurance.

The second effect of the limited supply of war risk insurance that results from monitoring aggregates is that a floor is placed under prices. Because each insurer has finite country capacity, the PRI market does not suffer from the extremes of price competition that drive the cycle of most insurance classes. Pricing of war risks by the PRI market will have the same characteristics as other PRI products. Insurers will be able to hold out for a price that reflects the risk, or save their country aggregate for a better opportunity.

6. Cooperation with the Government Sector

Cooperation with government schemes and insurers has always been a feature of the PRI market. While one has to go back a long way, cooperation between private and public insurers has been a feature of war risks insurance. For example, during the First World War business was shared between Lloyd's and the U.K. government. Lloyd's made profits on all sections of its war risk business. The U.K. government lost £7.5 million on its cargo business. However, the government more than made up for this on its hull and war on land account, netting a profit of £32 million overall. Again the two cooperated in the Second World War. There has long been a feeling at Lloyd's that writing a properly controlled war risk account can be very profitable, particularly in time of war.

Looking into the future, as the private PRI market develops as a writer of terrorism and war risk in emerging markets, there may come a demand for aggregate capacity beyond the prudent reach of private insurers. Reinsurance from governments might then seem sensible. If it does, MIGA would be ideally placed to deliver such reinsurance on a commercial basis. MIGA might need some time to think that idea through; happily it has some time, while the private PRI market uses its latent and underutilized internal capacities.

These principles for writing war risks are well-established PRI principles. They simply need applying to a new area, the writing of terrorism and war risks in emerging markets. The only principle some insurers need to revise is that paid losses should be recoverable over time. When writing terrorism and war risks, paid claims have to be met from premiums earned.

Learning from the Stand-Alone Terrorism Insurance Market

I have a reputation in London as a critic of the terrorism insurance market. It is true that I am a severe critic of the standard T3 wording being used for emerging market risks. I have kept on about the market's wording because T3 in the context of emerging markets is so wrong, and can so easily be put right.

That aside, I nevertheless recognize that the terrorism insurance market has been a spectacular example of the insurance industry at its best, responding rapidly to changed demand and filling an urgent need. Furthermore, it has made spectacular profits in the process. In doing so, it has reminded us that writing war risks in a controlled manner can bring rich rewards, particularly in time of war. After all, global terrorism is a war risk. In conclusion, the wind has shifted. Buyers of insurance are less interested in expropriation and the obsolescing bargain; they are more interested in terrorism and political violence insurance, which they sense is a greater geopolitical risk. The insurance market has so far not given them the right cover to deal with this risk, and only PRI policies can fill the void. The political risk investment insurance market needs to take advantage of this opportunity and shift tack. This shift does not mean abandoning other more traditional PRI covers: emerging market terrorism risk should be an additional reason for using the PRI market, not the only one.

To grasp the opportunity, one need only remember four key points:

1. In emerging markets terrorism cannot be separated from war risks and political risk.
2. Insurance buyers have never had, nor ever will have, effective terrorism insurance for emerging market assets within their general property insurance policy.
3. The T3/T3a terrorism cover and its variants do not provide effective terrorism insurance for emerging market risks.
4. Only specialist PRI insurers can provide effective terrorism and political violence cover for assets in emerging markets.

Notes

1. All premiums on policies bound in a particular year flow into that Year of Account. The four columns for each Year of Account show premiums received after two quarters (six months), six quarters (18 months), 10 quarters (30 months), and (for the 2003 Year of Account and earlier) the total received into the Year of Account by June 30, 2006.

2. An amended T3 wording was adopted by the Lloyd's Market Association on September 1, 2006 and is now known as T3 LMA3030. References to T3 in this paper are based on the latest LMA3030 version. However, I will simply refer to it as T3, the name the market recognizes.

3. On a historical note, confiscation and "takings" of property were considered by many as the main war risk. Marine insurers have long divided traditionally marine risks and war risks into separate policies. Prior to 1983, when the marine insurance wordings were rewritten, the war exclusion in a marine insurance policy was referred to as the FC&S Clause. This stood for "Free of capture and seizure," antiquated language, but highlighting confiscation and the like as the main source of war risk losses.

4. For the skeptics, this is not because claims have been denied under T3. Rather it is because the vast majority of assets around the world have no terrorism cover.

COMMENTARY

David Neckar
Willis

It is quite a challenge to try to draw together bilateral investment treaties and terrorism and see where there is a common thread. However, I hope to rise to the challenge. I will start by making some comments about the proposed BIT coverage, followed by some observations about terrorism coverage, and then step back a bit, draw them together, and share some thoughts about the future.

With regard to insurance based on bilateral investment rights, I think it is a great idea. However, I would like to go back to 1974 and to the immediate aftermath of the quadrupling of oil prices—a time when, I am rather embarrassed to admit, I started in this PRI business. This was one of the reasons why I think Charles Berry and I are here, and why we are all here in such numbers today, because it led to the flowering of the political risk insurance business.

One of the key outcomes of that period was that the Arab nations no longer required funding for their infrastructure projects—the hospitals, ports, and defense projects. They did not require buyer credits from the export credit agencies any longer. They were able to pay cash; but they required on-demand bonds to be lodged against the cash payments.

As far as U.K. exporters and contractors were concerned, this meant that they went to Export Credits Guarantee Department (ECGD) and said: "Can you give us cover because the banks are not going to lend us the money unless we have some insurance?" And ECGD said it would. But when the exporters looked at the details of how to make a claim, the question arose: "If the claim is unfair, how do we judge whether it is unfair?" To which ECGD replied: "We look to the contract."

What did the contract say? The contract said one goes to the Saudi Grievance Board (or its equivalent). At this point the exporter and the banks said to ECGD: "Well, how do we go about this? How do we collect on a claim?" And

ECGD said, "Well, you get a claim before the Saudi Grievance Board and you let them adjudicate."

It was at this time that a young David Neckar and a young Charles Berry were involved in trying to persuade the contingency market at Lloyd's to offer a political risk cover for unfair calling, based on using the insurance policy to arbitrate, and leaving the Grievance Board issues to be treated like subrogation issues.

I think that the historical lesson from that period is the key to looking at the BIT question today and answering Hansen's question: "Why?" The investors want certainty and they want it in a reasonable length of time. Most of the corporates, especially those of any size, are concerned with their quarterly income statements and with their annual balance sheets. So their key time frames are three months and 12 months.

Under a BIT award coverage, they may have to wait a long time to get certainty. They are not going to like it. So my broad comment on a proposed BIT coverage is that it is going to be difficult to sell because it is going to take a long time for investors to achieve certainty.

Turning now to terrorism, Charles Berry has painted a very strong Lloyd's perspective. I would like to organize my comments around three points: supply, demand, and then how this situation may evolve.

The points that Charles Berry makes about the rungs of the ladder are extremely well made, and effectively argue that the coverage is best provided from those political risk underwriters who understand emerging market political risk, and who see the continuum of terrorism through revolution. I think it is a strong logical point that this coverage ought to be written by those people who best understand those kinds of risk.

Fine. But turning to demand, it seems to me that demand—the buying decision—for this type of coverage is in the hands of people who are not familiar with the variety of insurance products and do not have sophisticated balance sheet views. Protection of fixed assets is in the hands of risk managers, and they understand the location of buildings, the health and hygiene of buildings, valuations, and physical problems. It seems to me that there certainly is a "turf" factor insofar as brokers are concerned. A clash arises with the property side of the insurance business, which has argued that terrorism is best handled by the risk manager. This is a wider issue for political risk underwriters, generally, in that the more one moves from physical assets coverage to intangibles, the more one moves from the turf of the risk manager to the credit manager, or to the chief financial officer.

So on demand, it is more a question of the real world: where is the locus of the decision-making process? While I think Charles Berry has made a strong argument based on the principles, there is more of a problem in reality.

And so I would give to both Ken Hansen and Charles Berry a French response: "Oui, en principle." Having worked for a French company, I can affirm that essentially means, "No, in reality"! In principle, these proposals sound great, but will they work in practice? I think they work in principle, in theory, but I just do not know how easy it is going to be to persuade investors to change their buying patterns with respect to these risks.

So I think it is market practices that may be a greater obstacle to their proposals than their intrinsic value.

One concluding point on terrorism, one needs to ask: "What added value can the insurer provide?" That seems to be the key to resolving the dilemma that Charles Berry has identified. If we take the parallel of kidnap and ransom insurance, the reason why a human resource or employee benefits person does not go to the life insurance market is because he or she recognizes that the underwriters who provide kidnap and ransom insurance have all sorts of additional training, and after-the-event and through-the-event expertise.

By analogy, this could be the key to resolving Charles Berry's dilemma for terrorism coverage: if the PRI markets can demonstrate they can add value to resolving the problem, they will get the business. (And that might also be true for the proposed BIT coverage.)

Allow me to step back to consider how to draw the subjects of these two papers together. I think one needs to start from the recognition that political risk investment insurance is simply not being bought—or being bought in the amounts that it once was. Why is that?

One particular client with extensive experience in this area volunteered that there were three main reasons. First, governments have gotten trickier and cleverer in their "takings," and the insurance product has not adroitly adapted to the new circumstances. Second, banks and other investors are not getting the regulatory relief in the way they used to, and insurance does not seem to fill their perceived needs. And third, investors have some concerns about how the coverage responded when they needed it (e.g., Argentina), and this has led them to utilize financial ways of reducing their exposure to loss. (Therefore, against an investor's capital base, potential losses are less important.)

I draw from these comments a few concluding remarks. I think I have seen why it is that I can talk about BIT and terrorism coverage in the same way. Here is a political risk investment insurance market that used to provide a lot of valuable coverage, and is no longer doing so in the volume that it wishes. And so the industry is asking itself: What is the next "new" thing? Where is the demand? How can we find business? How can we rejuvenate ourselves?

What is the real income value to an investor or a bank from a product if it is a complicated claim to administer and secure payment? I would suggest that if it does not seem to have real value to them on a profit and loss account, it is simply not going to be attractive.

My final point with respect to looking to the future is that I see from bank buyers a desire to use the insurance coverage as a way of mitigating their risk and getting capital relief. The PRI industry needs to develop products that enable its clients to have real credit risk management value. The bottom line is value—getting some profit and loss value rather than just pure asset protection.

COMMENTARY

Edie Quintrell
OPIC

These are two very different topics and I am not going to try to bring them together. I will give you a slightly different perspective on these topics from that which David Neckar just gave you. While he shared with us more of a London private market view, I will try to give you more of a North American public insurer perspective.

Let me start with Charles Berry's excellent paper and comment on some of his ideas about the terrorism market versus the PRI market. But before doing so, I would like to take exception to his point that the investment insurance industry is not doing well—that the market is not hot. Let me make two points in this regard.

At the most recent Berne Union meetings in Amsterdam,[1] it was reported that the industry is actually doing quite well. For the first six months of 2006, the total amount of business reported through the Berne Union was approximately $30 billion, and that compares with $34 billion done in all of 2005. So that is a very positive trend.

Second, I must point out that OPIC's premium income should not be seen as an indicator of the health of the market. OPIC does not evaluate or assess itself by premium levels, thank goodness. As many of you know, OPIC's focus is on particular segments of the market—supporting small business, supporting U.S. foreign policy, and complementing the coverages available in the private market. If anything, the fact that OPIC premiums are down is an indication that the private insurance market is actually doing quite well. While I understand that premiums in the private market are down, overall volumes of new business written are up.

But enough about the health of the PRI industry. I would like to talk about terrorism insurance versus political violence insurance, and why it is difficult to cross the line between these two markets.

As some of you know, OPIC tried to get into the business of terrorism insurance. Since the events of September 11, OPIC has been willing to provide stand-alone terrorism coverage at fairly attractive rates. But because terrorism coverage, as Charles Berry has pointed out, has traditionally been provided by the property market, OPIC has not been very successful, quite honestly, in the terrorism market.

There are many reasons for this. Some, but not all of them, are unique to OPIC. They are probably challenges that most public insurers face. Brokers want terrorism coverage for their clients very quickly; it sometimes needs to bound tomorrow. Terrorism insurance is often sought for existing assets in multiple countries, many of which may not, in our case, be eligible for OPIC coverage. OPIC simply does not have the ability to respond quickly or effectively to most terrorism inquiries.

Two years ago, OPIC entered into a pilot program with a reinsurance company based in Bermuda. The intent of the pilot program was to facilitate OPIC's issuance of terrorism coverage. After two years of effort, we have issued only one policy.

What is new and quite interesting about Charles Berry's paper and his comments is the image of the ladder of political violence, starting from terrorism at the bottom of the ladder, and going up to full revolution at the top of the ladder.

This image certainly rings true from OPIC's claims experience. In fact, one of the reasons OPIC went to the U.S. Congress in the early 1980s to expand our coverage from war, revolution, and insurrection to full political violence coverage was to eliminate the need to demonstrate whether an act was an act of rebellion or an act of terrorism—in other words, where it ended up on Charles Berry's ladder. With the broader definition of coverage, OPIC no longer had to be concerned with the ladder. As long as the violent act is politically motivated, then it falls within OPIC's definition of political violence.

Charles Berry argues that traditional investment insurers have not done a good job of writing political violence coverage. But, in fact, if one looks at OPIC's record, it has been very successful in providing political violence coverage, and has always been willing (since the early 1980s) to provide it on a stand-alone basis.

OPIC has paid 46 political violence claims since its inception in 1971, and has paid out about $32 million in political violence claims compensation. During the same period, OPIC has earned far more in premiums on the coverage (approximately $450 million).

The reason why OPIC has been so successful is clearly that these claims have tended to be quite small. When one looks at the OPIC political violence coverage, it clearly is a property coverage. Although it is linked to an equity investment, the basis of compensation is the value of the property and the cost of replacing or repairing the assets that are damaged or destroyed.

A good question for discussion might be: why are not more commercial political risk insurers willing to get into this business, given OPIC's very successful track record?

Turning to Ken Hansen's paper on the BIT, there are several matters I feel quite strongly about. He suggests that PRI could offer the investor who has succeeded in a BIT arbitration a means of shifting the enforcement risk to the insurer.

In principle, he is right. There is no reason for an insurer to be less willing to insure against nonpayment of an arbitral award based on a treaty right, than to insure against nonpayment of an award pursuant to a private contract right, which is what many insurers have been doing for many years under arbitration award default coverage.

However, there are many practical problems with this approach, cost and delay being the primary ones. If one looks at the ICSID website, one observes how ICSID claims move at a glacial pace. They take many, many years to resolve, and ICSID also has a built-in review process.

There are many unanswered questions about this proposed approach. At what point can the investor declare success? Will investors need to pay premiums for the entire time that the claim is going through arbitration? How will the premiums be initially set? What will they be? (Given that the value of the award is likely to be much greater than the value of the original investment, this is not an insignificant issue for both insurers and the insureds.)

I think an investor would be much better off making an expropriation claim against the insurer, based on the claim that it would have presented through an arbitration and letting the insurer try to collect from the foreign government through arbitration or through some other means, as in the case of the Ponderosa claim in Argentina that OPIC paid in 2006. It is an excellent example of an insurer seeking an alternative means of recovery while an ICSID claim was still pending. (I will come back to this point later.)

Requiring an arbitral award makes sense in projects where there are direct commercial agreements with the foreign government, such as power purchase agreements. In these projects, it is better to require the insured to pursue its remedies under the contract before it can claim on its insurance policy.

Only if the commercial arrangements with the government are silent with respect to arbitration, should insurers require the insured to pursue remedies under a BIT; OPIC has provided this kind of BIT coverage in at least one case.

BIT coverage is not an answer, however, to the ongoing debate about the relevance of PRI in addressing situations such as the Argentine economic crisis of 2001–2002. Investors are looking for clarity in their contracts, and they want to know that the political risk insurance industry is adapting to the risks of today's world.

There is no reason why an insurer should not be willing to offer such BIT award coverage, but I think we can do better.

Allow me to turn back to the Ponderosa claim in Argentina. I realize many of you may not be aware of it, but there is a public Memorandum of Determinations on the OPIC website about it. OPIC knew that the insured had a pending ICSID claim, but we made a determination that there had been an expropriation without waiting for the results of that process. If the investor had lost in ICSID, it might have affected OPIC's salvage rights against the government of Argentina, but in this case, OPIC was able to secure recovery without having to involve the government of Argentina.

The investor actually felt that the OPIC claim determination boosted its case in ICSID, which is still pending [as of the day of the Symposium, November 3, 2006—ed.]. So the determination may actually influence the arbitral process in ICSID, and it certainly gave the investor a reason to find value in its political risk insurance coverage.

Note

1. The referenced Berne Union meetings occurred the week before the November 3, 2006, Symposium.

DISCUSSION OF NEW PERSPECTIVES ON POLITICAL RISK INSURANCE PRODUCTS

Symposium Panelists and Participants

The discussion initially focused on the two papers and the commentators' observations on them, but subsequently addressed a number of related issues.

Question: Are there any "trapdoors" facing an investment insurer (who pays a claim and then seeks recovery from a host government) in terms of the arbitral process and the execution thereof if one wins?

Second, while one can see potential value for equity investors in such BIT-based arbitral award coverage, what are the implications for lenders?

Hansen: Potential "trapdoors" for insurers under such proposed coverage definitely exist. However, such technical issues can and should be addressed in the subrogation provision of the insurer's contract. One would need to make it clear that if for some reason the award could not be assigned under the terms of the BIT, then the insured will forward the funds from the award to the insurer.

There are potentially even bigger subrogation issues if an insurer pays a claim up front and then seeks to use a BIT as its salvage mechanism, because the ability of parties, other than the original party of interest to pursue a BIT claim, is a very open, and hot, topic. There does not seem to be much jurisprudence on this matter. So, as with traditional PRI coverage, one would need to keep the insured available up front through the process in case one needs them for jurisdictional reasons.

With respect to the issue of debt vs. equity interests under such a new BIT-based coverage, there certainly are some differences. One of the great problems for lenders under the traditional PRI contract or awards coverage, is that the lenders to a project rarely have step-in rights; they are at least one step removed from those rights. To the extent that lenders might have direct access under a BIT, actions could be taken to give lenders the right to initiate action. (There are a few precedents for such action.)

There will always be differences in the situation and treatment of lenders vs. equity; but, all else being equal, I would estimate that the comparative disadvantage to lenders could be less under a BIT coverage than the traditional breach of contract coverage.

Question: I would like to ask the insurers on the panel and in the audience if they give consideration in their underwriting procedures to the specific existence and terms of a BIT? And would you offer better terms if an investor came in with a brief on the likely benefits of such a BIT?

Quintrell: We would consider the existence of a BIT to be a proactive factor in our risk analysis; it obviously is a broad indicator of government support for foreign investment. However, I would point out that there are many countries in which OPIC operates where the United States does not have a BIT.

MIGA Representative: MIGA has long considered the existence of a BIT between the home country of the investor and the host country to be a positive factor in its underwriting process.

Question: Would the proposed scope of the BIT coverage be much broader than would be covered under current political risk insurance policies?

Hansen: The investor and the underwriter may agree on a relatively narrow scope of coverage, or alternatively on a broader coverage. There may be relatively few issues to be addressed in drafting the coverage—or many. Much also obviously depends on the scope of the BIT. The model U.S. BIT was originally relatively brief, but now it is over 90 pages—so there may be many possible issues to consider. However, let me be clear that I am not suggesting that PRI coverage of a BIT award is an alternative to, or substitute for, traditional PRI coverage. The point is rather: might it be a useful supplement to the traditional coverage? There may be circumstances where an investor should consider the possibility—especially if it is available at an attractive price.

Question: In terms of the potential effectiveness of a BIT, if the alleged offender is a subsovereign or provincial regulatory authority, how might that affect an investor's ability to obtain justice?

Hansen: One obviously needs to begin by closely reading one's contracts with the various governmental entities. Like most PRI policies, which make it very clear that "the government" includes other entities than just the central government, the BITs that I have looked at make it very clear for whose actions the government will take responsibility and for whom it will not. But, in principle, are the actions of subsovereign entities covered? The answer is yes.

Question: You asserted that the proposed scope of coverage under the BIT could be much broader than that under the traditional PRI policy. Could you explain this further?

Hansen: The answer to this type of question really depends on the particular BIT that you are reading and the particular coverage that was written. The U.S. model BIT used to be about 12 pages long and is now about eight times that length. The new model U.S. BIT is a very complex document. I think that you can infer that there are some rights in a 90-page document that are perhaps not to be found in a standard PRI contract. Hence, the coverage could be broader.

We have had some lengthy debates in this Symposium about when or under what circumstances a breach of contract by a governmental instrumentality is an expropriation. Well, a breach would very likely be the basis of a claim under a BIT, since a breach of contract is usually an explicitly enumerated subject in most BITs.

Having said that, in the event of a breach, one would still need to go through all the steps to prove your case and to win an award, then seek to secure payment from the government. This whole process can take a shocking amount of time. However, this is exactly why it may be quite interesting for an investor to consider getting such coverage in some circumstances.

Question: In broad terms an insurer needs to add value and provide a certain and fast solution for a corporate need. How would this proposed coverage do so?

Hansen: I agree; fast and certain is good. I would not argue that this proposed BIT award coverage is an alternative to traditional PRI, but rather as an extension to it. If someone has a good claim of traditional expropriation or traditional arbitration award coverage, that is great. But this proposal is meant to provide coverage in situations in which: (1) one does not have traditional arbitral award coverage—perhaps because one's contract does not have an arbitration provision; or (2) one is concerned about disputes that could arise with entities that are somehow not captured by your contract; or (3) some other special circumstances.

Fast and certain is a good thing. But going to one's insurance company may be shorter and more certain than dealing with a host government.

Concluding Observation: The discussion on the potential coverage of BIT awards concluded with the observation by a representative of a public PRI entity that there clearly needs to be more inputs from investors on this proposal. Is there really a demand for such coverage? If there is, why are important investment insurers not hearing from them? If there is no apparent demand, why is that the case? Investors' inputs will be critical if this coverage is ever to be developed.

Question: I would like to ask Charles Berry to perhaps provide us with a little more clarity on the nature of the "gaps" in coverage. Is the gap because standard commercial insurers will not cover stand-alone political violence, or is it because the business interruption and war losses that are covered in the PRI markets are on a much longer term, permanent basis and the property insurers are providing a more short-term coverage?

Second, with respect to your Lloyd's market statistics, I was thinking along the same lines as Edie Quintrell. How much of the premium decrease is due to soft market pricing conditions and how much is due to lower levels of coverage being written?

Berry: The gaps are real. As I note in my paper, the standard Lloyd's terrorism language (T3) is the right policy form, but with the wrong perils and exclusions. The standard PRI political violence coverage (in lenders or equity form) covers the right perils, but in the wrong policy form. Neither provides effective policy insurance.

As noted in some examples in my paper, it should be acknowledged that the standard PRI policy will pay some of the losses. It does pay the cost of repairing or replacing the damaged or destroyed property for the insured investor's portion of the project, but often not 100 percent—and that is a problem.

Many projects, of course, do not have standard PRI equity coverage. When they go to the terrorism market for coverage of terrorism loss (or repair and replacement and business interruption), they simply do not get the right coverage. We look at these coverages all the time and I can assure you that there are real gaps.

With respect to your second question, there are admittedly some data problems, and one might wish to round the numbers. However, where you see a dramatic drop in the PRI business is in the expropriation area. I would stick to my point: the expropriation-led investment insurance business is not hot, certainly in comparison with stand-alone terrorism coverage. One can simply look at the size of the premiums paid into Lloyd's on these two covers: about US$75 million on investment insurance, and US$500 million on terrorism.

Question: With respect to the proposed terrorism coverage, could you address issuance and distribution issues?

Berry: Certainly. There are going to be some challenges for investment agencies writing this coverage, as Edie Quintrell has noted. One does need to write it like a property insurance, which is to say writing it swiftly, making quick underwriting decisions, and being flexible. This may make it very difficult for some public sector investment insurers to participate. Some private insurers also need to be persuaded that they can profitably write a political terrorism book of business. There is certainly historical evidence that this is the case; and the stand-alone terrorism market is providing that evidence at the moment.

There is historical evidence going back as far as the First World War of the interplay between private insurers writing war risk coverage and the government supporting those efforts. The Lloyd's marine market had an 80 percent quota share reinsurance from the British government. In the end, I recall that the British government made a considerable profit from that reinsurance. When one writes this kind of coverage in a disciplined and sensible way, one can make money. More importantly, it provides a valuable service.

Finally, with respect to distribution, political violence coverage is bought by risk managers. There is a challenge for BPL and entities like us, because we do not have a natural distribution channel to reach them. However, when we do reach risk managers, they certainly understand the terrorism ladder and the shortcomings of some of their extant coverages. They also understand that their emerging markets assets require something better than they are typically receiving now. They particularly appreciate that better coverage often does not cost as much as they are currently paying for inferior coverage.

Question/Observation: I would like to make a comment about the OPIC Ponderosa claim settlement. If a claim by a government agency or any other insurer is admitted because there is a suitable settlement arrangement made prior to the actual dispensation on the merits of that claim, then there is a big problem. That can create some very bad jurisprudence as to the merits of that claim and gives us real problems in the marketplace for PRI. It is important to have disposition of claims on the merits and not simply on the basis of potential recovery that obviates discussion of the merits of the claim.

Quintrell: I would like to correct misleading statements and the record on the matter of the OPIC settlement of the Ponderosa claim. OPIC made a determination on the merits of the claim first, based on an extensive analysis of the insured investment and international law. After more than six months of analysis, OPIC determined that there had been a violation of international law based on a repudiation of a contract. The contract was a license agreement between the Government of Argentina and TGS.

Subsequent to the positive determination that there had been an expropriation claim, OPIC then commenced extensive negotiations with the investor concerning how we were going to settle the claim. Those settlement discussions did include several options, including pursuing the ICSID claim, but also including holding the shares for the custody of OPIC. In the end, OPIC was able to recover based on the sale of those shares to a third party. We absolutely did not determine the claim based on the sale of those shares to a third party.

Part Two

PRIVATE POWER PROJECTS IN EMERGING MARKETS: NEW MODELS FOR FINANCING AND RISK MANAGEMENT

OVERVIEW

Theodore H. Moran and Gerald T. West
Editors

Part Two is devoted to an examination of private power projects in emerging markets and the lessons from past experiences that might guide new power project investments in those markets. The first paper is by Erik Woodhouse of the Program on Energy and Sustainable Development at Stanford University; the second is by Jeff Safford, a seasoned veteran of many AES positions in China and Latin America. Finally, drawing on his own extensive experience in Asia, Barry Metzger, a partner with Baker & McKenzie's Global Banking and Finance Practice Group in New York City, comments on both papers and adds his own perspective on old vs. new models for financing power projects.

In the first paper, "Managing International Political Risk: Lessons From the Power Sector," Erik Woodhouse asks how the risks associated with private power projects might be mitigated more effectively in light of recent experience in the power sector. Noting that many key stakeholders remain wary after the well-known troubles faced by many power projects in the late 1990s, he proceeds to empirically analyze the recent experiences of a large cohort of private power projects in search of prescriptions for the future. In many ways, his paper is the apex of a large pyramid of research that dates back several years. The immediate underpinning of this paper is a large empirical study of 34 power projects in 13 emerging markets.[1] While Woodhouse summarizes the underlying methodology of that study and discusses the factors that seemingly have determined project outcomes, the intention of his paper is to extract lessons for the future.

Woodhouse groups the key findings that have determined project outcomes into three categories. First, country-level factors—while significant determinates of stress that can affect a project—do not explain project outcomes with meaningful detail or consistency. (This suggests that innovations at the project level were able to mitigate the risks faced by long-term investments in uncertain markets.)

Second, and contrary to expectations, the "ironclad" contracts, security mechanisms, and other tools that were seen as central to the 1990s infrastructure boom, were not the dominant factors that determined project success. Third, rather than ex ante "risk engineering" into contract provisions and discount rates, a range of strategic management practices provided the best determinates of success, particularly in the face of crisis.

In the third segment of his paper, Woodhouse discusses each of these key findings in greater detail. With respect to country-level factors, this includes treatment of the effects of macrolevel shocks on project outcomes, market conditions in the host electricity sector, the effects of corruption, and the impact of power sector reform efforts.

With respect to project-level factors that contribute to project outcomes, Woodhouse examines those "risk engineering" tools that investors in the 1990s thought were crucial for investment—including more precise contracting, guarantees and other security mechanisms, involvement of critical international partners, and international arbitration to settle disputes. He also considers "strategic management," a group of measures designed to anticipate and manage risks that are likely to arise, but difficult to manage through contracts. In broad terms, the first group of actions was found to be necessary, but not sufficient to preserve project outcomes, but the somewhat amorphous strategic management actions have more often played a key role in successful projects.

Woodhouse argues that one of the key lessons learned from this study of 34 power projects was that the risk management tools favored by the largely Western infrastructure investors of the 1990s enabled a great deal of private investment. However, the promise that in weak institutional settings, risk can be engineered into precise contractual formulations that will robustly hold through inevitable crises has crumbled. In the end, projects that were able to address their vulnerabilities with specific, tailored responses tended to be more successful. Woodhouse acknowledges that the distinction between "risk engineering" practices and "strategic management" practices blurs, especially when examining any particular project. He also notes that the core "risk engineering" method—the project finance structure itself—can, when properly structured, help enforce the incentives that make strategic management by key stakeholders possible.

In the fourth section of his paper, Woodhouse asks: what lessons does recent experience provide that can be used by investors interested in future, mutually beneficial infrastructure projects? This question is addressed in two ways. First, the limits of the classic independent power project (IPP) as an investment model are considered; and second, the possibility is explored that investors can be more "strategic" in the future both in structuring their projects and in subsequently managing them.

With respect to limitations on the "classic" IPP model of the late 1990s, the inability of many host governments to bear the risk burdens assigned to them in times of crisis has been clearly evident. Over the long term, the reduction and management of these risks depends on meaningful reform. However, as Woodhouse notes, ongoing reform brings many problems for host governments, including attempting to integrate existing IPPs into a more liberalized market.

With respect to whether investors can be more "strategic" in their ability to plan, execute, and manage IPPs in the future, Woodhouse broadly argues that they can. He notes that there is now some 15 years of experience with scores of projects that can be drawn upon to better equip stakeholders to evaluate and plan projects. He proceeds to discuss specific recommendations under three headings: (i) bidding, transparency, and social risk; (ii) host country governance and reform; and (iii) project governance and stress. There is unfortunately not a set of universal "cookie-cutter" recommendations as to what should be done. Woodhouse argues that the appropriate project structure and the nature of government participation will depend critically on existing institutions and market structure. In some cases, these considerations can be built into a project, while in other cases innovation after a dispute arises will be required.

Woodhouse concludes by asking: if the "classic" IPP is limited in the future to a niche role, how can countries get the most out of an IPP program, while laying the foundation for an effective transition to investment models that are more sustainable on a larger scale? Part of the answer to this question is technical, and comes down to effective reform, both in the electricity sector and the economy more generally, in a fashion that reduces risk. But even if one understands the necessity of such reforms and how they might happen, one should ask if current and likely future market conditions will encourage such reforms.

Woodhouse notes that older, developed, country-based multinational firms willing to venture into the turbulence of developing country electricity markets now face competition from new, local, and developing country-based firms. The appetite some of these new actors have for projects stems in part from their access to concessionary financing, greater flexibility with respect to accounting rules, and confidence in their ability to engage smoothly with local politicians and governments. Ironically, if developing countries can meet their short-term investment needs by dealing with such new actors, some of whom may have little interest in meaningful reform, the inefficiency and politicization that characterizes the electricity sector in many countries will continue.

Woodhouse suggests that the persistent turbulence that has characterized long-term electricity sector investment in developing countries will likely continue. Nonetheless, new projects will be built to meet the ever-growing demand.

However, nearly everyone will become more sensitive to the complex and dynamic realities of reform. Those countries that demonstrate a commitment to reform will disproportionately benefit from the attention of private investors. Future projects will benefit from taking a broader perspective on the relationships among host country conditions, reform efforts, and successful private investment.

In "AES's Experiences in Developing Countries," Jeff Safford presents both an overview of AES's experiences in emerging markets and seeks to relate, at least partially, those experiences to Erik Woodhouse's findings.

Safford starts with a brief overview of AES's global activities. Looking forward, he notes that AES has a strong development pipeline with 10 projects in the engineering and construction phase in seven countries, another seven projects in five countries in the advanced planning stage, while another 93 projects in 32 countries are in the early development stage. AES is strongly committed to emerging market countries, in part because that is where the greatest growth is expected.

Safford acknowledges that AES considers a host of macro-and structural factors before venturing into a project: the economy, its vulnerability to external shocks, monetary and fiscal policies, the political and judicial systems, the regulatory and tax policies, and the "workings" of all these systems. However, he also stresses the importance of project-level factors and of management's ability to address challenges and work through them until a solution is found.

While Safford finds Woodhouse's paper "pretty much on point" with the ways AES thinks about projects in emerging markets, he notes that, on the project level, the importance of being the least-cost producer is considerable because one is less likely to be exposed to political pressures. And while contracts do not necessarily protect the project from everything, a good set of contractual arrangements means that should one need to renegotiate, those negotiations start from a much better base.

Safford asserts that AES intends to maintain its project finance mentality: he articulates 12 components of that approach and cites the recent $1.4 billion Maritza project in Bulgaria as an example of such an approach.

Noting AES's commitment to growth in emerging markets, he concludes by noting AES's focus in three areas: traditional development (which will be greenfield projects, platform expansions, acquisitions, and privatizations), new and adjacent markets (which will include alternative energy LNG gasification), and portfolio management (which will include asset sales and the sale of minority interests to partners).

Barry Metzger, in his commentary, notes the contrast in tone between the two presentations. While Jeff Safford is cautiously optimistic and expansionist, Erik Woodhouse is far more cautionary. While AES sees many new opportunities in the developing world, Woodhouse seeks to draw lessons from the history of significant losses for sponsors over the last 10 years.

Looking at the structures of new vs. old IPP projects, Metzger asks: what has been learned from the past and how has it been reflected in the structure of new IPP projects?

He notes that he is struck by how little the conceptual framework for projects—the risk engineering piece—has changed over time. The biggest change has been the availability of local currency financing; this has allowed foreign companies to reduce the mismatch between foreign currency financings and local currency revenues.

However, Metzger argues that what has changed the most is the "strategic management" of the projects. More projects are being financed in the public sector rather than by private investors. Second, private sponsors are increasingly and deliberately seeking to diversify their portfolio over as broad a group of countries as possible. Third, the profile of the active sponsors has changed; some private international players have withdrawn; emerging market companies have stepped into the breach, led by national oil companies. The profile of the financial investors and lenders who are participating in these new projects has also changed; some international banks that had been active in project finance have withdrawn, but domestic lenders and financial institutions have become more active. Projects are now accessing the public markets and retail investors through infrastructure funds.

The entry of these new players—as sponsors, as financial investors, and as lenders to projects—is what has significantly changed in the strategic management of private power projects in emerging markets. Metzger notes that these new players, with their different geopolitical perspectives and their mix of economic and noneconomic motivations, may create an environment that is less conducive to domestic reform of the power sector and less hospitable to private investment.

Note

1. See Woodhouse, Erik J. 2005–2006. "The Obsolescing Bargain Redux? Foreign Direct Investment in the Electric Power Sector in Developing Countries." 38 *N.Y.U. Journal of International Law and Politics,* 121. This study was developed and sponsored by the Program on Energy and Sustainable Development at Stanford University (PESD). The full methodology and results of the study are reported at PESD's website, http://pesd.stanford.edu/ipps.

MANAGING INTERNATIONAL POLITICAL RISK: LESSONS FROM THE POWER SECTOR

Erik J. Woodhouse
Program on Energy and Sustainable Development, Stanford University

I. Introduction

In 1995, the title of an article in a prominent international business journal queried: "Is Foreign Infrastructure Investment Still Risky?"[1] The question captured the prevailing sense that the era of expropriation was over and that the risks for foreigners of long-lived developing country investment had abated or were manageable with layers of protection and leverage built into new projects. By the end of the decade, this confidence had evaporated (as trenchantly anticipated by the authors of the 1995 article) in the wake of successive economic crises and high-profile disputes that left both private stakeholders and host governments disillusioned.

Having relearned that private infrastructure investment is risky, the question for this article is how the architects of private investment regimes can mitigate those risks more effectively, in light of recent experience. With developing countries facing the need to mobilize staggering amounts of capital to meet projected infrastructure demand in the coming years, the question is critical.[2] Key stakeholders, however, remain wary after the well-known troubles in infrastructure markets beginning in the late 1990s. Exhaustive analysis of recent experience, moreover, has not yielded clear prescriptions for the future.

This paper draws upon a recent study of the IPP experience in 13 developing countries (referred to simply as the "IPP study" in this paper)[3] to offer insight and lessons from the last round of investment that can inform future efforts. Part II of the paper briefly summarizes the underlying IPP study, focusing on the methodology.

Part III discusses the central conclusions of the study regarding the factors that determined project outcomes. The goal is not to fully explain or defend these conclusions, which is done elsewhere.[4] Rather, the intention is to set the stage for the discussion in Part IV, which translates these conclusions, at times possible only in hindsight, into lessons for the future.

II. Methodology

The central task of the IPP study was to explain the wide variation in outcomes for private power projects across countries and across projects, and to identify the factors that contributed to success and failure.[5] The study considered outcomes from the perspective of investors ("investment outcomes") and host countries ("development outcomes"). This work began with a series of rival explanations—hypotheses—about the IPP experience, that reflected the academic literature in the area as well as interviews with investors, builders, operators, regulators, and host country officials.

First, the study considered whether structural characteristics of large infrastructure projects make them irreparably vulnerable to opportunistic behavior. For decades (if not more), investors have been sensitive to the fact that their bargaining position changes once concrete is poured and equipment bolted to the ground. The study revisited this classic "obsolescing bargain" hypothesis, asking whether the central dismal conclusion remains valid and exploring the efficacy of strategies adopted by investors to avoid host country opportunism. Second, the IPP study considered whether outcomes can be traced primarily to characteristics of the host countries. This inquiry included the significance of macroeconomic shock, the political and social context for private investment, and the legal and regulatory framework for power investment in particular, as well as the physical and commercial characteristics of the electricity market and underlying fuel markets. Third, the IPP study considered whether project outcomes are not determined by structural factors primarily, but rather by the behavior and vision of project managers and stakeholders. This inquiry included the overall characteristics of each country's IPP program, the financial arrangements for projects (primarily power sales arrangements and financing), fuel selection and fuel arrangements, the composition of key project stakeholders, and the impact of ongoing operations and management. Finally, the IPP study was sensitive to the possibility that the crucial determinants of project outcomes are located not within countries or projects at all, but reflect merely the fickle, yet often devastating, impact of external shocks and contagions such as the Asian financial crisis of the late 1990s or the collapse of Enron.

To unpack the impact and dynamic interplay of these factors, the study selected a set of 13 countries and 34 projects. From the full set of over 50 developing and transition countries that have had at least one IPP, the study selected a sample of countries that demonstrated variation across key country-level factors. From the universe of all IPPs in each of these 13 countries, the study selected a smaller set of 34 projects that demonstrated variation across project-level factors as well as unique country characteristics.[6] Based on initial reviews, the study selected eight countries for in-depth treatment, including field visits: Brazil, China, Egypt, India, Kenya, the Philippines, Tanzania, and Thailand.[7]

This sample allowed a substantial level of detail regarding the experience of each project, while also allowing comparison across projects, countries, and relevant time periods.[8] At the same time, the study faced limitations. Except in rare (and carefully controlled) cases, researchers did not have access to nonpublic financial performance indicators for projects, meaning that one core outcome for investors—whether they earned a reasonable return—had to be approximated using the best available data. Additionally, the level of detail reported for each project and country varied as research priorities evolved. One manifestation of this is that some potentially important questions are not fully addressed, such as differentiating between the interests of debt and equity holders among private stakeholders.

III. Key Findings

Three crucial findings have emerged from recent experience. First, country-level factors, while significant determinants of stress that can affect a project, do not explain project outcomes with meaningful detail or consistency. This suggests that innovations at the project level were, as hoped, able to mitigate the risks faced by long-term investments in uncertain markets. Second, and contrary to expectations, the "ironclad" contracts, security mechanisms, and other tools that were seen as central to the 1990s infrastructure boom, were not the dominant factors that explain this success. Third, rather than ex ante "risk engineering" into contract provisions and discount rates, a range of strategic management practices provides the best determinants of success, particularly in the face of crisis. This section summarizes the analysis underlying these three findings. Subsequent sections consider their implication for future projects.

A. Country-Level Factors: The Context for Investment

1. How did Macroeconomic Shock Affect Project Outcomes? The most prominent single explanation for the collapse of the IPP market in the late 1990s is a succession of macroeconomic crises. Six of 13 sample countries in this study suffered a substantial macroeconomic shock; all six saw severe stress imposed on

IPPs as a result of the macroeconomic shock. The reasonable expectation is that as electricity becomes both more expensive due to currency devaluation and less needed due to depressed industrial and economic activities, the outcomes for IPPs would correspondingly fall.

For governments and host countries, this is largely true—the dramatic local currency price increases associated with such shocks often led to mixed or negative development outcomes. For investors, the dismal expectation is only partially true. Where contracts were maintained or marginally renegotiated—which occurred in a series of significant cases—investors have seen their reasonable expectations met. While, as a general matter, the investment outcomes for IPPs are consistent with the conventional wisdom about how macroeconomic shock should affect investments, such broad patterns do not provide a full explanation for observed outcomes. On the one hand, the worst experiences often correlated with the most severe shocks in countries deeply vulnerable to currency devaluation—Argentina, Indonesia, and Pakistan being prominent examples. A number of countries have weathered crises with their IPP sector intact, including Thailand, Malaysia, and Egypt. At the same time, some countries were similarly exposed to crisis and were able to secure contracts or cooperative renegotiations that preserved investment outcomes and navigated a middle ground for development outcomes. The Philippines is a key example in this category, perhaps forfeiting gain from aggressive pressure on foreign infrastructure investors, but preserving long-term prospects for electricity sector financing.

2. Did the Market Conditions in the Host Electricity Sector Contribute to Positive or Negative Performance? Macroeconomic shock is not, of course, the only factor affecting a country's ability or willingness to pay for contracted electricity. Theory would predict that adverse changes in the host country electricity market would have a similar effect on IPPs if they made electricity more expensive or less necessary. In the IPP study, pressure on project arrangements was generally, but not always, correlated with the commercial health of key offtakers or consumers. This apparent opportunism has done much to inspire cynicism on the part of investors.

The severity of this pressure generally reflects the electricity system's capacity to generate revenue (reflecting aggregate demand and tariff levels) to cover the contracted supply (the fixed costs of the generation, transmission, and distribution). This hypothesis holds true both across cases and over time. The IPP study examined subnational experiences in India and China to (mostly) isolate these commercial variables. Neither country had a major macroeconomic shock in the late 1990s; both countries also have electricity sectors that are organized at the state or provincial level, allowing comparison across cases while controlling for country-level factors. In both countries, the outcomes for projects across different states or provinces are largely consistent with the relative financial health of the local electricity authorities, considering factors such as cost recovery and fluctuations in demand.[9]

Over time, the pattern is similar. Adverse changes in the commercial context for power sales (independent of macroeconomic shock) preceded controversy or stress in the IPP sector in another five of the 13 sample countries. The hydroelectricity-dependent countries—Brazil, Kenya, and Tanzania—each developed thermal IPPs during periods of poor hydrology. In each case, the return of normal rainfall left the thermal projects looking unnecessary and expensive. In many cases, too, political interference is often close to the surface, notably so in the Philippines and Thailand, which in delicate political moments took action that exacerbated the financial pressure on offtakers, such as limiting the costs that a state utility was able to pass along to consumers.[10]

3. Were IPPs in Countries with Higher Levels of Perceived Corruption More Vulnerable to Social or Political Risk? Corruption, whether perceived or real, is high on the list of ills affecting infrastructure investment in the minds of both investors and civil society.[11] However, in the IPP experience, operating in an environment perceived to be corrupt does not appear to be a major explanatory variable—either for the amount of investment or for project outcomes. The ability of a country to attract investment was not constrained by perceived corruption; investors in IPPs did not shy away from embracing countries perceived to have corrupt business environments.[12] At the same time, to date, no allegation of corruption related to an IPP in any of 13 sample countries has resulted in a full public adjudication.

Given the lack of enforcement, the risk of corruption is not yet a legal risk per se, but rather primarily a social risk. Without a reliable investigation and enforcement mechanism capable of identifying corrupt deals, suspicion easily propagates to the entire sector—without identifying the "bad" deals, there is no way of knowing the "good" deals. This explains why transparent project procurement appears to offer the most effective protection against the pressure of corruption. In Mexico, Thailand, and Egypt, countries that utilized transparent bidding for their IPPs, no serious concerns regarding corruption were encountered in the IPP study, despite wide variation in perceived levels of corruption among these countries. In Brazil, Tanzania, Turkey, Kenya, and the Philippines, projects allocated via competitive bid have remained immune to allegations of corruption that have plagued other projects in the same country that were allocated otherwise. In these countries, general suspicion did erode outcomes for host governments to varying degrees and created a more hostile (and likely costlier) operating environment. But with the exception of specific projects that did end up in messy disputes over corruption charges, actual project outcomes were not significantly affected by corruption (or, at least by the imperfect measures of corruption that are the only available proxy).

4. Did the Structure of Underlying Fuel Markets Affect IPP Performance? A striking, yet little explored, factor in promoting stability for power investment is transparency in fuel markets. Investors are highly attuned to the risks that may flow from fuel supply arrangements, both because the price of fuel is the principal cost component of electricity and because fuel markets offer fertile grounds for manipulation and opportunism. However, the topic has not attracted significant scholarly attention, leaving the field with a vast body of anecdotal experience but little systematic analysis.

In the IPP study, the characteristics of host fuel markets undermined project outcomes in country after country. Most often this occurred where fuel selection for projects was warped by political interference,[13] or where lack of transparency in the markets themselves left planners with little reliable information regarding prices or supply.[14] In addition to the problems that inherently follow supply interruptions or price spikes, such episodes made projects more vulnerable to host government pressure, notably in India and China. In contrast, many of the "model" IPP markets owe their success in part to mechanisms that essentially bundled all fuel risk into government books. Often, these have been master gas supply arrangements between state electricity utilities and state gas suppliers, although direct subsidy is also utilized.[15] Such arrangements—which notably exist at the project level, not the country level—have at time proven costly for national fuel companies, but have proven successful in attracting investment and sustaining project arrangements through difficult times.

5. Were Power Sector Reform Efforts Successful at Reducing Risk and Uncertainty? Investors were not unaware of these myriad risks. Most, if not all, private investment programs were accompanied by efforts to improve the legislative and regulatory framework in the electricity sector, a factor that ranked among the most important for investors considering a project.[16] Disentangling the effect such efforts had on IPPs, however, is a difficult task, largely because aggregate investment in IPPs bears little correlation to the extent or quality of legal or regulatory reform.[17] In most cases, IPP investors did not look for an ideal legal or regulatory system; rather, they sought particular arrangements that apply to their investment and risk profile. Conspicuously, early best practices manuals for private participation in generation explicitly stated that a coherent legal framework was not necessary so long as a few core provisions were present, while detailed regulation was left to project specific documentation.[18]

This approach isolated IPPs from the surrounding country environment, largely by reducing the investor-government relationship to a small set of contracts that, if they held, would ensure the viability of the project. Paradoxically, market-oriented reform often disrupted these careful arrangements. The correlation between formal reform indicators and successful country performance in the IPP sector is ambiguous, if not negative. For example, the three most successful IPP countries—Egypt, Mexico, and Thailand—had relatively unreformed electricity sectors during most of the bidding and structuring of projects (in those countries, ministry-based regulation has proven sufficient). On the other hand, core aspects of the reform process have increased risks for IPPs (even where the incompatibility of long-term contracts is overlooked), including efforts to create a comprehensive legal framework for electricity, establishing new regulators, and unbundling generation from transmission and distribution. These troubles largely reflect the fact that reform has almost universally ground to a halt in the political quagmire of domestic energy markets, ending in a quasi-reformed market that is uniquely difficult for private entrants. In Brazil, the dominance of the massive hydroelectricity sector led to a regulatory framework decidedly biased against new natural gas-fired power plants, making cost recovery difficult, even though the plants would have brought important fuel diversity to the generation sector.[19] In China, the devolution of authority over the electricity sector to local actors, while central government officials retained control over some sector planning, provided the authority and incentive for local officials to make life difficult for new foreign and private entrants that would be competing with local state-owned plants.[20]

Despite these challenges, available evidence suggests that where reform is effective, IPPs also benefit, largely because the same factors that foster effective reforms in the electricity sector often redound to the benefit of private generators as well. The most important of these factors are changes outside the electricity sector—particularly in financial markets, in the judiciary and legal system, and in critical factor markets such as labor and fuel.[21] For example, judicial reforms that increase the independence of the courts and the administration of justice have proven crucial in supporting fledgling regulatory authorities.[22] This is why, for example, India has reaped benefits from its state-level regulatory reforms, where those reforms have support and time to mature.[23] IPPs have benefited in parallel. For example, the key variable distinguishing the IPP experience in the Indian states of Andhra Pradesh, Gujarat, and Tamil Nadu, aside from electricity supply-demand fluctuations and available fuel sources, is the maturity of regulatory reform. Andhra Pradesh, with the most mature reform effort, has also been most able to generate and enforce meaningful regulatory decisions, while Tamil Nadu lags in both categories. Disputes between investors and local officials in each state have mirrored this distinction closely. In contrast, where regulatory decisions were not enforced, the level of reform would explain very little of the different experiences.[24] Such is the case in countries less known for their independent courts, such as China, Brazil, and the Philippines. In those cases, regulatory independence survives only so long as political will remains strong—in each case, regulatory authorities have seen their decisions reversed or undermined by political interference.[25]

More often, however, reform efforts take unexpected turns that undermine the political or economic sustainability of existing projects. As the process muddles along, electricity demand does not wait, and governments confront the need to attract investment on attractive terms, which requires insulating projects from the vagaries of reform. The awkward implication is that the twin goals of attracting investment and implementing meaningful reform are in tension—all the more so as investors seek higher risk-adjusted returns in the face of regulatory uncertainty.

B. Project-Level Factors: Risk Management and Uncertainty

Even where country-level factors contribute to project outcomes, they fail to fully explain success and failure. To supplement this gap, the IPP study explored the significance of two broad categories of project factors. The first is an arsenal of measures referred to as "risk engineering." This category contains most of the tools that investors thought were crucial for investment in the 1990s, including reliance on ever more precise contracting, guarantees and other security mechanisms, involvement of prominent international partners, and international arbitration to settle disputes. The second category—referred to as "strategic management"—includes measures designed to anticipate (and manage) risks that are likely to arise and gravitate toward vulnerabilities in a project, but are difficult to manage through contracts.[26] In broad terms, the first category has been necessary, but not sufficient, to preserve project outcomes, while the second category, amorphous as it is, has more often played a key role in successful projects.

1. "Risk Engineering" In response to the risks of IPP investment, investors adopted a canon of measures that revolved around four main elements: (a) supposedly airtight contracts that captured the key commercial bargain between government and investor, (b) payment security arrangements designed to ensure a regular flow of project income, (c) multi- or bilateral partners (as well as lenders and insurers) whose presence is thought to deter opportunistic breach by the host government, and (d) offshore arbitration designed to circumvent difficulties with local courts and improve the ultimate enforceability of contract terms.

Reliance on contracts, including purchase power agreements (PPAs), to mitigate transactional risks is, of course, not unique to the developing world. But the infrastructure investment boom of the 1990s grew out of a body of experience, including widespread expropriations in the 1960s and 1970s, and a dominant paradigm, Raymond Vernon's "obsolescing bargain" hypothesis, that primed stakeholders to look to contract stability as the bellwether of project success and government credibility. It is true that uninterrupted contract performance does, in general, correlate with project success for investors—in the IPP study, 92 percent of projects with stable contracts delivered positive investment outcomes. However, this blanket conclusion obscures the turbulent reality of long-term contracting. And it completely overlooks the myriad avenues host governments have taken to reach amicable solutions when caught between contractual obligations and genuine economic hardship.

In raw terms, out of 34 projects reviewed for this study, 13 have undergone mutual or cooperative renegotiation,[27] eight have faced unilateral renegotiation or nonpayment,[28] and 13 have held in a strictly formal sense—a group dominated by cases where country characteristics shunted severe stresses away from the projects or where projects have been tailored closely (by accident or design) to the risks of the surrounding power market.[29]

To begin to excavate the relationship between contracts and project performance, the raw outcomes drawn from the IPP study are set forth in figure 4 below,

FIGURE 4 Contract Performance versus Project Performance

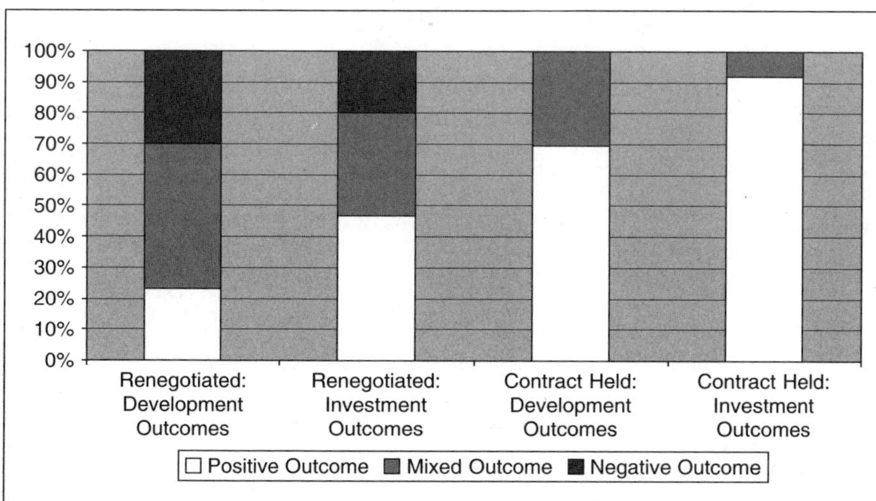

Source: Woodhouse, Erik J. 2006. "IPP Study Case Selection and Project Outcomes: An Additional Note." PESD Working Paper.

which tracks the development and investment outcomes for projects that were renegotiated and for projects in which the contracts held.

The broad result is that contract performance correlates with project performance, for both hosts and investors.[30] This is relatively unsurprising, as the contracts were designed to ensure investment success. Upon closer examination, however, there are two key questions raised by the results in figure 4. The first is to explain the proportion (47 percent) of renegotiated contracts that delivered positive results for investors. The second is to explain why development outcomes were lower than investment outcomes in projects that were renegotiated. Generally, that difference reflects the fact that renegotiation is spurred by adverse conditions affecting the host government, and that renegotiation often results in limited concessions, along with the long-term costs associated with public renegotiations. But this observation leaves a key question: what explains cases in which renegotiation did not erode outcomes for key stakeholders? As set forth in the sections that follow, the answer more often involves the "strategic management" practices described in the next subsection than the "risk engineering" methods detailed here.

Answering this question is important—the columns on the left side of figure 4 make up roughly two-thirds of the projects studied. Moreover, focusing on the "failed" contracts does not at all undermine the importance of clear and thorough contracting. After all, outcomes were best for all parties when contracts held—and in many cases this is because the IPP program was more sustainable from the start. But when country conditions generate stress, such as payment problems or civil society opposition to privatization, which can affect project arrangements, crucial vulnerabilities in contracts are often the first target. Thus, contracts are necessary; pressure focuses where gaps are allowed to persist, as in the case of China's annual tariff reviews or India's public gas contracts. But they are not sufficient; gaps are either unavoidable or unforeseeable, and intense risks can simply overwhelm any decent project structure. Contracts alone cannot hold the line when fuel is scarce and politicized, when regulators lack the capacity to resolve disputes, when social mistrust of private investors turns to suspicion and protest, or when laws and regulations are changing and uncertain.

Reliance on additional layers of protection, including sovereign guarantees, escrow arrangements, and letters of credit—all designed to bolster confidence around a predictable stream of payments from offtakers whose own financial or political situation gives cause for concern about credibility—did little to change observed outcomes. While lenders often demand such measures, the IPP experience reveals no more than a tenuous relationship between the layers of official credit support and capacity to withstand pressure to change a contract. For example, nothing in the study indicates that sovereign guarantees have been powerful determinants of project outcomes. While sovereign guarantees are associated with strong country performance in the IPP study, in light of competing factors it is difficult to conclude that sovereign guarantees are a significant factor. This is seen most clearly where the details of guarantees vary across projects within a country, notably in India and the Philippines; the explanatory power has been weak, as differing project outcomes have reflected variables other than security arrangements.

Another canon of the 1990s investment cycle was reliance on prominent international entities as partners, in the hope that the host government will avoid trampling on big toes.[31] The IPP study suggests that such partners are significant in managing renegotiations, where their connections and influence may facilitate a cooperative resolution. Where conflicts become intense, as in threatened or actual nonpayment, the cause is usually severe economic or other crisis, and the myriad other concerns that these entities have may erode their willingness to exert coercive force on host governments.[32] Strikingly, commercial banks appear to provide a much harder constraint on host government pressure than their multi- or bilateral counterparts.[33] Every government official interviewed for the IPP study who had been involved in a renegotiation identified debt payments as a hard constraint on their willingness to pressure a project. This observation offers a mixed diagnosis. On the one hand, prominent international actors do increase the robustness of project arrangements (although in ways that I will argue are more strategic than initially anticipated). Nonetheless, particularly where commercial banks are involved, equity remains vulnerable to persistent pressure, and the security of debt coverage will do little to comfort potential project sponsors.

Finally, aware of the risks posed by weak host country institutions, project participants sought to contract out of host country risk by moving dispute resolution offshore, to a variety of international commercial arbitration panels. The goal was increased enforceability and predictability of contracts when a dispute spins out of control. In the IPP study, three of 34 projects entered some form of arbitration; a striking figure, considering that 21 projects underwent some form of renegotiation.[34] This limited arbitration experience may reflect the high cost and relative uncertainty of enforcement mechanisms after an award is made, and continued churning in the law surrounding some of the thorniest issues surrounding expropriation and economic necessity.[35] As a result of these problems, while some investors have managed to enforce their awards, the reliance on arbitration provisions has most often been deployed as a means to gain leverage toward a negotiated settlement. Taking this perspective, the dismal image that one might draw by looking at the most famous arbitrations in the IPP universe is not borne out in the IPP study. In two of the arbitrations—Independent Power Tanzania Ltd. (IPTL) and the Philippines' Casecnan—the threat of arbitration (Casecnan) or an actual arbitral decision (IPTL)[36] was part of a broader negotiation in which key terms were adjusted in an attempt to salvage the project for both parties.[37] In the other case (India's PPN Power), the ongoing dispute makes it difficult to disentangle the role of arbitration in project outcomes thus far.

For each element of risk engineering discussed here—strict contracts, prominent partners, official credit support, arbitration protection—the IPP experience reveals little evidence of magic partners or arrangements that mitigate political risk to equity investors in a systematic way. Anecdotal evidence abounds, and the halo effect that such measures carry is likely effective in some cases. Yet, projects—in particular, the equity portion of investment—remain exposed without the use of other risk management tools.

2. Strategic Management A second category of project factors—"strategic management"—plays a large role in explaining final project outcomes. In general terms, these tools structure the project in a manner that reduces vulnerability to particular risks. As noted previously, this category of risk management tools has been proposed by a range of analysts, yet never fully populated.[38] The IPP experience offers a range of practices that fit this description and are systematically related to successful projects. This section focuses on three overarching factors: (i) project selection and cost, (ii) local partnerships, and (iii) project governance.

Under the right circumstances, project selection through competitive bidding may deliver a number of benefits—including low prices[39] and increased transparency[40]—that bolster the sustainability of projects. While experience is mixed regarding when and under what conditions a transparent bidding process can deliver these benefits,[41] in the IPP study, bidding is highly correlated with stable project arrangements, even in the face of stress. Notably, IPPs in Egypt, Turkey (the build-operate-transfer rights, or BOTs), and Thailand weathered macroeconomic shock after well-organized and transparent bidding. In contrast, direct negotiations have resulted in projects that prove costly—in economic, political, or social terms. In India, for example, the issue generating the most consistent controversy in the IPP sector is costs and cost overruns for early projects that were selected through negotiations rather than bidding, with tariffs set according to a cost-plus system.[42] Moreover, direct negotiation intrinsically suffers from low levels of transparency, which left these early Indian projects (among myriad examples across the 13-country sample) exposed to the criticism that costs were inflated because these projects were allocated to firms with special connections rather than through market discipline. While there are examples of negotiated deals that have been stable—many of the early Philippine and Kenyan projects, for example—the political turmoil surrounding these deals has been qualitatively different from that surrounding bid projects.

Over the long run, in addition to transparency, cost is a dominant determinant of outcomes. In seeking investment, governments often espouse goals for IPPs that imply tolerance for IPPs that have higher costs than incumbents. Such goals include improving technological or environmental performance or introducing new fuels. In reality, these myriad (and often important) benefits are rarely weighed heavily when cost differences become apparent. Projects that compare favorably with incumbents in raw commercial terms (usually price/kWh) outperform those that do not, regardless of the other benefits such projects may bring. The specific benefit desired varies, but the result does not. In China, it was *foreign* capital and *foreign* technology; in Brazil and Kenya, it was thermal generation capacity to offset reliance on the dominant hydroelectricity generators. In all three markets, the benefits were delivered, but played little role in the controversy surrounding high prices when country conditions took a turn for the worse; of course, in Kenya the thermal units regained the affection of their hosts when hydrological conditions took a second turn for the worse. By contrast, IPPs have been able to play a key role in moving away from dominant incumbent fuel sources only where they have compared favorably with the incumbent, which was the case in Mexico and the Philippines where IPPs could compete with relatively expensive incumbent oil-fired plants. While IPPs can play a role in meeting unique needs, they must remain competitive with the incumbent grid-connected system.

Similarly prominent on the list of lessons from the 1990s—and often cited by those burned by the Dabhol supernova—is reliance on local partnerships. This is seen as a way to facilitate communicating and operating in a foreign environment; it is also prized as a way to mitigate the political risks inherent in being a foreigner, and in some cases to recruit influential local actors to defend the project from government or other interference. The need to manage these risks is particularly acute when, as in electric power, the investment is prone to a high degree of politicization. In the IPP study project sample, 14 of 34 projects were wholly foreign-owned and the balance had some local equity partnership. In confronting the most common problems that face IPPs, projects with local partners were more likely to successfully mitigate that risk than those that are wholly foreign-owned. These benefits, however, decline as project risk becomes more acute and more political. Thus, local partners are most valuable addressing mundane challenges such as understanding local electricity and fuel markets, but have a less striking impact in the classic political risk areas of nonpayment; areas that often require confrontation with government officials or a broader political strategy to alter the behavior of central government agencies. Strikingly, however, some of these "mundane" issues, such as turbulent and opaque host fuel markets, are among the most important zones of risk for new IPPs, as set forth above.

Differences in the capacity of individual projects to navigate stress are explained not only by partnering strategies, but also by the governance structure of the project. One of the reasons that the project financing structure has been robust in so many different contexts is that it is highly attuned to any changes in circumstance. This sensitivity plays a key role in keeping stakeholders' attention focused on the project; where it is abandoned, poor outcomes may result due to weak oversight by key participants and consequent mismanagement.[43] But this sensitivity comes with a price—with rights and obligations spelled out with such specificity, it is deceptively easy to end up with a contractual web that locks up under stress or creates problems of its own.

In this regard, three trends emerged in the IPP experience. The first is a project structure that insulates key participants from uncertainty. Disputes regarding performance, for example, are difficult to resolve when the operator is paid regardless of performance and the board of the project company is evenly divided.[44] The second is with respect to a project structure that unnecessarily concentrates risk on the wrong counterparty. Where a middleman is inserted between generator and offtaker, and is required to buy fixed amounts of electricity in hard currency but to sell the same electricity in variable amounts in local currency, the full weight of currency and demand risk may fall upon a single, small, marginally involved counterparty, rather than on larger, more committed participants.[45] Such structures run counter to the proposition of allocating risk to the party most able to bear it, and are hardly a recipe for success.

The third trend is positive, and reflects project structure that facilitates cooperative renegotiations, particularly with respect to government stakeholders. Countries that have vested a central authority with control over the relationship with private generators generally have been more able to manage stresses that arise for IPPs—which was the case in Thailand and the Philippines in the aftermath of the Asian financial crisis. Severe problems in prominent private investment programs are more likely to be resolved when critical counterparties are under the control of reformers in the central government, who likely harbor a greater long-term interest in sustaining private investment. Such reformers also have access to the resources and strategic vision to devise sustainable cost-sharing arrangements that arise, for example, during contract renegotiations following a macroeconomic shock.

C. In a Nutshell: What Was Learned?

The first goal of the IPP study was to determine, in raw terms, what happened to the projects built out during the recent infrastructure boom. The answer was striking. Contrary, perhaps, to the dismal mood in the wake of successive economic shocks and investment controversies, the experience with private investment in IPPs has been quite varied. For investors, projects in Thailand, Malaysia, the Philippines, Turkey, Egypt, Kenya, and certain projects in Brazil and India have seen stable investment outcomes even in the face of considerable stress. For governments, reality has hewn closer to popular perception. Because standard risk allocation for IPPs left country risk with the host governments, a "successful" contract meant that adverse changes in circumstance often increased the local currency cost of electricity substantially, and invited related political and social turmoil. But it has proven possible to craft project arrangements that are robust in difficult circumstances.

A second key goal of the study was to determine whether the innovations of the 1990s, sometimes referred to as the "new international property rights" (and discussed here as "risk engineering"), were effective in addressing the risks of long-term contracting in developing countries. With certain exceptions, the study indicates that these measures were necessary, but not sufficient conditions for success. The reasons for these shortcomings are as varied as the tools themselves, but rest on a common denominator: when stress-tested, ex ante, bright-line protection proved ill-suited to address specific challenges that arose. The myriad vulnerabilities of a power plant—from fuel sources to environmental liability to rising local currency costs during times of macroeconomic shock—provide ample targets for opportunistic pressure. The risk management tools favored by the infrastructure investors of the 1990s—hailing mostly from the Western industrialized nations—enabled a great deal of investment. But their false promise—that in weak institutional settings, risk can be engineered into precise formations that will hold through inevitable crises—has crumbled. In the end, projects that were able to address these vulnerabilities with specific tailored responses, as many were, were more successful.

A third (and related) goal was to add depth to our understanding of these factors. Three broad categories provide the best guide to success and failure. The first includes measures that minimized the exposure of the host country to IPP obligations. While minimizing foreign exchange exposure is important, it is also difficult without sufficiently mature local capital markets.[46] A measure, however, that is more readily accessible is simply limiting the IPP sector to a small share of total generation. The second includes measures to minimize a project's vulnerability to pressure that almost inevitably arrives, including competitive and transparent project procurement to lower prices and forestall suspicions of corruption, and protecting a reliable fuel source (to the extent possible). The third includes measures that maximize the coordination and decision-making capacity of project stakeholders in times of crisis. Among the factors improving host governments' ability to coordinate a response were allowing minimal reforms in the electricity sector, and utilization of a single buyer close to central government reformers; those for private stakeholders included integrating effective partners among local and international constituencies, and keeping incentives aligned to respond to changes in circumstance.

While drawing a clean distinction between practices that depend on "risk engineering" and those that comprise "strategic management" is methodologically cleaner (and necessary for analysis), in practice, the distinction blurs when examining any particular project experience. This conclusion is illustrated, in part, by looking to the participation of prominent international partners. Such partners did have a positive impact on projects' ability to withstand pressure. Anecdotal evidence, however, suggests that this effect was as much for the due diligence in planning potential projects and their ability to facilitate cooperative solutions as for the much anticipated arm-twisting ability that such entities may command. And the core "risk engineering" method—the project finance structure itself—can, when properly structured, enforce the incentives that make strategic management by key stakeholders possible.

In the end, the large early capital outlays and long time horizon necessary to recoup the investment mean that IPPs remain vulnerable to Vernon's classic obsolescing bargain dilemma. Despite this unifying characteristic, outcomes for individual projects have varied considerably. While country characteristics and macroeconomic forces largely determined the level of stress that projects faced, a significant subset of individual projects was able to weather even intense stress and "beat" the curve set by their environment. Will future projects be able to emulate this success? The next section considers the lessons that can be drawn from the 1990s round of private power sector investment.

III. What Is Next for Infrastructure Investment?

The conclusions summarized in the previous section do not translate clearly into action. After all, project developers cannot predict the future, and it is precisely such uncertainty that detailed contracting aims to remedy. And, while hindsight may reveal crucial factors and trends that underlie success, the role of serendipity cannot be denied in explaining why some projects were able to discover favorable ground relative to others once specific risks, out of endless possibilities, actually materialized.

Thus, the question remains: What lessons does recent experience provide that can be used by investors and other stakeholders interested in mutually beneficial infrastructure projects? Near-term investment needs, after all, outstrip any single source of capital—as developing economies grow, demand for new investment will also grow, along with offers of answers to the ever-present need for stability and credible commitments.

This section addresses that question in two parts. The first part explores the role that IPPs may play in the newly reforming electricity sectors in developing countries. The second part explores the ways in which developers evaluating a particular project might directly apply the lessons of the past to evaluating future investment opportunities.

A. *What Are the Limits of the IPP as an Investment Model for Developing Countries?*

The "classic" IPP of the 1990s facilitated enormous capital mobilization for power sector investment in developing countries by providing a risk management framework that foreign sponsors and lenders could stomach. These qualities have not been called into doubt by the experience of the past decade. Rather, by illuminating its drawbacks, recent experience has provided guidance as to the limits of a classic project-finance model for projects in developing countries undergoing a transition from a state-dominated to a privately financed electricity sector. This limitation is illuminated by two interlocking tensions that project architects must navigate more consciously.

First, a project-financed IPP, particularly one supported by a sovereign guarantee, requires a long and sustained repayment period that, from the host country perspective, is more like a debt obligation than prototypical inbound foreign equity investment. These obligations convert country risk—which, to the extent that it affects prices for fuel and other crucial inputs, previously had been absorbed in the massive and nontransparent ledgers of state enterprises and softened with subsidized capital—to hard payments that are essentially "due" to project companies (and which can inflate precipitously when risks are realized). The same rule applies to noncountry specific risks such as financial contagion and fuel price risk. Experts may debate whether it really is more or less expensive to capture this risk in payments to IPPs than to aggregate it on state books. But the real question is not whether private ownership is better; rather, one must understand the circumstances that make private investment an attractive option (and recognize that it is not always so). Indeed, without tackling an array of more fundamental reforms, such as rationalizing tariffs, requiring efficiency from state enterprises, and making accounting practices in fuel markets and in the public sector more transparent (to name a few), private investment is most likely to raise immediate costs, reduce flexibility, and generate controversy.

Unfortunately, the pattern just described was too often the experience of reform and private investment in the 1990s. While leaving country risks with the host country makes theoretical sense, countries often proved unable to manage their "own" risk when it was bundled into hard payments to foreign investors. Private sector enthusiasts now ask whether the risks of the 1990s infrastructure projects exceeded the risk-bearing capacity of the contracts and extracontractual security mechanisms that were commonly deployed. A better question is whether a given project exceeds the risk-bearing capacity of the host government, regardless of the rings of containment arrayed around it. This explains why one of the key benefits of an IPP program—rapidly expanding generation capacity—is limited. The more IPPs, the greater the exposure of the host government or host consumers will be.

Over the long term, the answer to the management of these risks is to reduce them with sustained and meaningful reform. The second major lesson, however, is that the characteristics of successful IPP programs exist in tension with many key tasks of electricity sector reform. The countries that have had the most successful IPP experience have utilized a single-buyer model with long-term contracts, formal or informal guarantees, and substantial risk assumption by the public sector counterparty (notably including fuel supply and price risk). Under these circumstances, investors are able to commit substantial sums, while mitigating the risk premia that otherwise might accrue. But such commitments do not blend well with ongoing reform and liberalization in electricity and fuel markets, which involve tinkering with rules and warring with entrenched interests, and demand that efforts be sustained over many years of uncertainty. Indeed, ongoing reform brings problems for host governments attempting to integrate IPPs into a more liberalized market.[46] It also increases risks for existing projects in myriad ways, from eroding the financial welfare of key state counterparties, to opening the door to political interference in the electricity markets.

These two overlapping tensions suggest that foreign-sponsored IPPs will be limited to a niche role in developing country power grids in the near term. Even so, that niche role may be important. The 1990s-model IPPs proved able to attract investment, along with new technology and managerial expertise to a wide array of countries around the world exhibiting vastly divergent characteristics. With near-term investment needs exceeding any single source of capital, both countries and investors will remain interested in building projects in uncertain conditions. With the limitations on the IPP model in mind, the next section considers how stakeholders can maximize its benefits.

B. Can Foreign Investors Be More "Strategic"?

The question sounds quaint, but is worth asking. The project models developed in the 1990s were highly sophisticated. Investors thought they knew what they were doing then; is there any reason to expect that future investors will be able to do better? The results of the IPP study suggest that the answer is "yes." The body of experience that has been accumulated, studied, and analyzed over the past 15 years offers several lessons that promise to better equip stakeholders to evaluate and plan projects. Rather than presenting a laundry list of brief recommendations, this section is organized around three broad thematic topics.

1. Bidding, Transparency, and Social Risk Part of the problem for IPPs was that they were persistently vulnerable to criticism, whether founded or unfounded, of being too expensive and of being laden with corruption. The social and political pressure that built up around projects, while difficult to tie directly to specific outcomes in all but the most egregious cases, undoubtedly caused substantial problems for both investors and host governments.

Responding effectively to this risk involves two distinct facets. The first is actually pricing projects competitively and transparently. The second is to maintain the appearance of doing so. The two aspects are sometimes difficult to disentangle. Competitive bidding is not always possible, nor does it always secure lower prices. In such cases, some models of direct negotiation have proven successful at lowering prices.[47] But when stress washes over a country, any lack of transparency or of specific prices that appear expensive makes IPPs become large, vulnerable targets.

An important addendum to this point is that, among the myriad benefits according to which an IPP may be measured, cost is dominant for maintaining public support when conditions change. Where government officials have professed a desire for particular characteristics in a power plant at the expense of higher prices, the importance of the "other" benefits often fades from memory quickly. Except where new technology or innovative fuel selection enable cost reductions, the most stable IPPs do not change the electricity sector—they fit within it. This means that IPPs will have to walk a fine line between cost management and investment in the social function that the electricity sector often plays in developing countries, such as provision of low-cost electricity to local communities, environmental protection, and research into new technology.[48] While such policies can be part of a successful risk management strategy (and are often critical, even when times are good), they must remain highly visible.

2. Host Country Governance and Reform To reap the benefits of strategic management practices, stakeholders must draw upon in-depth familiarity with host country institutions. Crucially, stakeholders must recognize the limits of reform and become savvy to its common pitfalls. Power sector reform efforts over the last two decades have almost universally been initiated in response to crisis, either financial or electrical. While the myriad plans, frameworks, regimes, and advisory papers that define a country's reform agenda envision a long-term process, the political needs driving reform are universally short-term. Concomitantly, reform often grinds to a halt when crisis abates and politics reclaim their natural prominence. The result is that reform efforts often end in unpredictable stasis somewhere between the old, state-dominated system and the envisioned private regime. This can be a very uncomfortable environment for private investors who entered early in the process to form the vanguard of reform.

Where electricity sector reforms did meet expectations, at least partially, the determinants of success were reforms *outside* of the electricity sector. In particular, reforms in the judiciary and legal system, public finance, local financial markets generally, and in fuel and labor markets have proved to be crucial elements of successful reform.[49] Experience suggests that, at the margin, these kinds of basic reform—which are notably contrasted to the "textbook" reforms of the 1990s, such as full unbundling, privatization, and establishing competitive generation markets—have also signaled credible commitment to an IPP program. The fact that this experience is marginal is not surprising, given the rarity of successful power sector reforms and the low correlation between IPP investment and reform in any event; the challenge for the future is to build on this experience.

The first area is the extent to which the political will for private infrastructure projects is transformed to a legal obligation, particularly the ability of courts to enforce regulatory decisions. As noted previously, Indian states that have attempted to raise tariffs under the auspices of newly established regulatory commissions have often been successful, in part, because courts have enforced those orders (albeit with long delays). This helps explain why states furthest along in the reform process, such as Andhra Pradesh, have actually reaped the benefits of reform, and similarly have proven most able to sustain IPP commitments.[50] In contrast, the reversal of regulatory decisions during delicate political moments in countries less known for independent courts has been a key driver of IPP disputes.

The second domain is the state of fuel markets, particularly the transparency of reporting and decision making. In country after country, poor information about fuel sources and prices has routinely undermined project outcomes by leading to poor fuel choice, unpredictable supply, and wildly fluctuating prices. This suggests that improvements in financial reporting and transparent fuel source management will benefit electricity reformers and investors by allowing more accurate planning and decision making. In the past, countries that have mitigated such risks have done so largely by bundling all fuel risk into master fuel supply agreements, or by allowing projects to craft unique solutions. So long as domestic fuel markets, and particularly the operations of national oil and gas companies, remain opaque, such measures (which are often drastic) will be necessary. Efforts to combat these tendencies should be seen as evidence of a more credible commitment to sustainable infrastructure investment.

Third, the state of public finance, particularly the ability of host governments to impose hard budget constraints and real capital costs on state enterprises and agencies plays an important role. The accounting games that are common in government bureaucracies make life difficult for new, private, entrants to the market in myriad ways: obscuring the solvency of key counterparties,[51] helping local competitors appear cheap, and, most importantly, holding open a wide window for political interference in the sector. By contrast, where capital is liberalized and hard budget constraints are imposed on state firms, the financial health of crucial counterparties becomes more transparent, and most importantly, the playing field is leveled.[52]

While the technical aspects of sector reform remain important—there are as many ways to get it "wrong" as to get it "right"—investors should look to these related reforms in gauging the likelihood that electricity sector specific measures will be robust. Increased sensitivity to these risks will help investors evaluate better where to invest and will add urgency to the search for more sustainable solutions.

3. Project Governance and Stress IPPs, and any long-lived infrastructure investment, must be structured to respond to changes in circumstance. This adaptability, however, is more operational and financial than contractual. Indeed, the search for a "flexible" contract has, thus far, not turned up viable options. But recognizing the critical importance of clear and precise contracting need not obscure the reality that successful projects have almost universally faced and overcome adverse changes in circumstance by changing fuels and fuel sources, refinancing project debt, accepting some level of deferred payment, and rearranging various project elements in order to approach renegotiation as a give-and-take, rather than a zero-sum game.

The sample of projects examined in the IPP study did not yield strong conclusions as to whether the project finance model is well suited to this task or not. Certainly, precise allocation of risk and responsibility keeps key stakeholders focused on identifying and resolving problems. The bare fact that a majority of the projects in the IPP study changed some significant contractual, financial, or operational terms attests to a robust capacity for adaptation. And the relative rarity of identifiable problems with project structure that locked up under stress[53] further supports this conclusion. But available information does not indicate whether these adjustments were made reasonably efficiently or whether the most effective adjustments were, in fact, made. For now, the lesson for private stakeholders may simply be to avoid problems in project structure (some of which are identified in this paper and in more detail in the larger report on the IPP study).

For host governments, recent IPP experience has provided a rich tapestry of narratives describing how government stakeholders responded to stress. Prominent on this list is identification of project counterparties. In the absence of truly independent and effective regulation—which is notably contingent on an independent and effective judiciary—political will is critical. While a concept as amorphous as "political will" is inherently unpredictable, it may be possible to identify actors more likely to sustain commitments. Such is the case, in part, in China and India's decisions to establish regional offtakers for IPPs that are not tied to provincial or state politics. It is also seen in the Philippines renegotiation, where an incendiary report on IPPs was handed, for implementation purposes, to a body that was populated by private sector professionals and tasked with privatizing the state utility—both features that likely moderated the renegotiation and led to an amicable resolution.

Unfortunately, there is no cookie-cutter recommendation that can summarize these observations. The appropriate project structure and government participation will depend critically on existing institutions and market structure. In some cases, these considerations can be built into a project, while in others innovation after a dispute arises will be the best available option.

IV. Conclusion

The points raised above present an important question: if the "classic" IPP is limited to a niche role as suggested, how can countries get the most out of an IPP program while laying the foundation for an effective transition to investment models that are more sustainable on a large scale? Part of the answer to this question is technical, and comes down to effective reform, both in the electricity sector and in the economy more generally, that reduces risk and increases the availability of local capital. But, even if we understand how such reform might happen, it is worth asking whether current market conditions will encourage these positive and sustained efforts.

Persistent turbulence and politicization in developing country electricity markets have favored actors who are relatively more able and willing to deal with renegotiations and navigate uncertain markets. Increasingly, this means local or foreign developing country firms, along with a small handful of developed country firms that have a long-term commitment to an emerging market presence. Many characteristics of the new actors are laudable, including a long-term commitment to the home or regional markets (with the equally important fact that profits are more likely to remain in the domestic economy), an ability to engage more smoothly in a give-and-take with local government officials, and the ability to navigate the continued churning in electricity and fuel markets that comes with long familiarity. However, the new local actors present some concerns as well. Some of the new appetite for projects may reflect access to concessionary finance that obscures the real cost of capital and the real risks of particular projects. Similarly, much of the new actors' flexibility may reflect different, or looser, accounting rules than those that apply to publicly traded companies in developed countries. Developing country firms' connections with local government may invite suspicions of transparency and corruption similar to those that plagued foreign firms. If the disadvantages of the "new" IPP investor come to outweigh the advantages, the consequences could be difficult; if countries continue to be able to meet short-term investment needs by working with sponsors and lenders with little demand for meaningful reform, the inefficiency and politicization that characterizes the electricity sector in many countries will persist.

This panorama infuses new urgency for sponsors and lenders to become sensitive to the complex realities of reform in developing countries. Specifically, by channeling investment to countries that demonstrate substantive commitment to reform across a range of crucial areas, including public finance, fuel markets, the judiciary, and (within the electricity sector) basic tasks such as raising tariffs. This process will likely unfold as a decentralized search mechanism involving private and public sector actors making self-interested decisions about where to commit resources. But, in contrast to the 1990s, when governments learned that investment would follow a relatively narrow set of specific contract terms, future projects will benefit from incorporating a broader perspective on the relationship between host country conditions, reform efforts, and successful private investment.

By drawing on detailed experience across 13 countries and dozens of projects, the IPP study aimed to produce generalizable conclusions that will guide the architects of future projects in this effort. The IPP study illuminated the persistent turbulence of long-lived infrastructure investment, and in that sense, the picture is not rosy, particularly for foreign investors navigating unfamiliar markets. Nonetheless, new projects will be built to meet ever-growing demand. These projects undoubtedly will rely on new forms of legal and financial engineering to make the risks palatable to lenders and insurers. In the simplest of terms, the basic lesson from recent IPP experience is that these measures cannot stand alone, but must be complemented by a realistic appreciation of the political economy of reform in developing countries, and of the diverse paths to success that prior projects have paved.

Notes

1. Wells and Gleason. 1995. "Is Foreign Infrastructure Investment Still Risky?" *Harvard Business Review* (September/October).

2. International Energy Agency. 2003. *World Energy Investment Outlook 2003,* at 364.

3. See Woodhouse, Erik J. 2005–06. "The Obsolescing Bargain Redux? Foreign Direct Investment in the Electric Power Sector in Developing Countries," 38 *N.Y.U. Journal of International Law and Politics* 121. The study was developed and sponsored by the Program on Energy & Sustainable Development at Stanford University (PESD). The full methodology and results of the IPP study are reported at PESD's website, http://pesd.stanford.edu/ipps.

4. See Woodhouse, supra note 3.

5. The study's approach followed the case study methodology set forth in King, Gary, Robert O. Keohane, and Sidney Verba. 1994. *Designing Social Inquiry: Scientific Inference in Qualitative Research.*

6. Each country displays its own pattern of IPP characteristics in terms of sponsors, fuel, and other arrangements. The task of accounting for individual country characteristics means that not every project-level variable is reflected neatly in each project.

7. More than 200 interviews were conducted in these countries and in the United States, including with host government officials, project sponsors and other equity investors, project advisors and

lenders, academic and civil society representatives, and multilateral officials. Because of the sensitivity of key data and information, interviewees are not identified by name in the text.

8. The raw material from this research is reported in a series of working papers—one paper per country, with appendixes reporting on individually selected projects, along with a series of analytical reports and a stand-alone summary of the countries and projects studied and the outcomes for each project. Each of the working papers is available online at http://pesd.stanford.edu/ipps. A summary of country and project outcomes and brief analysis is presented in Woodhouse, Erik J. 2006. *IPP Study Case Selection and Project Outcomes: An Additional Note*. PESD Working Paper, also available on the PESD website.

9. See Woodhouse, supra note 3.

10. See Woodhouse, supra note 3.

11. See, e.g., Japan Bank for International Cooperation and the World Bank. 2005. *Connecting East Asia: A New Framework for Infrastructure, Joint Study of the Asian Development Bank;* Lovei, Laszlo and Alastair MacKechnie. 2000. "The Costs of Corruption for the Poor—The Energy Sector, Public Policy for the Private Sector." Note No. 207, World Bank, Washington, DC.

12. For example, foreign direct investment generally is less likely to include local partners in countries where corruption is perceived to be widespread. Smarzynska, Beata K. and Shang-Jin Wei. 2000–2006. "Corruption and Composition of Foreign Direct Investment: Firm-Level Evidence." World Bank Working Paper, at 14. IPP investment demonstrates no such pattern.

13. de Oliveira, Adilson. 2006. "The Political Economy of Brazilian Power Sector Reform." In *The Political Economy of Power Sector Reform: The Experiences of Five Major Developing Countries,* ed. David G. Victor and Thomas C. Heller, Cambridge University Press (discussing political pressure backing the Bolivian gas pipeline); Woodhouse, supra note 3 (discussing the decision to allocate naphtha to IPPs); Woo, Pei Yee. 2005. "China's Electric Power Market: The Rise and Fall of IPPs." PESD Working Paper No. 45, at 37.

14 . See Barroso, L.A., B. Flach, R. Kelman, B. Bezerra, S. Binato, J.M. Bressane, and M.V. Pereira. 2005. "Integrated Gas-Electricity Adequacy Planning in Brazil: Technical and Economical Aspects." Paper presented at IEEE General Meeting, San Francisco, June 15–16 (discussing the disconnect between the regulation of natural gas markets and electricity markets in Brazil); Woo, Pei Yee. 2005. "China's Electric Power Market: The Rise and Fall of IPPs." PESD Working Paper No. 45, at 19 (discussing the impact of Chinese coal market instability on IPPs); Woodhouse, supra note 3 (discussing the development of natural gas fields in the Philippines and the impact on IPPs); id. (discussing the challenges of navigating Indian coal, gas, and naphtha markets and the effect on IPPs).

15. Eberhard, Anton, and Katharine Nawaal Gratwick. 2006. *From State to Market and Back Again: Egypt's Experiment with Independent Power Projects*. Managing Infrastructure Reform & Regulation, University of Cape Town, at 23. Available at http://www.gsb.uct.ac.za/mir.

16. Lamech, Ranjit, and Kazim Saeed. 2003. "What International Investors Look for When Investing in Developing Countries." Energy and Mining Sector Board Discussion Paper No. 6 (May), at 9; Price-Waterhouse Coopers. 2005. *Under Pressure* 6.

17. This pattern is observed in several areas of foreign direct investment outside of the power sector. See, e.g., Perry, Amanda. 2000. "An Ideal Legal System for Attracting Foreign Direct Investment? Some Theory and Reality." 15 *Am. U. Int'l L.* Rev. 1627, 1646–48 (illustrating the disparity between theory—that more efficient legal systems will attract and sustain more investment—and reality with a case study of investment in Sri Lanka, and discussing a series of hypotheses that might explain the comfort level of investors in an environment that provides little systemic legal certainty).

18. See, e.g., World Bank. 1994. "Submission and Evaluation of Proposals for Private Power Generation Projects in Developing Countries." IEN Occasional Paper No. 2 , at 6. ("If the basic enabling legislation exists, private projects can be structured, and obligations can be clearly defined and established in contractual agreements between the private power producer, the purchaser of power, and the government.")

19. They did this by ensuring that power plants were dispatched according to short-run marginal cost. A hydroelectric plant, with no fuel cost, has very low short-run costs, but the price of power does not reflect the true cost of building or operating the facility. A thermal plant, by contrast, has short-run marginal costs that reflect fuel prices, and are much higher.

20. Woo, Pei Yee. 2005. "China's Electric Power Market: The Rise and Fall of IPPs." PESD Working Paper No. 45, at 27; and see also Berrah, Noureddine, Ranjit Lamech, and Jianping Zhao. 2001. "Fostering Competition in China's Power Markets." World Bank Discussion Paper No. 416, at 9. Out of three projects reviewed in this study (Miezhouwan, Shandong Zhonghua, and Shajiao C), none has operated pursuant to the terms of the original contract. Tariffs in China are set according to a straight energy payment at a price of fen/kWh to be calculated according to a formula in the power sales agreement—each project has seen this formula disregarded.

21. Victor, David G., and Thomas C. Heller. Conclusion. In *The Political Economy of Power Sector Reform,* supra note 13.

22. Id.

23. Id.

24. See Woodhouse, supra note 3.

25. See Woodhouse, supra note 20 at 22–23 (China); Woodhouse, Erik J. 2005. "The Philippines Electricity Market Investment Context." PESD Working Paper No. 37, the Philippines, at 21–22; Victor & Heller, supra note 21 (Brazil).

26. The tools that comprise this second approach to risk management have been described in a variety of ways. See Moran, Theodore H. 1998. "The Changing Nature of Political Risk." In *Managing International Political Risk,* ed. Theodore H. Moran, 7, 11 (noting the prevalence of "legal and financial" risk management that seeks to price risk appropriately and lock in absolute terms, as opposed to strategic management that seeks to anticipate and reduce risks); Lessard, Donald, and Roger Miller. 2002. "Mapping and Facing the Landscape of Risks." In *The Strategic Management of Large Engineering Projects: Shaping Institutions, Risks, and Governance,* 85–86 (distinguishing between "decisioneering" approaches to risk management, which attempt to calibrate discounted cash flows to predictions about future risk, and "managerial" approaches to risk management, which attempt to "match risks with strategies" in order to "influence outcomes"); See also, Miller, Roger and Xavier Olleros. "Project Shaping as Competitive Advantage." In Miller & Lessard, supra, at 93–112 (arguing that large engineering projects, including power plants, that are successful are not "selected"—i.e., dependent wholly on external variables—but rather are "shaped"—a process that entails constant adaptation, innovation, and adjustment by key managers who understand and react effectively to evolving risks).

27. "Mutual" or "cooperative" renegotiation refers to a renegotiation that does not appear to have a significant financial impact on the project. Use of these terms does not imply that the renegotiation was wholly amicable or pleasant.

28. "Unilateral" renegotiation refers to a renegotiation that is undertaken with substantial government pressure, nonpayment, or other coercion, and which produces a result that has a significant financial impact on the project.

29. These are dominated by projects in Mexico, Turkey, and Egypt, but also include certain projects in Brazil, the Philippines, and Kenya.

30. For a definition of outcomes in the IPP study, see Woodhouse, supra note 3, at 141–43. For a discussion of each project's outcomes, see generally Woodhouse, supra note 8.

31. See, e.g., Wells, Louis T., and Eric Gleason. 1995. "Is Foreign Infrastructure Investment Still Risky?" *Harvard Business Review* (September-October); ("A number of foreign investors in developing countries have sought to involve international institutions in their investments. They believe that a government that acts against a project that includes, say, the International Finance Corporation, recognizes that it risks being cut off from further funds by the World Bank Group").

32. A bump in success rates in managing operational risks for projects with prominent international partners, likely reflects the fact that many of these entities focus substantial attention on ensuring commercial viability in projects they lend to, meaning that dispatch and fuel risk is "managed" in advance.

33. This theme is a familiar one in the foreign direct investment literature. See, e.g., Wells and Gleason, supra note 31; Moran. "Lessons in the Management of International Political Risk from the Natural Resource and Private Infrastructure Sectors." In *Managing International Political Risk,* supra note 26, at 70, 78.

34. The arbitrations are PPN (India), Casecnan (Philippines), and IPTL (Tanzania).

35. For a broad discussion of these problems, see Jenney, Frederick E. 2001. "Breach of Contract Coverage in Infrastructure Projects: Can Investors Afford to Wait for International Arbitration?" In *International Political Risk Management: Exploring New Frontiers* 45, ed. Theodore H. Moran; Kantor, Mark. 2001. "International Project Finance and Arbitration with Public Sector Entities: When is Arbitrability a Fiction?" 24 *Fordham Int'l L. J.* at 1122.

36. See Tanzania Electric Supply Co., Ltd. v. Independent Power Tanzania, Ltd., Case No. ARB/98/8, available at http://www.worldbank.org/icsid/cases/awards.htm.

37. See Woodhouse, Erik J. "The Philippines Electricity Market Investment Context," supra note 25, at A14; Gratwick, Katharine, Rebecca Ghanadan, and Anton Eberhard. 2006. "Generating Power and Controversy: Understanding Tanzania's Independent Power Projects, Managing Infrastructure Reform & Regulation." Working Paper, University of Cape Town, at 21. Available at http://www.gsb.uct.ac.za/mir.

38. See references supra note 26.

39. Albouy, Yves, and Reda Bousba. 1998. "The Impact of IPPs in Developing Countries—Out of the Crisis and Into the Future." Public Policy for the Private Sector Note No. 162, at 6. World Bank, Washington, DC (December).

40. Klein, Michael. 1998. "Infrastructure Concessions—To Auction or Not to Auction?" World Bank Viewpoint Note No. 159, at 2–3.

41. Guasch, J. Luis, Jean-Jacques Laffont, and Stéphane Straub. 2003. "Renegotiation of Concession Contracts in Latin America." World Bank Policy Research Working Paper 3011 (April).

42. Such pricing systems often lead to projects with excessive capital expenditures. This is the well-known Averch-Johnson effect that has been observed in regulated utilities in the United States and elsewhere. Averch, H., and L. L. Johnson. 1962. "Behavior of the Firm Under Regulatory Constraints." *Am. Econ. Rev.* (52, December), at 1053–69.

43. The details of the Spectrum case are related in Lamb, Peter M. 2005. "The Indian Electricity Market: Country Study and Investment Context." PESD Working Paper No. 48, at 44. Available at http://pesd.stanford.edu/ipps.

44. Woodhouse, supra note 3.

45. Woodhouse, supra note 3.

46. See, e.g., Woolf, Fiona, and Jonathan Halpern. 2001. "Integrating Independent Power Producers into Emerging Wholesale Power Markets." Mimeo.

47. In Thailand, the public bidding process was followed by a period of intense direct negotiation. See Woodhouse, supra note 3. Some reports cite Chinese projects as securing low prices via negotiation, although the IPP study did not specifically observe such outcomes (except perhaps where a project was renegotiated). See United States Agency for International Development, Energy Program: South Asia Generation Pricing Study, at 36 (November 2003).

48. Victor, David G., and Thomas C. Heller. Introduction. In *The Political Economy of Power Sector Reform,* supra note 21.

49. Id.

50. Similarly, in Mexico, radical reforms to bolster the independence and efficiency of the judiciary preceded a crucial Supreme Court decision upholding the IPP contracts against constitutional challenge.

51. The general bankruptcy of state electricity utilities is often assumed, but this does not suggest an analysis precise enough to support project design. For example, everyone involved in early privatization efforts in India knew that the state electricity board in Orissa was bankrupt, but investors were nonetheless surprised to learn the extent of the problems—after they had sunk their capital. Rahul Tongia, *The Political Economy of India Power Sector Reforms,* in Victor and Heller, *Political Economy of Reform,* supra note 13.

52. It is more common for local private or state-owned firms to adopt cutting edge management practices and technology while retaining their privileged status as domestic insiders. As local firms have begun to resemble national "champion" companies, foreigners grow increasingly wary—as is the case in China, Thailand, Malaysia, India, and to a certain extent, even Brazil.

53. For a discussion of selected examples, see Woodhouse, supra note 3.

ANNEX 1 Project Details[1]

	Selected Specifications						Sponsors		Outcomes	
Project Name	Country	Fuel	MW	US$M	$/MW	COD[2]	Foreign	Local	Inv't	Dev't
Termoceará	Brazil	Nat'l Gas	290 MW	$100	$345	2001	MDU Resources	EBX Capital	Mixed	Negative
Norte Fluminense	Brazil	Nat'l Gas	780 MW	$887	$1,137	2004	Electricite de France	—	Positive	Mixed
Uruguaiana	Brazil	Nat'l Gas	600 MW	$350	$583	2000	AES Corp.	—	Mixed	Mixed
Caña Brava	Brazil	Hydro	450 MW	$426	$947	2002	Tractebel Energia	—	Positive	Positive
Shajiao C	China	Coal	1,980 MW	$1,870	$944	1996	CEPA → Mirant	Guangdong Gov't	Positive	Mixed
Miezhouwan	China	Coal	724 MW	$755	$1,043	2001	Intergen, El Paso, Lippo	—	Negative	Mixed
Shandong Zhonghua	China	Coal	3,000 MW	$2,200	$733	2003	CLP, EDF	Shandong Gov't	Mixed	Mixed
Sidi Krir	Egypt	Nat'l Gas	685 MW	$418	$610	2002	Intergen	—	Positive	Positive
Suez	Egypt	Nat'l Gas	683 MW	$340	$498	2003	EDF	—	Positive	Positive
Port Said	Egypt	Nat'l Gas	683 MW	$338	$495	2002	EDF	—	Positive	Positive
GVK Jegurupadu	India	Nat'l Gas	216 MW	$261	$1,208	1996	CMS	GVK	Positive	Mixed
Lanco Kondapalli	India	Nat'l Gas	250 MW	$285	$1,140	2000	CDC Globeleq	Lanco	Positive	Mixed
Essar Power	India	Naphtha/Gas	515 MW	$514	$998	1995	—	Essar Steel	Positive	Positive
CLP Paguthan	India	Naphtha/Gas	655 MW	$734	$1,121	1998	Powergen → CLP	—	Mixed	Mixed
PPN	India	Naphtha/Gas	330 MW	$252	$764	2001	El Paso, PSEG, Marubeni	Reddy Group	Negative	Negative
ST-CMS	India	Coal	250 MW	$320	$1,280	2002	CMS	ST Power	Negative	Negative
IberAfrica	Kenya	Diesel	44 MW	$65	$1,477	1997	Union Fenosa	KPLC Pension	Positive	Mixed
Tsavo	Kenya	Diesel	75 MW	$85	$1,133	2001	Cinergy, CDC, Wartsila, IFC	IPS (Agha Khan)	Positive	Mixed

(Continued)

ANNEX 1 Project Details[1] (*Continued*)

	Selected Specifications						Sponsors		Outcomes	
Project Name	Country	Fuel	MW	US$M	$/MW	COD[2]	Foreign	Local	Inv't	Dev't
Monterrey III	Mexico	Nat'l Gas	1,190 MW	$610	$513	2001	Iberdrola	—	Positive	Positive
Rio Bravo II	Mexico	Nat'l Gas	568 MW	$234	$412	2002	EDF	—	Positive	Positive
Merida III	Mexico	Nat'l Gas	530 MW	$260	$491	2000	AES, Nichimen	Grupo Hermes	Positive	Positive
Navotas I	Phil.	Diesel	210 MW	$40	$190	1991	CEPA → Mirant	—	Positive	Positive
Pagbilao	Phil.	Coal	700 MW	$888	$1,269	1996	CEPA → Mirant	—	Positive	Positive
Quezon	Phil.	Coal	460 MW	$895	$1,946	2000	Intergen, Ogden	PMR Resources	Positive	Positive
Casecnan	Phil.	Hydro	140 MW	$495	$3,536	2001	CalEnergy, Peter Kiewit	LA Prairie, San Lorenzo	Mixed	Negative
Cavite	Phil.	Diesel	63 MW	$22	$349	1995	CMS → Covanta	—	Negative	Negative
ENS	Poland	Nat'l Gas	116 MW	$132	$1,138	2000	Enron (Prisma)	JAC International	Positive	Mixed
Elcho	Poland	Coal	220 MW	$324	$1,473	2003	PSEG	EC Chorzow	Mixed	Negative
Songas	Tanzania	Nat'l Gas	190 MW	$130	$684	2004	OTC → AES, IFC, CDC	—	Mixed	Mixed
IPTL	Tanzania	Diesel	100 MW	$127	$1,270	2002	Mechmar	VIP Engineering	Mixed	Mixed
Eastern Power	Thailand	Nat'l Gas	350 MW	$250	$714	2003	Marubeni	GMS	Positive	Positive
Independent Power	Thailand	Nat'l Gas	700 MW	$369	$527	2000	Unocal, Westinghouse	Thai Oil	Positive	Positive
Gebze, Adapazari, Izmir	Turkey	Nat'l Gas	3,860 MW	$2000	$518	2002	Intergen	Enka	Positive	Positive
Trakya Elektrik	Turkey	Nat'l Gas	478 MW	$600	$1,255	1999	Enron (Prisma)	Gama	Positive	Mixed

[1]Full discussions of each project are available in the country studies posted at http://pesd.stanford.edu/ipps. A brief summary of the selection criteria and analysis for each country and project is provided in Woodhouse, Erik J. 2006. "IPP Study Case Selection and Project Outcomes: An Additional Note." PESD Working Paper.
[2]Commercial Operations Date.

AES'S EXPERIENCE IN DEVELOPING COUNTRIES

Jeffery A. Safford
AES

It is usually difficult for me to figure out what the best opening for a presentation or paper might be. Today it is a little easier, but first, as there are forward-looking statements, I need to note certain disclaimers.[1] Opening remarks are a little easier because when I picked up yesterday's, November 2, 2006, emerging markets research report by Bear Stearns, I noticed that it actually summarized well some of the day-to-day issues faced by AES. These include an electricity tariff revision and expansion requirement in Brazil, the importation of electricity to Argentina from Brazil, and challenges faced in respect to the privatization of EDC (Electricidad de Caracas) in República Bolivariana de Venezuela. These are all typical challenges faced by a global power company.

AES, as most of you know, is one of the largest global power companies and, accordingly, we have a strong and broadly spread development pipeline. This means that we are looking to develop businesses in many of the markets that we are discussing here today, existing and new markets. We are developing business not only in our traditional lines of generation and distribution but in new lines of business as well. AES has a strong development pipeline with 10 projects in the engineering and construction phase spanning seven countries, another seven projects spanning five countries in the advanced planning phase, with another 93 projects spanning 32 countries in the early development stage.[2] Therefore, the whole topic of risk assessment and risk management is very important to us.

From a risk perspective, in most situations, AES considers the standard list of structural macro- and microeconomic concerns and drivers. None of these are new to anyone in this business. A country's focus and policies in these areas may not always work in concert with foreign investment, but when properly balanced, it should lead to a least-cost scenario for the country, lower risk premium, enhanced competition, enhanced investment, developed capital markets, and other positive benefits.

We look at many macroeconomic factors, including inflation, GDP growth, foreign exchange reserves, etc. On the judicial side, we look at how the political system functions, the separation of powers, the legal system, the basis of law, and probably the most important and most difficult to find, the swiftness of government processes. Needless to say, we would also look at many tax issues, the incentives for investment and regulatory policies. We look at whether there are transparent and clearly defined rules and regulations; this is often a difficult area for some developing markets. Finally, we would also examine monetary and fiscal policy, corporate law, labor law, the education system, and the pension and health care systems.

As I relate some of AES's experiences, I will more heavily weight my remarks toward Asia and South America, with which I am more familiar. However, in relating some of the lessons or experiences that we have had in various markets, the first one I would note dealt with questions over pertinent requirements in the hearing process where there were allegations made of improper testing or studies being performed and how we conveyed that message. That situation ultimately led to our losing that asset. The interesting thing here is that this happened in the United States on one of our projects in our earlier days, and hence, as we venture into developing markets, when questions arise about political risk, we always recall that operating in the United States is not without risk.

My personal experiences in other places, starting with AES China Generating, where we raised money upfront to invest solely in projects in China, yielded some interesting lessons. First, in order to raise the money upfront, one needed to figure out how to invest those funds and, as one might imagine, there were a lot of gray areas involved in Chinese laws and regulations in the 1990s. We needed to understand how to effectively deal with such a situation.

The other interesting thing about the overall transaction was that we ended up developing a 2,100 MW project called Yangcheng in which we had a minority stake; the project delivered power from a coal site in Shanxi Province to Beijing. This was not something that we would typically have done at that point, but we felt it was an important project from a China policy standpoint. In that project, we learned how to deal and interact with local partners and investors. As we developed more in China, we ended up doing nine projects. As people know, the situation of capacity constraint quickly moved to overcapacity. But our experience in China has, over time and in hindsight, been very good.

We then moved into privatizations in Argentina and Brazil. And thinking back, the Argentine regulatory policies were the ones that were very well designed, very well respected, clear, transparent and well communicated; whereas in Brazil, the policies were less defined and more subject to interpretation, which caused investors to exhibit a tendency to irrational exuberance in the overall process.

We also got into situations where we entered into bridge or short-term financing arrangements, where we were eventually affected by the financial markets because we never were able to look at longer-term arrangements, and needed to renegotiate not only the financing arrangements with the lenders, but also in some situations, arrangements with various government organizations.

Unsolicited tender offers in República Bolivariana de Venezuela and Chile were interesting from the standpoint of learning about their respective legal systems and particularly how their corporate laws and tender offer rules work. At the end of the day, these transactions do not get done without the full support of the government.

Rationing has affected us and demonstrates how market conditions can change rapidly. We have learned from the electricity rationing in Brazil and we could also refer to the gas curtailment situation in Argentina that has affected us both positively and negatively in both Chile and Brazil and in Argentina, as well. Finally, of course, we have all had our experience with macroeconomic shock and sector reforms.

I take away a number of things from all of these experiences. Erik Woodhouse has talked about the obsolescence bargain chip. There was a Cambridge Energy Research Association presentation that referred to this same phenomenon as the capital trap, where Lucy is holding the football for Charlie Brown, and as he runs up to the football, she pulls it away. We have learned quickly that there is a real difference between being committed to these markets vs. being involved. Let's not forget that at breakfast, the pig *is committed* because he *is* the bacon, and the chicken *is involved* because she just provided the eggs. So, we have had to learn how to address challenging situations and figure out how to manage them.

The second thing that we have learned is that the capital markets have a short-term memory of the past, despite what may subsequently happen. Some of the developing markets do tend to come back and, in some cases, come back fairly quickly.

I found Erik Woodhouse's paper to be very intriguing and I would say pretty much right on point with the way AES thinks about things. However, what I came out with based on the paper was that the things that were important, or of concern, are macroeconomic shocks, fuel supply constraints, and other country-level factors. I would stress the importance of project-level factors: changes in market condition, power sector reform, competitive bidding, and robust contracting. These are things that I have grown up learning to concentrate on and what AES focuses on in many situations, particularly in competitive bidding situations. If you are the least-cost producer, you are less likely to be exposed to political pressures. Also, although contracts do not necessarily protect you from everything, the fact that you have a good set of contractual arrangements means that, if you need to, your renegotiation can start from a good basis; this is very, very important.

With respect to country-level factors, we have been exposed to each and every one of those things. Trade policy has affected us, sometimes positively and sometimes negatively, but we have been able to renegotiate or get through those effects. Corruption has not had a significant effect on us.

Let me note one anecdotal story in China with respect to robust contracting. We did nine joint ventures there, and it was ingrained in our heads: "Western contracts. Western contracts. Western contracts." We had many difficulties of translation and communication on the principles. So, when we subsequently encountered our first problem, we sat down with our counterparty and said: "Well, we have terms in the contract," the other party said, "No, that's just the basis of negotiation." This is when you realize your starting point on your renegotiation.

Looking forward, the case for global investment is very clear to AES. The U.S. Energy Information Administration (in its "International Energy Outlook 2005") notes that the growth areas, in terms of energy consumption from the present to 2030, are not primarily in the developed OECD markets, but rather in the emerging markets of Asia, South America, Africa, the Middle East, and Eurasia. As I said before, AES, in particular, is very committed to these developing markets.

The International Energy Agency's "World Energy Outlook" estimates an energy sector market of US$5.5 trillion through 2015, some 61 percent of which is claimed by the electricity sector. AES sees this as a tremendous opportunity to provide that $3 trillion of new generation capacity that is expected.

The other thing, I think, that is significant as we look forward is that there is a new world economic order in the emerging economies. Some of them are no longer borrowers, but rather lenders at this point. Government revenues are growing. Many of them are more financially stable, and many are ripe for political change.

In the developed economies, some countries have become borrowers and not lenders; some are economically stable and others face growing indebtedness; their populations and workforces are aging, and some are struggling with immigration problems; and yet many of them are flush with capital.

Just to illustrate this new world, one can look at the current account balances, or imbalances, over the 1996–2004 period. One can see how the developing markets have become stronger and more financially stable relative to the United States and the euro area. This is reflected as well in the emerging markets bond index, as the premium has come down significantly from its rise, starting with the Mexico "tequila" crisis. Credit quality has clearly improved in many developing countries, but this raises concerns and questions as we look forward.

Broad economic growth together with strong commodity demand is supporting unprecedented financial stability in emerging markets. However, I would suggest that high commodity prices are behind many of the imbalances that we are currently seeing. As the commodity markets fall, that could create some upheavals. Any growth slowdown will transmit to commodity markets, and their fall could potentially stimulate political upheaval. The risk to global imbalances is always potentially destructive. The United States may not be the financial conduit forever and currency crises are far less likely than before, but the bigger question, I think, is the potential for political instability.

From an AES perspective, we will seek to maintain our project finance mentality; that is, we will:

- Focus on the legal, judicial, and regulatory frameworks in the host country and on any reform processes that are underway
- Seek to allocate risk appropriately
- Seek to enter into robust contractual arrangements
- Conduct competitive bids (i.e., be the low-cost provider)
- Utilize multilateral and large international institutions when appropriate
- Utilize local partners, stakeholders, and advisors
- Remain open to balancing all stakeholder interests (i.e., create win-win situations)
- Scrutinize all project opportunities carefully
- Use risk-adjusted return rates (i.e., ones that reflect regulatory uncertainties and other factors)
- Seek to enhance our image, reputation, and customer satisfaction
- Be socially responsible
- Be concerned with governance, ethics, values, and principles.

These are factors that are probably not new to anybody in this room, but it is our focus to maintain our project finance standards. Of course, in order to compete, we will need to figure out different ways to manage our risks and concerns from those we may have used in the past, but this is the basis from which we will start.

Probably the most recent example of maintaining strict project financing standards is at our new greenfield plant in Bulgaria. Maritza is a US$1.4 billion, 670 MW lignite-fired power plant, with strong commercial and financing terms, including a 15-year contract with the national utility, a letter of support from the government, and a 15-year fuel supply agreement. A €790 million nonrecourse financing closed in December 2005 with commercial and multilateral institutions. It should be in service in 2009–10.

Finally, as I said before, AES needs to grow. We think we can do this effectively in developing markets. We believe that we have a good footprint throughout the world. We want to leverage ourselves in markets that we—it's to be hoped—understand better these days, and we are going to focus on three areas from an investor's standpoint: traditional development (greenfield projects, platform expansions, acquisitions, and privatizations); new and adjacent markets (alternative energy and LNG gasification); and portfolio management (asset sales and the sale of minority interests to partners).

Much of this is happening in the United States. But certainly when tapping into new and adjacent markets, given our platform that we have throughout the world, it will also lead us into developing economies. We intend to leverage our market opportunities. We are going to utilize our platform. We are going to think globally and act locally. And I think maybe the most important thing that will help us balance our risks, including some of the political risks, is that we are going to take more of a portfolio management approach, not only selling when prices seem to be high in nonstrategic positions, but also trying to balance our risk portfolio throughout AES globally.

Notes

1. Editors' Note: Mr. Safford noted that certain statements in his presentation and paper regarding AES's business operations may constitute "forward-looking statements." Such forward-looking statements include, but are not limited to, those related to future earnings, growth, and financial and operating performance. Forward-looking statements are not intended to be a guarantee of future results, but instead constitute AES's current expectations based on reasonable assumptions. These assumptions include, but are not limited to, continued normal or better levels of operating performance and electricity demand at our distribution companies, and operational performance at our contract generation businesses consistent with historical levels, as well as achievements of planned productivity improvements and incremental growth from investments at investment levels and rates of return consistent with prior experience. For additional assumptions, see the AES website: www.aes.com. Actual results could differ materially from those projected in AES's forward-looking statements due to risks, uncertainties, and other factors. Important factors that could affect actual results are discussed in AES's filings with the Securities and Exchange Commission, including, but not limited to, the risks discussed under Item 1A, "Risk Factors" in the Company's Annual Report on Form 10K for the year ended December 31, 2005, as well as other SEC filings. AES undertakes no obligation to update or revise any forward-looking statements, whether as a result of new information, future events, or otherwise.

2. Additional information about AES's business activities and performance is available at www.aes.com.

COMMENTARY

Barry Metzger
Baker & McKenzie LLP

I am struck by the contrast in tone between the two presentations.

Jeff Safford's presentation about AES's view is a cautiously optimistic and expansionist view, seeing many new projects and many new opportunities in the emerging markets. I am reminded that several months ago, I was at the Asian Development Bank's annual meetings in Hyderabad and was sitting in on a presentation by an Indian government minister on private investment in the power sector. Having just arrived in Hyderabad after traveling halfway across the world, at one point this sort of jet-lag fog came over me, and I lost my concentration. But then my concentration came back, and I was listening to the minister's presentation. I knew I was in Hyderabad, but I thought it was 1994, hearing what he had to say about Indian government policies to encourage private sector development in the power sector. The Indian government's policies in the early 1990s to encourage private sector development in the power sector had failed, but that history was not being addressed in the renewed efforts to promote new investment in the sector.

In contrast, Erik Woodhouse's presentation is far more cautionary. He is telling us that, as one looks at the experience of the last 10 years of IPPs in the emerging markets, that the record is one of significant losses for sponsors. Project success is a difficult thing to measure unto itself, but by one measure in the study that he reported on, a third of the projects were not successful, at least for the sponsors, and other studies done by the World Bank and other multilateral institutions put that number somewhere around 40 percent.

So, let us look at the new IPP projects to see how they differ from the structure of projects that were being done 10 years ago. What are the lessons that have been learned from earlier project failures that we can actually see in structures and approaches of new projects?

One noteworthy thing is the risk engineering piece—the contractual framework of these projects—actually has changed very little over this period. Probably the most significant element is that far more of the projects are being totally or partially financed in local currency, dealing with the significant problem of a mismatch between foreign currency financings and totally local currency revenues. It is also a reflection of the further development of the local financial markets in many countries that has made this possible. In many emerging markets, financial sector reform has permitted local banks, insurance companies, and pension funds to lend to (and, in some cases, to invest equity in) private sector infrastructure projects. Foreign companies have also gained freer access to local currency borrowings and the interest differentials between local currency borrowings, and borrowings in leading foreign currencies, have narrowed.

But the area where there has been the most change is in terms of what has been referred to as the strategic management of these projects. The most significant change is seen not in the specific contractual terms, but rather in the overall framework of such projects.

First, from the public sector point of view, what we are seeing is more power projects being undertaken in the public sector rather than through private investment. There was a dramatic fall-off in IPP investment after the Asian financial crisis and, in the intervening years, much more is being done in the public sector. This can be seen on the largest scale in China, where a great deal of new capacity is being built in the public sector. But one of the great ironies is that much of that new capacity may ultimately wind up—at least in part—in the private sector, as privatization progresses in the Chinese market.

Governments have learned one of the lessons pointed out by Erik Woodhouse in his study: that too great a reliance on private sector IPP in a country's overall portfolio of generating capacity can make the management of problems in that portfolio difficult in times of stress.

A second element of strategic management is that private sector sponsors are trying to diversify their portfolios over as broad a group of countries as possible, building or balancing portfolios, with a fairly high level of exposure in the developed world to balance emerging market exposure. During the years before the Asian financial crisis, it had been thought that having projects in a number of regional markets was a decent enough diversification, but the contagion of that regional crisis made clear that greater diversification was necessary and many sponsors now believe it prudent to carry only a small proportion of emerging market projects in their power sector portfolios.

But probably what has changed the most in terms of strategic management is the composition or profile of the most active sponsors—the people who are putting equity money at risk. AES remains a very active participant internationally and a significant competitor and yet, as one looks around the world, one sees the significant development of local and regional sponsors—companies from the host emerging market countries and from their neighboring countries. In many cases, such emerging market companies have stepped into the breach as international companies have withdrawn as sponsors. Most prominent among such new sponsors are the national oil companies, who are likely to be the 800-pound gorillas in this space over the years ahead.

An interesting illustration of these developments can be seen in Bolivia. President Morales is not yelling, "Yankees, go home!" If anything, he seems to be yelling, "Brazilians, go home!" because it is Petrobras, Brazil's national oil and gas company, which is the single largest investor in Bolivia's energy industry.

In addition to the change in the profile of emerging market power project sponsors, the profile of the financial investors and lenders who are participating in these projects has changed as well. Many of the international banks that had been active in project finance prior to the Asian crisis are no longer active in the sector, and we are seeing much more of the financing for private sector power projects in emerging markets coming from lenders and other financial institutions in the host countries who are far more comfortable with the political risks in their own country and in neighboring countries.

We also are seeing projects accessing the public markets and retail investors. For about 10 years now, particularly in Hong Kong and Singapore, we have seen listed vehicles that have provided opportunities for investors to invest in infrastructure companies that include power sector assets in their portfolios. We are now seeing similar developments in other markets, such as a recent Korean infrastructure fund listed by Macquarie Bank on the Korean and London Stock Exchanges. Whether one considers this an asset class appropriate for the level of sophistication of retail investors, I leave to the readers' own judgment.

My dominant observation about changes in strategic management of private sector power projects in the emerging markets focuses on the arrival of new players on the scene: as sponsors, as financial investors, and as lenders to projects. With respect to the countries concerned, they have a fundamentally different view of the level of political risk to which they are exposed, and price that political risk in ways that are fundamentally different from those employed by international investors and lenders. It remains to be seen what the impact of that pricing differential is going to be on the competitive position of the international players over a longer period.

One of the points made in the opening remarks of Ms. Omura was the role of the Chinese commitment to infrastructure projects in Africa. Such financing is the modern equivalent—in the context of the geopolitics of energy and commodities—of U.S. and Soviet foreign aid in support of infrastructure development that was part of the earlier geopolitics of the Cold War. One of the things that characterized much of that Cold War-era investment was that it was not driven by an economic analysis of the projects.

We should heed the point that Erik Woodhouse made about the importance of overall power sector reform within a country in terms of the stability of the environment for private sector investment. It may very well be that the new players, with a geopolitical perspective and the national oil companies as new investors, may ultimately create an environment that is less conducive to domestic reform of the power sector and less hospitable to private sector investment.

DISCUSSION OF PRIVATE POWER PROJECTS IN EMERGING MARKETS: NEW MODELS FOR FINANCING AND RISK MANAGEMENT

Symposium Panelists and Participants

The discussion following the Woodhouse and Safford presentations was initially dominated by the issues raised in Barry Metzger's commentary. In particular, the role of the "new players" in power sector investments, local equity and debt investors, was discussed at some length.

Question: I would like to pick up on the point made by Barry Metzger concerning the increased participation by local investors and lenders in power sector projects. I think many of the people who participated in the Dabhol project in India would agree that the participation of a syndicate of Indian banks in the project greatly complicated the resolution of the issues, at least for the foreign bank participants in the project syndicate. Could the panelists elaborate on whether this phenomenon has occurred elsewhere?

Woodhouse: Let me broadly respond to the concerns raised by the question concerning the involvement of local lenders and the involvement of national oil companies, a matter raised by Barry Metzger.

In the IPP study, we observed increased involvement by national oil companies either as local fuel providers or as owners and developers of plants within their own countries and, in some rare instances, outside of their own countries. We also observed increased local participation, whether local lenders, or local sponsors and equity holders. The growing role of these groups does raise some problems.

I noted in my paper that in the 1990s, developed-country investment flowed most often to where the right contract terms were offered, where the right combination of insurance and arbitration were offered, and where the right BITs were available to protect the investment. However, one of the findings was that these measures were not sufficient to support a successful outcome.

So the questions are: What is motivating the new players? What are they looking for?

They are not looking at contracts the same way that Western investors do. The new players, especially the national oil companies, may not be asking for stable markets and transparent decision making in the electricity sector. Their decision-making processes—why they are involved in certain projects—is not clear. Some of them are clearly interested in becoming regional investors and in many cases are rapidly buying or acquiring assets.

It may be that in five to 10 years they will face consequences similar to those Western investors faced in the mid-1990s. When stress washes over the sector again, the flaws in their investments will be revealed. Just as there were challenges hidden under the surface in the mid-1990s when the market for private power projects was booming and the cracks in the system had not yet begun to appear, we will need to understand the challenges hidden under the surface today.

Safford: Let me start by responding to some of the issues raised by Barry Metzger and then turn to other questions.

Barry Metzger noted that, when listening to an Indian government official recently, that it seemed as if he was back in the early 1990s. It is interesting that I actually had a similar experience several weeks ago as we were talking to Indian government officials. The focus was the same as 10 years ago—how to get projects done.

While I was somewhat optimistic in my presentation, I think that there was an underlying message as well that in this new economic order there are some significant risks to achieving as much expansion as we might expect. I think from an AES standpoint, there are certainly opportunities to leverage our capabilities to develop greenfield projects in targeted markets in which we are comfortable. Greenfield projects, I believe, are something that AES does best. There are certainly limited opportunities and there is a great deal of competition out there. However, as I described, we are expanding into different markets, into different types of businesses, and we are quite excited about some of them.

With respect to financing and global partners, we have learned, at least in China, the value of a local partner. The local partner does understand the political risks better. They provide the links on the political side that help you understand and figure out how to negotiate the curves in the road; they may make the difference between operating and not operating in a country. But while local partners are important, they do not necessarily provide all that is needed from a capital perspective, nor are they able to operate those businesses as efficiently as international players.

With respect to local financing, AES, at least in Brazil, has viewed it very positively. Having Brazilian banks involved in the transaction has not in any way disrupted anything. We look to them as partners with respect to our capital needs and possibly in other ways as well.

Metzger: Let me first respond to the question as to whether the involvement of local lenders complicates the process of dealing with troubled projects. I think, inherently, if you have a local bank syndicate and a foreign bank syndicate, the local lenders will always take a different view of political risk, particularly when specific problems arise. Local lenders tend to be more responsive to governmental pressure and more sympathetic to a government's view even in the absence of such pressure. So, yes, those will almost always be complicated situations and the potential for complication should be part of lenders' evaluations of such projects.

Increasingly, we are now seeing projects financed almost totally by local banks (providing both foreign currency and local currency financing) and global bank syndicates led by local banks. Going back to the Asian financial crisis, Thailand and Malaysia probably had the smoothest transition in terms of the renegotiation of power project contracts, and that was largely a reflection of the extent to which local lending institutions and financial investors were involved in those projects. As we look at projects that now have more local financing, there are many projects, including major projects, in which there are no foreign banks involved.

Woodhouse: I will address the matter of local equity holders since Jeff Safford and Barry Metzger have spoken about the role of local lenders. We found in our IPP study across several projects that local equity holders did provide some immediate benefits to foreign sponsors in terms of understanding the complexities of unfamiliar fuel markets and regulatory systems. The observed corporate governance problems or intractable disputes between local and foreign partners were striking, but relatively rare. There may have been some projects that flew under our radar, but we observed four or five cases in our sample where local investors helped the foreign partner decide how to respond to government pressure, whether to arbitrate or negotiate, or how to resolve construction delays or other challenges of that nature.

Question: I am wondering how much of the message of sobriety that comes from Erik Woodhouse's paper might lead investors like AES to think that their past business models are perhaps limited in their ability to respond to changing circumstances.

Is a different business model needed? Perhaps working more intensively with local partners is necessary. It is hard to see what niches exist for the old 1990s model.

Safford: I would not like to go as far as to say that the business model is broken, but that every business model needs to evolve. In AES's situation, we have determined that we need to operate our existing businesses well and to look at pockets of opportunities that are IPP-related, greenfield-related projects. Mergers and acquisitions are probably less likely because of the prices that are currently being paid.

Metzger: There is a certain contradiction or tension that exists between contract flexibility and leverage. We talk about IPP contracts as being long-term relationships with government in which the sponsors need a certain amount of flexibility to adapt to changing economic and political circumstances over time. Yet the reality has been that in limited-recourse, project-financed projects, the contracts make the structure quite brittle and there is not a lot of room for flexibility to deal with changed circumstances.

From one perspective, if one talked to a finance professor, he would say: "Well, more of this stuff should be equity financed and more of the debt should be financed against the balance sheets of the sponsors because this would create more flexibility over time to deal with contingencies and changed circumstances." Yet leverage, and particularly limited recourse leverage, is a very seductive thing. If it is an offer to the project sponsors and they calculate their return on equity investment, the more leverage the better. And there is still a lot of leverage being offered.

One of the key findings of the study that Erik Woodhouse directed is that in the failed IPP projects of the 1990s, the people who took the losses were the equity investors. The lenders, for the most part, received a full recovery of their interests. The problem of failure or horrific renegotiations of IPPs has largely been a story of the de-equitization of the projects. The comment is made in Woodhouse's paper that the ability of the troubled IPP project to continue to service its commercial debt is seen by governments as a hard negotiating constraint in dealing with such projects. Governments are concerned that "nailing it" to commercial lenders might affect other interests of the government in terms of financing projects and financing in the private sector.

There is still a willingness of lenders to participate in highly leveraged projects, and that high amount of leverage on a project-financed basis translates into a degree of brittleness in the structures that makes renegotiations particularly difficult when problems arise.

Woodhouse: With respect to the brittleness of the project financing structure, I noted in my paper that it was relatively rare that negative project outcomes could be directly linked to problems in corporate decision making among stakeholders or other issues. But because those problems reside in some of those delicate areas of project operations, one could not really determine whether the right adjustments had been made in a reasonably efficient manner.

So, while the project-managed structure has proven able to adjust when conditions change, it is not clear whether that is really happening as cost effectively as it could, and it may be that one is underestimating the overall costs in some cases of the adjustments that were made, given the coordination problems that Barry Metzger alluded to.

Question: I have two related comments and questions relating to the strategic management of projects. We have talked about how useful it is to have powerful outside partners who can cast a shadow forward over opportunistic behavior by the host government. What about some other kinds of powerful inside partners, not just the established equity players, but potentially in those countries that have enough institutional capacity, entities like pension funds, social security funds of the military or civil service, and others?

A pension fund trustee might roll his eyes at the idea of putting all pensions into one or two projects in a country, but if one could diversify those investments, perhaps across a region or even internationally, to the kind of securitized assets that Barry Metzger was talking about, might that be a constraint on opportunistic behavior that has not been explored enough here?

My second point is regarding the reform of the regulatory sector. Some work on water privatization suggests that the most stable projects are those where the local water costs have been brought to a market level first. Then, typically by the efficiencies that a private provider can produce, the provider can end up lowering water prices, rather than suddenly bringing up water prices to a market that has been unofficially subsidized. Is there any evidence of this kind of phenomenon in the power sector?

Woodhouse: With respect to the experience of the water privatization, where private investment might go in after the prices have been raised to market levels, the problem is that in the power sector that almost never happens. So, while it might be conceptually promising—and this is one of the points I mentioned earlier—it has rarely happened. If host governments had been successful at raising or rationalizing tariffs and enforcing those regulatory orders in litigation, this is a very credible signal that they will be able to sustain those prices, and then the benefits of foreign or private investment become clearer.

The optics are totally different when the 800-pound gorilla in the room is the foreign or private investor who says we have to raise those tariffs because we are passing through the rising cost of fuel, or the costs of foreign exchange in the aftermath of a currency devaluation. That increase may be critical for having a sustainable private investment program, but the problem in the power sector is that it is extremely rare to actually see that accomplished without serious difficulties.

With respect to involving other prominent actors, such as pension funds, we saw several examples. The first was in Malaysia, where much of the funding for the IPP program came through the state pension fund, and there was a similar case in Kenya. In Malaysia, I think it definitely contributed to an amicable resolution of the problems following the Asian financial crisis, but we did not delve too far into that case because the workout was already accomplished very discreetly and not made public, as far as I could discern. The principal lender and the principal stakeholders across the board were all linked somehow to the government. So they found a solution that was not easy to discern from the outside.

In at least two other instances, pension funds played a large role in deterring host government opportunism. A challenge that a foreign investor faces is that in many countries, while pension funds should have leverage from being so close to the government, this may also mean that the those funds are more amenable to solutions that the foreign investor, particularly a Western investor, would not really desire.

Another point is that I do not think the experience of the last 20 years is going to undermine the value of the project-financed IPP model. It simply illustrated some of the limitations. Contracts certainly are important and will remain so. However, unless one wants to find oneself facing continual renegotiation pressure or cancellation pressure, the focus has to be on the commercial viability of the project, the long-term prospects, and the sustained ability of the host government (or the host consumers and the government), to pay for the project. Alternatively, there may be other strategic ways of placing the project where it will continue to be valuable enough to the host country to deter opportunistic governmental behavior.

So contracts are important, and one cannot attract financing without them. I have not found a promising means for creating a "flexible contract." One renegotiates contracts in the United States all the time. But how does one renegotiate so that the key stakeholders are able to preserve the returns they originally expected?

Safford: I cannot add anything of significance to Erik Woodhouse's comments with respect to contracts. To the extent that one has the standard IPP contracts in place, then one should be able to attract financing. All the parties, whether private lenders, equity holders, national or multilateral entities, need to add something positive to the project initially, as well as subsequently, in the event one needs to renegotiate.

One could end up in situations such as the ones Erik Woodhouse has mentioned, where there is a party in a losing situation, a non-win-win situation, where the government has all the winning cards. So one has to come back to the negotiating table, but when coming back, it is important who is coming along, and who was there initially. Depending on what the renegotiation is about, the partners may be the key to a satisfactory resolution.

With respect to the involvement of pension plans, I also agree with what Erik Woodhouse has said. With reference to Brazil in particular, I think it is an attractive idea to pool some of the pension fund money, but because interest rates have been so high, it would be difficult. Pension funds are more typically geared toward just investing in higher yielding debt securities.

Finally, I have a last comment on raising tariffs, if I am interpreting the question correctly. It is the regulator's job to keep rates down, to make sure that the entity that is operating the concession or the plant itself does so in a cost-effective and efficient fashion. The reality is that negotiating a raise in tariffs is always going to be a challenge in any location.

Metzger: On the point of pension fund investors, another recent example would be the Korean private equity infrastructure fund managed by Darby that closed about the same time as Macquarie floated its Korean infrastructure fund. In Darby's fund, the lead investor was the Korean social security system; the other investors included a large number of other Korean institutions.

But more broadly, the phenomenon that we are seeing of local banks, local insurance companies, and local pension funds in the emerging markets becoming involved in private investment and lending to infrastructure including power, is, in part, a tribute to reforms that the World Bank, the Asian Development Bank (ADB), and the other multinationals have encouraged in the financial sectors of many of these countries. Historically, these local financial institutions had been required to invest heavily in government securities—and often in government securities alone. The categories of permitted investments and the levels of permitted lending to private infrastructure projects and to public-private partnership projects have increased, making it possible for these institutions to play a more significant role in private infrastructure financing.

Finally, there is yet another dimension of pension funds, namely investments by American and European pension funds investing their citizens' pensions in private infrastructure projects in emerging markets. Ms. Omura referred to the role of monoline insurers earlier. While pension funds in the developed world have been very modest investors on the equity side in private infrastructure, internationally they are becoming far more involved on the debt side, with monolines "wrapping" debt instruments coming out of private infrastructure projects, including private power projects. They are taking unrated project debt and, through the monolines, bringing it up to AAA status and placing it in the portfolios of conservative pension funds that—it's to be hoped—are going to pay for our retirement.

Part Three

THE CHALLENGE OF MANAGING REGULATORY RISK

OVERVIEW

Theodore H. Moran and Gerald T. West
Editors

Leading off on this topic, Peter Choharis, an experienced Washington lawyer, argues in "Regulatory Takings Under International Law: A Brief Legal and Practical Guide," that foreign investors have some good news when it comes to the law protecting their property against government interference. But, he concludes, international law should still be a last resort for those who want results quickly and efficiently.

Emerging from long debate there is widespread agreement, Choharis suggests, that international law does protect foreign investors against unlawful regulatory actions that deprive them of their property rights. These regulatory actions are referred to as "regulatory takings," because they take away property rights even though the government refrains from taking possession of the property itself as would happen in a traditional expropriation.

But there is still considerable uncertainty, he asserts, about the nature of the property rights, about what government acts are now permitted, about rationales that might excuse government actions with regard to property rights, and about how much property loss must occur to qualify as an unlawful taking under international law. At the same time, there are procedural difficulties that hinder legal solutions. Even bilateral investment treaties between the investor's home and the host country for the investment that specify mandatory arbitration may result in drawn-out, costly, public arbitral processes. The possible participation of third parties adds more challenges, and the competence of the arbitrators cannot be taken for granted.

Choharis begins by reviewing some treaties and arbitral decisions that address regulatory takings in the context of international law. While they try to offer guidance for analyzing regulatory takings under international law, they are, in fact, far from adequate. They exhibit weaknesses in research, reasoning, and exposition, and lead to even greater uncertainty about basic legal issues surrounding expropriation.

To be sure, he points out, treaties must always be rather general, but recent efforts to provide more specifics are also deficient. These efforts should be given credit for helping to establish that there are international protections against regulatory takings, even though they do not provide clear guidance on the nature and extent of those protections.

The United States, with its strong history of protecting private property and vast legal community, has generated a substantial body of law dealing with regulatory takings. Nonetheless, U.S. jurisprudence covering regulatory takings remains unclear, with many inconsistencies—well acknowledged by U.S. Supreme Court justices themselves. Recent U.S. government attempts to incorporate U.S. jurisprudence on regulatory takings into international treaties suffer from grave deficiencies (an argument that is elaborated in the discussion section).

Choharis aims at responding to the uncertain status of international legal protections for foreign-owned property on both substantive and procedural levels. On substance, he outlines a new analytical approach for judging government interference of foreign-owned property under international law. Beneath detailed examination of many specific factors, he offers a three-part test that addresses: (i) the property rights at issue, (ii) the relevant government actions, and (iii) the degree of property loss. If the foreign property owner established that host authorities have interfered with recognized property rights, the next step is to determine whether, in the particular circumstances of the case, the government's actions are allowed under international law. If they are not, then the issue becomes whether the loss suffered by the property owner was large enough to justify compensation.

Turning to procedure, Choharis recommends that foreign investors take preemptive action to block or reduce host government interference with their operations. He examines why approaches typically chosen by international lawyers—such as relying on local foreign counsel or resorting hastily to international arbitration—may not work out well. He concludes by suggesting "nonlegal" measures to preempt or settle disputes at low cost, quickly, and discreetly.

In "Are You in Good Hands with Your Insurance Company? Regulatory Expropriation and Political Risk Insurance Policies," Mark Kantor, a former partner at Milbank, Tweed, Hadley & McCloy, LLP, who teaches at Georgetown University Law Center and serves as an arbitrator, continues by noting that claims of regulatory expropriation have gained visibility as countries shift from state-owned enterprises toward state regulation of privatized (or partially privatized) enterprises.

Kantor draws attention to the specific provisions of a PRI policy and asks: "Is the regulatory expropriation claim covered by the policy?" The answer is far from clear. Kantor joins Choharis in observing that the very definition of "regulatory expropriation" remains the subject of much discussion, as do the related concepts of "indirect expropriation" and "creeping" expropriation." Therefore, the scope of coverage of a PRI policy in this area starts from an uncertain base. In addition, PRI policies typically contain confidentiality provisions and dispute resolution clauses calling for private arbitration proceedings. As a result, little practical information exists about the claims practices of PRI insurers with respect to regulatory expropriation claims. Only OPIC makes publicly available its claims determinations and related arbitration rulings, and other insurers do not feel bound to follow OPIC's practices.

Kantor employs provisions from an illustrative private political insurance policy (his "sample private policy") to explore a number of coverage provisions to determine the kinds of arguments a claim of regulatory expropriation may face. With respect to a PRI policy's scope of expropriation cover, common definitions of the term "expropriation" itself give rise to a number of issues. Some policies cover only affirmative acts by the host government ("acts or series of acts"), while others, such as the MIGA Contract of Guarantee, expressly cover "inaction" as well. Coverage of failures to act may, of course, be affected by whether the host government had a duty to take action in the circumstances. The definition of "expropriation" in many PRI policies may also call for "total cessation" of an investment's "operations." A company may suffer severe losses by virtue of the government's regulatory conduct, but its operations may continue to limp forward. Thus, the host government's conduct may rise to the level of a "deprivation" of "fundamental rights" or "effective control," as called for by some PRI policies, but not "total cessation" as required by the text of other policies. The interpretation of these provisions is made even more difficult if the company in question is a start-up or development-phase business; has it begun "operations" within the meaning of the PRI clause?

PRI policies also differ in how they treat multiple sources of causation and ultimate causates—what caused the injury suffered by the covered investment? Kantor's sample private policy requires that an insured's loss be caused "*principally* and directly" by the expropriation. In contrast, other PRI policies may require the loss to be caused "*solely* and directly" by the expropriatory event. Since alleged expropriations often occur within the context of larger economic, political, and social change, the causation standard set forth in the PRI policy will be crucial in deciding whether a claim will be successful. The causation issue, of course, arises in both the scope of cover and policy exclusion provisions. Common exclusions in PRI policies include those for "provocative acts" by the insured and "financial default" by the covered investment.

These exclusions, Kantor suggests, create difficult questions of "which came first, the provocative act/financial default or the expropriatory conduct?" Resolving these causation issues will be affected in significant measure by the standard of causation set out in the policy itself. The very definition of "host government" in the PRI policy may also be controversial. If a state enterprise has legal authority or practical control over access to essential "network" assets such as a pipeline, an electricity transmission line, or a telecommunications interconnection system, is the state enterprise acting as a commercial party or as a state authority when setting the terms for access by the covered investment to the asset? That interpretive problem will be exacerbated in transition economies where state officials may have moved into corporate positions, or sit on the supervisory board of a partially privatized, state-controlled enterprise.

Regulatory expropriation claims also pose especially difficult questions under the exclusions from coverage found in policies, notes Kantor. PRI policies typically exclude losses caused by a failure of the investor or investment to comply with host government law or permitting requirements. Yet, regulatory expropriations will often constitute instances of "creeping expropriation." At some point during that process of "creep," the covered enterprise may have fallen out of compliance with host government requirements—is that sufficient, Kantor asks, to trigger the policy exclusion, even if it later becomes apparent that the circumstances were part of the conduct that matured into an expropriation over time? Also, PRI insurers often divide coverage into expropriation and state breach of contract. Some, like OPIC, hold that state breach of contract can, in the appropriate situation, rise to the level of an expropriation under international law and the policy. Others exclude from their PRI policies "a material breach by the host government of any contractual agreement with the insured or the foreign enterprise."

Cause and effect come into play here too, Kantor points out: if the expropriatory conduct has caused the breach of contract, or if the breach constituted the expropriatory act, is the loss still excluded by the language of the policy exclusion? In addition, the distinction between commercial and governmental functions is also important. For example, the MIGA Contract of Guarantee excludes from coverage circumstances where the host government is "acting in a commercial capacity." If the distinction between "commercial" conduct and "governmental" conduct of a host government entity is not employed in the "contracts" exclusion, Kantor notes, then regulatory expropriation claims involving concession contracts and other investment agreements may be excluded from cover merely because the government's obligations were embodied in a contract. More generally, both international law and PRI policies treat acts by the host government in a commercial, rather than governmental, capacity as outside the scope of compensable expropriations. Some insurers, like OPIC (as reflected in its *Bank of America, as Trustee*, claims determination involving the Dabhol power project), focus on the capacity in which the host government acted, not the motives underlying the government's actions. Therefore, a state's expropriatory motive effected by means of the commercial capacity of a state-owned enterprise would be excluded from expropriation coverage. However, an arbitral panel reviewing a separate OPIC claims determination involving Dabhol (brought by GE and Bechtel as equity investors) rejected that view. The arbitrators held instead that the government's motives were properly considered in determining if the conduct of the Indian government was a covered expropriation. This issue remains unresolved, since arbitral awards are not binding precedents for other disputes.

PRI policies, Kantor observes, also customarily contain exclusions for bona fide nondiscriminatory acts that a government normally takes in the public interest. Examples often cited of such bona fide acts include regulating economic activity, ensuring public safety and health, raising revenue, and protecting the environment. The potential conflict between a regulatory expropriation claim and the exclusion for bona fide nondiscriminatory acts is obvious. PRI policies do not, however, always employ the same terms to describe this exclusion. The MIGA Contract of Guarantee, for instance, limits the bona fide exclusion if the host government has "designed" the measure to have a confiscatory effect. Kantor's sample private policy, on the other hand, does not contain a similar limitation. Indeed, international investment law does not always offer a consistent description of the principle of bona fide nondiscriminatory governmental acts. The U.S. Model Bilateral Investment Treaty, illustratively, says that the exclusion does not apply "except in rare circumstances," perhaps drawing on U.S. Supreme Court experiences with the analogous "takings clause" of the U.S. Constitution.

In addition to scope of coverage issues and potentially applicable policy exclusions, Kantor points out, PRI policies also contain covenants for the insured to disclose information about circumstances that could give rise to losses under the policy and to minimize losses. Failure to comply with these obligations entitles the insurer to terminate coverage. To what extent must an insured disclose the inevitable regulatory uncertainties and ambiguities unearthed in the process of developing a project? And how does the insured balance the obligation to minimize losses with its other obligations in the PRI policy, such as the obligation to avoid provocative acts? There are no simple answers to these and similar questions, Kantor concludes, and therefore a candid conversation between insurer and insured is a prudent course of action before issuance of the policy.

Like his predecessors, Frederick "Rick" Jenney, of Morrison & Foerster LLP, observes, in "A Sword in a Stone: Problems (and a Few Proposed Solutions) Regarding Political Risk Insurance Coverage of Regulatory Takings," that investors in developing countries face the constant threat of regulatory change, which in extreme cases can constitute a type of expropriation known as a "regulatory taking."

Jenney explains that political risk insurers have always intended to cover wrongful regulatory takings, but not legitimate takings. He notes that, unfortunately for the PRI industry, it is extremely difficult to find an appropriate legal standard that distinguishes between "wrongful" and "legitimate" government regulatory actions.

Because an insurer that pays an expropriation claim must have a corresponding claim back against the host government, argues Jenney, it is crucial for a political risk insurer who wants to cover a regulatory taking that the host government regulatory action be a violation of international law. Normal change of law is not an insurable event, because it is not a wrongful action under international law. Legitimate regulatory actions do not give rise to a right of recovery against the government; if they did, no government could afford to make changes to a regulatory regime.

In practice, it is difficult to draw the line between normal regulation and a regulatory taking, observes Jenney, and claims can be determined only on a case-by-case basis. But a recent series of North American Free Trade Agreement (NAFTA) and BIT cases have developed new theories of regulatory takings under international law, based on such concepts as inducement and breach of representation by the host country, investors' legitimate expectations, and breach of the duty of "fair and equitable treatment."

Jenney concludes that the challenge for political risk insurers is: (i) for a regulatory action to be insurable, it must be compensable by the host government; (ii) for it to be compensable it must be wrongful, as opposed to legitimate; (iii) the only workable definition of "wrongful" is that it be a violation of international law; and (iv) international law on the subject is hopelessly vague, inconsistent, evolving, political, and (ultimately) unclear.

Jenney sets out five principles for political risk insurers to consider in covering regulatory takings. First, to be insurable, a regulatory action must be a violation of international law. The amount that an insurer pays as a claim gives must rise to an equal right of recovery against the host government. Second, political risk insurers should not be put in a position of having to determine whether a regulatory action is a violation of international law. If arbitral tribunals cannot draw a clear line, it is unreasonable to expect political risk insurers to do so.

Third, investors should get no more than they bargained for at the beginning. Investors who fail to structure their arrangements with the host government to protect against regulatory change in a highly regulated industry should not expect to turn to their insurers to compensate them for a normal business risk that they could have anticipated.

Fourth, for investor rights to be protected by insurers, they must be protected by the host government. Investment agreements and stabilization clauses, which are agreements by the government to compensate the investor for the consequences to it of changes in the law or the investment regime (for example by exempting the enterprise from tax increases, whether legitimate or not), have existed in the international investment world for years.

Fifth, where a host government has made an agreement in a concession or a contract, arbitral award default coverage, which ensures payment by the host government of an arbitral award, is available to backstop enforcement of that agreement. In this coverage, it is the arbitral panel, not the political risk insurer, that determines that the host government has wrongfully breached a stabilization clause in an investment agreement and what the damages are.

From these principles, Jenney offers three possible solutions for the PRI industry:

- First, insurers could provide arbitral award default coverage of contractual stabilization clauses. For political risk insurers, international arbitration also serves to sort out the political actions of the host government from its legitimate contractual claims. Arbitral panels can sort out fact-specific questions with respect to regulation, including in connection with investment agreements containing stabilization clauses protecting against the effects of regulatory changes.
- Second, insurers could provide arbitral award default coverage for other international arbitral awards. Jenney suggests that political risk insurers could use arbitral award default coverage more broadly to cover awards resulting from international arbitrations arising from treaties, rather than from direct agreements with the host government. International arbitral awards, including those arising from treaty-based disputes, have the force of law and are enforceable without judicial review, and so are generally insurable.
- Finally, insurers and insured investors (or brokers) could establish a standing pool of regulatory takings experts who would be available to address international law issues, drawn from the large (and growing) group of international arbitrators and other experts specializing in the area. Such international law experts, concludes Jenney, should be in the best position to draw the line between legitimate regulation and wrongful regulatory taking, avoiding some of the steep learning curve in analyzing regulatory takings.

REGULATORY TAKINGS UNDER INTERNATIONAL LAW: A BRIEF LEGAL AND PRACTICAL GUIDE

Peter Charles Choharis[1]
Principal, Choharis Global Solutions

Executive Summary[2]

Foreign investors have some good news when it comes to the law protecting their property against government interference. However, international law should still be a last resort for those who want results quickly and efficiently.

After decades of debate, there is now a strong consensus that international law does protect against unlawful government actions that deprive foreign investors of their property rights. Such government actions are commonly called "regulatory takings," because they deprive owners of their property rights even though the government does not seize the property outright as in traditional expropriations.

So much for the good news. Unfortunately for investors, there is still a lot of uncertainty about what kind of property rights are protected; what kind of government actions are impermissible; how exigent circumstances may justify government interference with property rights; and the amount of property loss necessary to comprise an unlawful expropriation under international law. Beyond the uncertainty over substantive international law, there are also serious procedural obstacles to seeking legal redress. Even when an investment treaty between the foreign investor's country and the host country provides for mandatory arbitration, international arbitrations have become increasingly time-consuming, expensive, and public. In some cases, third parties can participate, further complicating the process—and, of course, the quality of arbitrators continues to vary to an uncomfortable degree.

The first part of this paper identifies some treaties and arbitral decisions that recognize regulatory takings under international law. However, although some of these authorities have tried to provide guidance for analyzing regulatory takings under international law, they have fallen short. Many arbitral decisions are disappointing in terms of research, reasoning, and writing—yielding more, not less, uncertainty about fundamental legal issues governing expropriation. And while treaties by their nature must be general, recent attempts to provide greater guidance have also fallen short. Still, these authorities should be credited for helping to establish that there are indeed international legal protections against regulatory takings, even as they have left the nature and extent of those protections uncertain.

Not surprisingly, with huge numbers of lawyers and a strong tradition of protecting private property, the United States has developed a substantial body of law governing regulatory takings. Yet, for all of the sophistication of U.S. courts and the legal bar, U.S. jurisprudence on regulatory takings remains unclear, inconsistent, and ad hoc—as a number of Supreme Court justices have candidly admitted. Accordingly, the second part of this paper argues that recent American attempts to incorporate U.S. regulatory takings jurisprudence into international treaties are ill-advised and will be counterproductive.

The remaining two parts of this paper provide a substantive and procedural response to the uncertain state of international legal protections for foreign-owned property.

Substantively, the third part sets forth a rough outline of a new analytical approach for evaluating governmental interference of foreign-owned property under international law. Although it is fairly detailed with respect to the specific factors it takes into account, this framework is basically a three-part test that examines: (i) the property rights at issue; (ii) the relevant government actions; and (iii) the degree of property loss. In brief, if a foreign property owner establishes that a host government has interfered with recognized property rights, then the inquiry shifts to whether, under the circumstances, the government's actions were permissible under international law. If not, the question then becomes whether the property loss was severe enough to warrant compensation.

Procedurally, the fourth part argues that foreign investors should consider preemptive action to prevent or minimize government interference with their investments. It explains why traditional international lawyers' approaches—like overly relying on local foreign counsel or too quickly resorting to international arbitration—can be inappropriate. It then presents a "nonlegal" approach to preempt or resolve disputes quickly, discreetly, and cost effectively.

1. *There Is No Current Consensus on the International Law of Regulatory Takings*

1.1 U.S. Regulatory Takings In the United States, the Supreme Court long ago recognized that legislation or regulation that has the effect of "appropriating or destroying" property is the constitutional equivalent of a taking, and thereby warrants compensation.[3] Subsequently, the Court has made clear that there is a "per se" taking—meaning that compensation is due and no further analysis is necessary—where the regulation or legislation has deprived the property owner of *all economically viable* use.[4]

Where there is less than a complete taking, the Supreme Court, in *Penn Central*, identified three factors "that have particular significance."[5] Although the Court emphasized that there is no "set formula," subsequent courts and many international arbitrators have reduced *Penn Central* to a three-part test: (i) the economic impact of the regulation; (ii) the owner's reasonable investment-backed expectations; and (iii) the character of the regulatory action.[6]

1.2 International Law The recognition of regulatory takings under international law has developed more recently. In the 1960s and 1970s, a few scholars argued that international law should recognize "indirect" expropriations as well as direct seizures, but there were few authorities to buttress their arguments.[7] Eventually, however, scholars, arbitrators, bilateral treaties, and then multilateral treaties began to recognize that governments may expropriate the property of foreign investors both by outright seizures and by indirect measures that were tantamount to a seizure. For example, Article 1110 of NAFTA, January 1, 1994, provides that "[n]o Party may directly or indirectly nationalize or expropriate an investment of an investor of another Party in its territory or take a measure tantamount to nationalization or expropriation of such an investment," unless the government's action is: (1) for a public purpose; (2) is nondiscriminatory; (3) meets due process of law and minimum treatment accorded to the government's own nationals; and (4) pays compensation fully, promptly, and in a convertible currency.[8] The Central America-Dominican Republic-United States Free Trade Agreement (CAFTA), signed August 5, 2004,[9] and modern U.S. BITs contain similar provisions. Nor is this view purely an American one. For example, the 1994 European Energy Charter Treaty, to which the United States is not a signatory, similarly requires compensation for investments "nationalized, expropriated or subjected to a measure or measures having effect equivalent to nationalization or expropriation."[10]

1.3 NAFTA Cases While these treaties helped establish that a regulation, legislation, or other government action may constitute an expropriation in violation of international law, it was far from clear when such a "measure [was] tantamount to nationalization or expropriation."

A handful of NAFTA cases have tested the boundaries of government regulatory authority. Under Chapter 11, foreign investors may challenge regulatory measures that impair the value of their property before international tribunals.[11] Although NAFTA directs that the international tribunal's governing law shall be the NAFTA Agreement as well as "applicable rules of international law,"[12] it is unclear whether arbitral decisions assessing the regulatory regimes of three advanced, industrial economies are applicable to less developed countries. In fact, the deference that most NAFTA tribunals have accorded the Mexican, Canadian, and American governments with respect to their regulatory prerogatives is not commonly shared by other tribunals assessing the behavior of emerging market countries. Nonetheless, because NAFTA arbitral decisions are public and among the most recent decisions addressing regulatory takings under international law, a brief review of a few cases will identify some doctrinal developments as well as shortcomings.

The *Metalclad* case involved a local Mexican government that refused to grant a hazardous waste landfill permit to a Delaware corporation that had received assurances from the Mexican federal government that it could proceed with operations. Subsequent to those assurances, the governor declared the area an ecological preserve and Metalclad sued for damages.[13]

As a preliminary matter, the tribunal affirmed that NAFTA recognized a regulatory taking as an expropriation under NAFTA's Article 1110:

> expropriation . . . includes not only open, deliberate and acknowledged takings of property, such as outright seizure or formal obligatory transfer of title in favor of the host state, but also covert or incidental interference with the use of property which has the effect of depriving the owner, in whole or in significant part, of the use of reasonably-to-be-expected economic benefit of a property even if not necessarily to the obvious benefit of the host State.[14]

The particular claims of the case, however, concerned when a government's denial of an investors' reasonable investment-backed expectations was expropriatory. Because the Mexican federal government had represented to the claimant that it met all of the requirements necessary to construct and operate a landfill, and because the municipal government had denied the claimant a construction permit without a good faith basis relating to the site or construction, the Mexican authorities "effectively and unlawfully prevented the Claimant's operation of the landfill."[15] Because the actions of the Mexican authorities resulted in the "complete frustration" of the claimant's operation of the landfill and "negate[d] the possibility of *any meaningful return* of Metalclad's investment," the tribunal held the Mexican government liable for $17 million.[16]

The *Pope & Talbot* decision addressed both discrimination and the degree of loss necessary to be compensable.[17] In that case, an American lumber company alleged that Canada's allocation of softwood export quotas constituted an expropriation as well as violated other NAFTA provisions. The United States and Canada had entered into the Canada-U.S. Softwood Lumber Agreement, which governed softwood export quotas. The claimant alleged that Canada's administration of that agreement, specifically its quota allocations, discriminated against it (and its Canadian subsidiary) relative to other softwood producers, thereby unfairly limiting its access to U.S. markets, or, as Pope & Talbot phrased it, "deprived [it] of its ordinary ability to alienate its product to its traditional and natural market."[18] In an interim decision, the tribunal dismissed the expropriation claim.[19] Initially, the tribunal made a highly questionable holding that "access to the U.S. market is a property interest subject to protection under Article 1110."[20] The tribunal then recognized that regulatory takings can be a violation of international law: "Regulations can indeed be exercised in a way that would constitute creeping expropriation. . . . Indeed, much creeping expropriation could be conducted by regulation, and a blanket exception for regulatory measures would create a gaping loophole in international protections against expropriation."[21] However, the tribunal held that there was no regulatory expropriation because there was no "substantial deprivation" of Pope & Talbot's property rights, since a partial loss of profits was not sufficient.[22]

In *S.D. Myers*, a more restrictive standard of regulatory takings was announced, holding that government regulation, while not immune from liability, enjoyed a presumption in favor of legality:

"The general body of precedent usually does not treat regulatory action as amounting to expropriation. Regulatory conduct by public authorities is unlikely to be the subject of legitimate complaint under Article 1110 of the NAFTA, although the tribunal does not rule out that possibility."[23]

Explaining this deferential standard, the tribunal stated, "expropriations tend to involve the deprivation of ownership rights; regulations a lesser interference."[24] Although this reason merely restates a factual test that a claimant's property loss must be complete or close to it, from this, the tribunal announced a general principle of regulatory takings that would insulate most governments from such claims: "The distinction between expropriation and regulation screens out most potential cases of complaints concerning economic intervention by the state and reduces the risk that governments will be subject to claims as they go about their business of managing public affairs."[25]

As discussed below, there is no internationally recognized rule that all value must be lost in order for an expropriation under international law to occur. Indeed, there is no such rule in U.S. jurisprudence, where one federal circuit court has repeatedly recognized partial takings. Nonetheless, even though there is no res judicata generally under international law, and even though NAFTA tribunals are not bound by previous tribunal precedents, *S.D. Myers* clearly intended to shut down most NAFTA regulatory takings claims.

1.4 U.S. BITs and CAFTA Despite *S.D. Myers*'s attempt to limit regulatory challenges, the NAFTA experience of the parties led the U.S. government to two conclusions. First, the treaty language still left substantial uncertainty with respect to the substantive elements of a regulatory taking. Second, claims were being brought for what many considered to be reasonable regulatory actions.[26] In response, the U.S. State Department, with the assistance of the U.S. Department of Justice, adopted an audacious strategy: take the three "significant" factors from *Penn Central*, convert them into a three-part test, and then call the test part of customary international law. Not only would the *Penn Central* "test" add some substantive specificity, it would also discourage claims by erecting a high barrier.

As a result, Article 6 of the 2004 U.S. Model BIT and Article 10.7.1 of CAFTA reproduce the NAFTA definition of direct and indirect expropriations, with the four exceptions that will render the government action permissible. But in addition, Annex B of the 2004 Model BIT and Annex 10-C(4) of CAFTA go further, adding the three *Penn Central* factors:

> [An] indirect expropriation [is] where an action or series of actions by a Party has an effect equivalent to direct expropriation without formal transfer of title or outright seizure.
>
> (a) The determination of whether an action or series of actions by a Party, in a specific fact situation, constitutes an indirect expropriation requires a case-by-case, fact-based inquiry that considers, among other factors:
>
> (i) the economic impact of the government action, although the fact that an action or series of actions by a Party has an adverse effect on the economic value of an investment, standing alone, does not establish that an indirect expropriation has occurred;
>
> (ii) the extent to which the government action interferes with distinct, reasonable investment-backed expectations; and
>
> (iii) the character of the government action.

And lest the intent of the United States to limit regulatory takings claims by incorporating the *Penn Central* factors be missed, both Annex B of the 2004 Model U.S. BIT and Annex 10-C(4) of CAFTA contain this further proviso:

> (b) Except in rare circumstances, non-discriminatory regulatory actions by a Party that are designed and applied to protect legitimate public welfare objectives, such as public health, safety, and the environment, do not constitute indirect expropriations.

2. Penn Central *Is Not, and Should Not Be, International Law*

The aspiration of the United States to bring greater clarity to the international law of expropriation governing regulatory takings is laudable. And U.S. government officials undertook that effort pursuant to Congress's directive that U.S. investment treaties provide foreign investors with private property protections against U.S. government regulatory takings that are no greater than the protections provided by the United States Constitution.[27] One must be sympathetic to those charged with fulfilling that congressional mandate in the absence of a well-established international standard. Unfortunately, the U.S. government's strategy of incorporating the *Penn Central* factors in subsequent international treaties is misconceived.

2.1 Not International Law The language of both CAFTA and the 2004 U.S. Model BIT seems to say that the standards that they establish reflect customary international law. CAFTA Annex 10-C says, "The Parties confirm their shared understanding that: 1. Article 10.7.1 is intended to reflect customary international law concerning the obligation of States with respect to expropriation." Similarly, the 2004 U.S. Model BIT, Annex A says, "The Parties confirm their shared understanding that 'customary international law' generally and as specifically referenced in . . . Annex B ["Expropriation"] results from a general and consistent practice of States that they follow from a sense of legal obligation."

If the United States and specific trading partners wish to establish treaty-based standards governing expropriation, and specifically regulatory takings, they are free to do so. But to suggest that their approach to regulatory takings reflects customary international law is simply untenable.[28] If, on the other hand, the United States is trying to make *Penn Central* into customary international law, that approach is unwise. For one thing, arbitral tribunals that must interpret these treaties are now stuck with having to decide what the "customary international" law of regulatory takings is, and then whether to apply that law or U.S. jurisprudence interpreting the *Penn Central* factors. For another, even after decades of case law, many issues under the U.S. *Penn Central* jurisprudence remain unclear or unresolved.[29] Emulating *Penn Central* will hardly advance the interests of foreign investors or host countries—though it will prove a boon for the international legal profession.[30]

2.2 Uncertain and Ad Hoc From the start, the U.S. Supreme Court has been quite clear that the three *Penn Central* factors require an "essentially ad hoc, factual inquiry."[31] And to be fair, both CAFTA and the 2004 U.S. Model BIT recognize this.[32] While there is nothing wrong with factual inquiries—after all, both courts and arbitral tribunals are experienced at fact-finding—there are a host of issues that remain unclear or unresolved as to the meaning of these three factors. As Justice John Paul Stevens has observed, "Even the wisest of lawyers would have to acknowledge great uncertainty about the scope of this Court's takings jurisprudence."[33] As a result, rather than promote the development of a coherent body of international law, this uncertainty will likely retard it, with tribunals struggling to interpret factors that have confused and divided U.S. courts for years.

To take one example, on the threshold issue of how much loss is necessary in order to make out a regulatory takings claim, U.S. courts are divided. Subsequent to *Penn Central* and its application of the multifactor test for "partial" (not per se) regulatory takings, the Supreme Court has declined to find a taking in any case where the property owner's loss was less than total.[34] Although the Court has never established a bright-line test as it has with per se (total) deprivations, in *Lucas* it suggested that 95 percent would likely qualify.[35] Similarly, the Second Circuit and the district courts in that circuit uniformly hold that, in order to establish a regulatory taking, the plaintiff must show either that the regulatory imposition has deprived it of *all* economically viable use of its property, or that the regulation does not advance legitimate state interests.[36]

By contrast, unlike the traditional takings jurisprudence articulated by *Penn Central* and followed for the most part by the Second and other Circuit Courts, the takings decisions by the Federal Circuit and the Court of Federal Claims have occasionally indicated that *partial* takings may be compensable. The number of cases that have so held, however, is limited.[37]

To take another example, a second basic question that is also the subject of great confusion is how to identify the "property" that has allegedly been taken—sometimes referred to as the "denominator" or "remainder" problem—especially after the property-holder has taken steps to modify the property interests. As Justice Antonin Scalia noted, "the rhetorical force of our 'deprivation of all economically feasible use' rule is greater than its precision, since the rule does not make clear the 'property interest' against which the loss of value is to be measured."[38] This issue is difficult in realty takings; in regulatory takings, it can be especially thorny.

Given the uncertainty of U.S. takings jurisprudence about such basic questions, it would be prudent at least to explore a different approach when trying to formulate international legal standards.

3. *A New Analytical Approach*

One of the deep-rooted problems with U.S. regulatory takings law is that it has evolved from realty takings jurisprudence. This is understandable in the United States, where both common law constraints and the need for a constitutional textual basis led to imperfect judicial metaphors to graft one kind of takings law onto another.[39] But international law is not, and need not be, so constrained. Recent U.S. efforts to shoehorn realty concepts and multiprong tests onto regulatory takings analyses in international law should be rejected.

The following is a rough outline of how to evaluate whether a governmental action constitutes an expropriation (regulatory taking) under international law. This approach would be suitable for an arbitral tribunal to consider, or for incorporation in an investment treaty or PRI policy. If incorporated in PRI coverage, this analytical approach to regulatory takings can be modified to reflect the particulars of an industry, country-specific regulatory risks, or deal-specific considerations.

3.1 Property Interests While Western legal writers usually refer to a "bundle" of property rights without explaining which specific sticks comprise that bundle, in the foreign direct investment context, investors are mainly concerned with five basic rights: (i) title, (ii) management and control, (iii) exclusivity—the ability to prevent others from using or having access to property without permission, (iv) profit or return on investment, and (v) alienability—the ability to sell, barter, give, bequeath, or otherwise exchange or dispose of property, including converting profits to freely traded currency at a reasonable or market rate.[40] In order for there to be a regulatory taking under international law, then, a governmental action must impair one or more of these rights.

3.2 Kinds of Government Interference Although a regulatory taking may take a variety of forms, there are three broad requisites for it to be expropriatory under international law: (1) the alleged expropriatory action or failure to act must be by a state actor; (2) the state actor must be acting pursuant to state authority; and (3) the state actor must be performing an exclusively governmental function—either legislative, adjudicative, administrative, or (in some cases) investigative.[41] If the government or government instrumentality acts pursuant to its market powers, just as a private, commercial actor might, then its actions are not expropriatory in violation of international law.

3.3 Degree and Kind of Loss or Property Interference Recognizing that foreign investors hold multiple property rights, two questions arise: (i) how many of these rights must be affected by state action, and (ii) to what degree must the government interfere with these rights in order to amount to an expropriation in violation of international law?

How to draw the line both with respect to the number of property rights and the amount of loss has challenged triers of fact for decades. Most arbitrators[42] and U.S. courts[43] have held that total or near-total deprivation of all property rights or—in what may be a different way of measuring the deprivation—of the property's value is necessary for there to be an expropriation or taking. This approach has significant advantages. Triers of fact need not parse through all the different kinds of "rights" that a particular property may or may not possess.[44] Similarly, they can avoid having to speculate on the value of one or more such rights. And requiring a near-total loss of value is an easy line to draw, both in evidentiary terms for proving the loss and conceptually in order to avoid a slippery-slope critique.

I explore a different approach: deprivation of all property interests is unnecessary in order for there to be an expropriation under international law; complete deprivation of one property right may be sufficient.[45] Similarly, a partial deprivation of one or more property interests that collectively is severe may be sufficient, depending on the number of property rights and the degree of deprivation. Finally, a complete deprivation of value would amount to a per se expropriation warranting compensation, as it would under U.S. constitutional law.

3.4 Discrimination against Foreign Investors? Although not necessary in order to establish an expropriation claim under international law, discrimination against a foreign investor is a strong indicator that the government's actions or inactions violated international law. Thus, although this fourth element is not required to make a regulatory takings claim, proving discrimination would go a long way toward prevailing.

How should a trier of fact determine whether a government's actions or omissions were discriminatory toward foreign investors? As I have done in an earlier law review article,[46] I argue that discrimination should be measured both by intent and effect. But even if the government's action is discriminatory, there may be affirmative defenses available. I further argue that discrimination is an indicium of, but not a requirement for, expropriation under international law.[47]

As explained in Part 4.1, if the foreign property owner establishes discrimination and no affirmative defenses are available to justify that discrimination, then the host country must show that its actions were taken in response to an emergency, or to achieve important systemic reforms in order to evade liability.

4. A Shifting Burden, but a Limited Inquiry

If a foreign property owner can meet the first three criteria above, then the owner has made out a prima facie case that a host government has interfered with a property interest protected by international law. The burden of proof then shifts to the host country to show that its actions fell within one or more of the permissible types of governmental interference with property rights.

Although the government has the burden of proof, this does *not* mean that the government must justify its actions, or establish that the public benefits outweigh the private deprivation. The Restatement (Third)[48] and other authorities direct that triers of fact inquire into the "purpose" of the government's actions in order to assess whether they are permissible under international law.[49] Others, and I, have argued that such an inquiry is both impractical and inappropriate.[50] Moreover, triers of fact should stay clear of any *Lochner*-type inquiry that evaluates the substantive merits of government policy.[51] Rather, the government need only prove that its actions were of the kind that fall within one of the three types: (i) a general regulatory measure; (ii) a response to a grave public need or emergency; or (iii) a systemic reform. It need not demonstrate the wisdom or value of its actions. Rather, if the government has acted within one of these broad frameworks, then its actions are permissible unless there is a total deprivation of value, that is, unless there is a "per se" taking.

4.1 General Regulatory Action General regulatory action is in many ways the flip side of the discrimination inquiry. If the foreign property owner establishes discrimination and the host country cannot establish an affirmative defense, then the host country will not be able to show that its actions were pursuant to a general regulatory framework. If, however, there is no showing by a claimant of discrimination, then the host country can try to show that its actions were pursuant to a general regulatory scheme.

Thus, absent discrimination, a governmental action that diminishes a foreign investor's property rights may still be permissible if taken as part of the sovereign's general police powers.[52] In other words, if the state action is pursuant to a general regulatory scheme that "adjusts the benefits and burdens of society," then it is generally permissible under international law, provided the government complied with due process of law. Court and arbitral decisions often hold that there is no regulatory taking when a sovereign acts to protect the public health, safety, or welfare. However, government action should be designed to minimize the intrusiveness of the property rights of foreign investors.

4.2 Grave Public Need or Emergency Even if not pursuant to a general regulatory framework, a government action that responds to a grave public need or emergency is afforded substantial deference under international law.[53]

4.3 Systemic Reforms There is not much international law on this subject, but its importance seems likely to increase as the World Bank and other institutions aggressively pursue government reforms as part of their agenda.[54] I argue that, to the extent not covered by a general regulatory framework analysis, sovereigns may pursue systemic reforms, even at the expense of foreign investors, in order to foster transparency, competition, privatization, market efficiency, and to fight corruption. This is particularly important in the deregulation context.[55]

If a foreign investor-claimant prevails on the first three (or four) factors, and the host country is unable to prevail on any of the last three factors, then compensation is required. (If there has been a total deprivation, compensation is also required.)

4.4 Compensation Required Finally, triers of fact must measure the type[56] and degree of property rights deprivation,[57] and determine how to calculate damages based on this loss. U.S. courts interpreting international law have not yet developed a consensus regarding the appropriate standard of compensation or method of valuation under international law.[58] However, these American cases are anachronistic, because the international law governing compensation has developed substantially and largely reached consensus. The old international debate between developing countries and capital exporting countries regarding valuation methods and compensation standards[59] has largely disappeared due to the demise of communist and socialist constructions of international law;[60] developing countries' pursuit of foreign investment;[61] and the rise of multinational corporations in some of the leading, formerly less developed countries, such as China and India, that have now evolved into foreign investors themselves.

As a result, international law recognizes that restitutio in integrum, or full restitution, is now the standard of compensation required.[62] In the words of Professor Elihu Lauterpacht of Cambridge University, international law has evolved so that there is an "increasingly wide acknowledgment that the proper standard of compensation to be paid upon the taking of foreign property is that of prompt, adequate and effective compensation," i.e., the traditional standard under the Hull Doctrine.[63]

5. When Things Go Bad, Don't Just Call a Lawyer

5.1 Shortcomings of Traditional Dispute Resolution Foreign investors face numerous problems if they rely exclusively on traditional dispute resolution mechanisms—litigation or arbitration—in order to protect or recover the value of their investments. Litigation may not be available because there is no effective forum—whether in the investor's own jurisdiction or in the host country. Arbitration may not be available where there is no contractual basis or BIT. Even if a forum is available, both arbitration and litigation can be time-consuming, expensive, intrusive, and uncertain. Foreign investors may also suffer severe opportunity costs while consumed with resolving disputes through conventional methods.

And, as discussed above, either the absence or lack of clarity of the international law governing regulatory takings makes arbitration and litigation uncertain.[64]

5.2 Alternative Strategy: Politics, Information, Coalitions ("PIC") Instead of just hiring the largest law firm in the host country's capital city and hoping for the best, foreign investors need to construct a comprehensive strategy to protect their interests. A "PIC" approach offers a number of advantages: greater speed, more privacy, and often better results. In addition, it can sometimes enhance legal claims if the dispute is not resolved.

By contrast, relying solely on overseas legal counsel to resolve disputes may present numerous limitations, including (i) inability—inexperience or a lack of capacity to assemble the appropriate resources to obtain (or even seek) redress from the host government or private parties (NB: "government relations" practices are practically unheard of in emerging markets); (ii) regional limitations—no contacts or relevant experience in the region in which the controversy exists; and (iii) personal limitations—lawyers and other professionals from the capital city may come from different groups, castes, clans, or tribes that predominate at the investment site.

The specifics of the particular strategy will depend on the nature of the dispute, the relevant parties, and the ultimate goal. The dispute could be a nonperforming loan, a distressed equity investment, a contractual dispute, a threatened adverse governmental action, etc. There may also be significant labor, environmental, or even human rights—so-called Corporate Social Responsibility (CSR)—components to an investment dispute. Finally, the goal can be financial, business, or governmental in nature: refinancing, restructuring, selling, partial payment, capping losses, limiting future liability, retaining reputational integrity, repealing regulation, obtaining tax exemption, permit approval, etc.

Throughout the process, investors should seek opportunities to enhance the potential for prosecuting claims—both substantively (e.g., additional claims such as denial of due process or denial of minimum standards), and procedurally (e.g., obtaining information as an alternative to formal discovery)—in case the dispute is unresolved. At the same time, investors must not compromise any potential legal remedies, for example, through inadvertent waiver.

5.2.1 Political and Regulatory Context—Develop Deep Understanding. In addition to the specifics of the immediate dispute, governments (and their bureaucracies) have larger political agendas and constraints into which a particular dispute fits. As a result, foreign investments and related disputes have different political profiles and raise different levels and types of local and national sensitivities. Opposition parties may be a source of information, leverage, or antagonism. The regulatory framework, including competing and overlapping jurisdictions, may present unexpected opportunities as well as perils. Regulatory reforms—including those in other industries—may also offer opportunities. The role of multilateral organizations in the host country's development agenda must also be understood. Local counsel usually can assist with some, but not all, of these issues. But understanding a host country's larger political framework—including the constraints imposed by foreign actors—is just as important as understanding the particulars of a dispute.

5.2.2 Information and Knowledge—Develop Broad Sources. To develop full understanding of the dispute and possible avenues of redress, a full range of information should be tapped, knowledge sought, and erudition cultivated. Sources include public and private, traditional and nontraditional. Depending on the host country, rather than the investor's own embassy, other countries' embassies may be more informed and better advocates. Foreign governments may also be engaged directly, rather than through their embassies, if warranted. In addition to lawyers in the host country, other professionals that may be able to assist include former diplomats, business executives, and former legislators and judges. Where available, private investigators may also be helpful. Contacts with U.S. and other intelligence agencies can sometimes be engaged.

Local counsel may be quite limited in its ability to tap many of these resources. The very common assumption that local counsel is best positioned to develop information, or provide the broader context on which to base a strategy is misplaced. Rather, depending on the type of challenge, foreigners may be much better positioned to assemble a broader and more detailed understanding of the problem and possible solutions.

5.2.3 Coalitions—Develop Powerful Coalitions. Coalitions may sometimes be of great value, whether formal or informal, public or private. Whether because of inexperience, lack of key contacts, or political sensitivities, local counsel is very often poorly positioned to assemble and deploy coalitions effectively. With greater access to foreign and even some host country institutions, and unencumbered by local political and cultural restraints or other clients' interests, foreigners are almost always better positioned to develop and utilize coalitions in emerging markets. Foreign entities that may be part of a coalition—or a subgroup of a coalition—include multilateral agencies, other foreign investors, embassies, rating agencies, and media. Local elements of a coalition might include host country banks, local chambers of commerce, industry allies, customers, suppliers, trade unions, and local media.

5.3 Case Studies The first three of these case studies are based on my experience representing one of the parties in the dispute. I have changed certain facts in order to protect client confidentiality. The last is a current dispute on which I have advised third parties.

5.3.1 West African Country Accused of "Expropriating" Property by Failing to Provide Adequate Police Protection and Judicial Due Process A U.S. investor entered into a joint venture in a regulated industry with a foreign national who had decades of experience in a West African country. After assisting in obtaining the necessary licenses, the foreign national allegedly defrauded the U.S. investor, and used the lower courts of the host country to assume control over the joint venture's books, bank accounts, and assets. Furthermore, the foreign national allegedly occupied the joint venture's headquarters, removing money, computers, and documents while the local police observed. Other facilities were also plundered before the foreign investor could obtain court authority for police protection. The U.S. investor alleged that the host country failed to protect its property, failed to arrest the foreign national, and failed to provide due process when it initially ruled in favor of the foreign national's claim of corporate ownership. There was no BIT available.

The U.S. investor threatened litigation in U.S. courts, and publicly accused the host country of an unlawful expropriation, to no avail. What other avenues were open to create leverage and achieve a satisfactory resolution? In order to develop leverage, the American investor could investigate whether the host country was receiving U.S. Africa Growth and Opportunity Act (AGOA) benefits, Millennium Challenge loans, USAID assistance, and U.S. and other arms sales. The host country's debt rating and political risk index were other sources of leverage. With upcoming national elections, opposition parties and press could provide further leverage. Alternatively, party officials of the ruling party might provide assistance. With respect to facilities outside of the capital city, local tribal and government leaders could also be recruited for help. Seeking support from other foreign investors, and their embassies, could also be helpful. Parallel with developing a leverage strategy, the U.S. investor could develop an exit strategy that did not require a financial expenditure from the host government, and certainly not an admission of liability. For example, with appropriate government guarantees and OPIC or other financing, the former joint venture could be recapitalized and rehabilitated. The American investor's former equity interest might be converted to secured debt or sold.

5.3.2 Central American Country Considers Adopting Mass Tort Legislation Targeting U.S. Pesticide Manufacturers and Plantation Owners Encouraged by U.S. plaintiffs' lawyers and their local counterparts, a Central American country considered changing its laws to adopt U.S.-style mass tort legislation for use against U.S. pesticide manufacturers and U.S. plantation owners. The American manufacturers and plantation owners maintained that, among other things, the legislation would be discriminatory, deny them minimum standards, and represent a regulatory taking. No BIT was available for bringing an arbitral challenge. But even if there were a BIT, for business reasons, the companies could not wait for the legislation to pass, lawsuits to be filed, and adverse verdicts to be entered so that damages could then be challenged. It was also questionable whether the manufacturers and plantation owners would prevail in challenging enforcement of the foreign judgments. How else might they protect themselves?

One strategy was to reinstitute lawsuits that had been dismissed in U.S. courts under forum non conveniens, thereby negating any need for plaintiffs' lawyers to proceed overseas. But a parallel strategy in the host country was also available. A coalition of constitutional scholars and retired Supreme Court justices in the host country could be recruited to opine on the constitutionality of the proposed legislation. Opposition party members and press could investigate the role of foreign plaintiffs' lawyers in promoting the legislation. Private investigators, the press, and even U.S. law enforcement might investigate whether any "corruption" had occurred with respect to influencing foreign legislators. On a different tack, local health facilities could be supported to treat directly the alleged tort victims, who would otherwise have to wait years for assistance. Local attorneys could explore settlements with potential claimants in order to provide for their families. And local families employed by the plantation owners could be recruited to oppose the legislation.

5.3.3 South Asian Country's Civil and Criminal Investigation A U.S. investment firm entered into a joint venture agreement with the first and largest mutual fund in a South Asian country. In return for providing marketing, management, and investment expertise, the U.S. firm would share in a portion of the foreign fund's profits. The president of the U.S. firm also agreed to serve on the board of directors of the foreign mutual fund, although he never attended any meetings. Less than a year later, before the U.S. firm had provided any significant assistance, the head of the foreign mutual fund embezzled hundreds of millions of U.S. dollars. The equivalent of the South Asian country's Securities and Exchange Commission began a civil and criminal investigation. Aware of a prior, high-profile precedent that held a U.S. company and its president criminally liable for a tort accident, the U.S. firm was worried that it would be used as a scapegoat to divert blame and reimburse investors. It wished to squelch an investigation as quickly and quietly as possible.

Due to a memorandum of understanding between the South Asian country and the United States to provide mutual assistance in criminal investigations, as well as to U.S. case law on enforcement of foreign subpoenas, the U.S. firm faced substantial hurdles to blocking witness and document subpoenas from the South

Asian agency. However, it would have been possible, as a peremptory strike, to inform agency officials that efforts to scapegoat the U.S. firm could expose the agency's own policing failures of the mutual fund. The firm could have also exposed the generally inadequate regulatory oversight of the South Asian agency. If need be, influential local financial writers and political observers could have been enlisted to highlight the government's failures with respect to policing the country's capital markets, as well as the shortcomings in the country's general regulatory regime governing financial institutions.

5.3.4 East African "Regranting" of Oil Exploration Licenses After a European company ("A") received a license to explore a substantial tract of oil and gas fields from the national government, a provincial government granted another European company ("B") licenses to explore many of the same fields. Members of the provincial government received substantial equity in B, and promptly passed local laws banning officers of A from conducting any activities in the region. Relations between the provincial and national governments were very tense, with a history of ethnic, religious, and tribal tension, and outright armed conflict. Moreover, the respective jurisdictions of the regional and national governments were not clear after a reconciliation agreement provided for shared responsibility for economic development.

Readers may consider: What are A's options? And what are the options for B?

6. *Conclusion*

International legal protections against government interference of foreign investors' property rights have improved. At a fundamental level, there is now widespread, though not yet universal, recognition that certain kinds of "regulatory" conduct—whether legislative, administrative, or otherwise—can constitute an expropriation in violation of international law. But the absence of any consensus on how to analyze whether such an expropriation has occurred has led the United States government to promote an American approach that is riddled with problems. As a result, even when foreign investors do have access to a mandatory arbitration process to resolve investment disputes, they still must face a substantive body of law that is either undefined or—in the case of recent U.S. investment treaties—conceptually flawed. In either case, international law offers a chance for relief—but not quick, inexpensive, or certain relief. Prudent foreign investors should consider earlier intervention to preempt disputes or mitigate damages before resorting to arbitration or litigation. When deals cannot be restructured, foreign investors need to develop a comprehensive strategy that extends far beyond the traditional role of local counsel to influence government behavior.

Notes

1. The author is also a Visiting Scholar at The George Washington University Law School. He wishes to thank Dean Susan Karamanian and the GW Law School for their generous support of his academic research and writing.

2. This paper is based on a longer, forthcoming law review article on the international law of regulatory takings. Some arbitral, scholarly, and even U.S. court authorities refer to "regulatory takings" and "creeping expropriations" as synonymous. I distinguish between the two, and limit "creeping expropriations" to discrete government actions that individually may not amount to an expropriation but that collectively may.

3. *Pennsylvania Coal Co. v. Mahon,* 260 U.S. 393, 415 (1922).

4. See *Lucas v. South Carolina Coastal Council,* 505 U.S. 1003, 1015 (1992).

5. *Penn Central Transp. Co. v. City of New York,* 438 U.S. 104, 124 (1978).

6. For a while after *Penn Central,* the Supreme Court developed a related inquiry—examining the legitimacy of the regulation—to determine whether a taking has occurred. *See Agins v. City of Tiburon,* 447 U.S. 255, 261 (1980) (imposing the requirement that the regulations at issue "substantially advance legitimate governmental goals" and requiring an "essential nexus" between the governmental interest at stake and the regulatory means utilized by the government); *Nollan v. California Coastal Comm'n,* 483 U.S. 825, 837 (1987) (same); *Dolan v. City of Tigard,* 512 U.S. 374, 391 (1994) (refining this legitimacy inquiry to require that the regulatory exaction be "roughly proportional" to the anticipated effect of the proposed development).

However, the Court recently abrogated this approach and held that "the 'substantially advances' formula announced in *Agins* is not a valid method of identifying regulatory takings for which the Fifth Amendment requires just compensation." *Lingle v. Chevron U.S.A., Inc.,* 544 U.S. 528, 545 (2005). The Court distinguished a takings analysis, which focuses on the magnitude or character of the burden on private property and how the burden is distributed among property holders, from a due process analysis, which focuses on "whether a regulation of private property is *effective* in achieving some legitimate public purpose." *Id.* at 541. While a due process challenge to a government burden on private property is subject to the very deferential "arbitrary or irrational" standard, *id.,* the Court affirmed that the Due Process clause provides an opportunity for U.S. courts to conduct a substantive review of government regulation.

7. See, e.g., Weston, Burns H. 1975–1976. "'Constructive Takings' Under International Law: A Modest Foray into the Problem of 'Creeping Expropriation'." 16 *Va. J. Int'l. L.* 103; Christie, G.C. 1962. "What Constitutes a Taking of Property Under International Law?" 38 *Brit. Y.B. Int'l L.* 307.

8. See North American Free Trade Agreement, NAFTA Secretariat, available at http://www.nafta-sec-alena.org/DefaultSite/legal/index.

9. Available at http://www.ustr.gov/assets/Trade_Agreements/Bilateral/CAFTA/CAFTA-DR_Final_Texts/asset_upload_file328_4718.pdf.

10. Energy Charter Treaty, Dec. 17, 1994, art. 13(1), 34 I.L.M. 360, 391.

11. In addition to "expropriation" claims (Article 1110), investors also frequently bring claims for denial of National Treatment (Article 1102), Minimum Standards of Treatment (Article 1105), and other NAFTA causes of action.

12. Article 1131(1). See Article 102(2) (providing that the Agreement be interpreted and applied "in light of its objectives . . . and in accordance with applicable rules of international law").

13. See *Metalclad Corporation and United Mexican States,* I.C.S.I.D. Case No. ARB(AF)/97/1, Award (Aug. 30, 2000) available at http://www.worldbank.org/icsid/cases/mm-award-e.pdf.

14. Id. at Par. 103, p. 195.

15. Par. 106, at 195.

16. Par. 113, at 197 (emphasis added).

17. See Statement of Claim, *Pope & Talbot, Inc. and Government of Canada,* Mar. 25, 1999, Pars. 10–11, available at http://www.appletonlaw.com/cases/STATEMENT%20OF%20CLAIM.pdf.

18. Id. at Par. 93–94.

19. Interim Award, *Pope & Talbot Inc. and the Government of Canada,* June 26, 2000, available at http://www.appletonlaw.com/cases/P&T-INTERIM%20AWARD.PDF. This interim award denied the Claimant's expropriation claim under Art. 1110. A subsequent award, Award on the Merits of Phase 2, April 10, 2002, found Canada liable for violation of Art. 1105 (fair and equitable treatment). Subsequent to that, the Award in Respect of Damages awarded the Claimant more than US$461,000 plus interest.

20. Id. at Par. 96. Although the ability to alienate property without undue restraint is traditionally recognized as a property right under international law, that is very different from market access constituting a property interest. The tribunal did not identify the source of this novel property right. If such a right does exist, it would have to be based in NAFTA alone, not customary international law.

21. Id. at Par. 99. In doing so, the tribunal rejected Canada's argument that its regulations were legitimate as a matter of law and thus immune from an expropriation claim.

22. Id. at Par. 102.

23. *S.D. Myers and Canada,* Partial Award, November 13, 2000, at Par. 281. *Available at http://www.dfait-maeci.gc.ca/tna-nac/documents/myersvcanadapartialaward_final_13-11-00.pdf.* The tribunal did, however, find violations of Article 1102 (National Treatment) and Article 1105 (Minimum Standards of Treatment, interpreted as fair and equitable treatment).

24. Id. at Par. 282.

25. Id. at Par. 282.

26. Numerous NAFTA critics feared that a flood of NAFTA challenges would undermine the ability of the party countries to protect their environments and otherwise promote the safety and welfare of their citizens. See, e.g., Been, Vicki, and Joel C. Beauvais. 2003. "The Global Fifth Amendment? NAFTA's Investment Protections and the Misguided Quest for an International 'Regulatory Takings' Doctrine." 78 *N.Y.U. L. Rev.* 30.

27. See Bipartisan Trade Promotion Authority Act of 2002, 19 U.S.C.A. § 3802(b)(3) & (D) (2002) (recognizing among the "principal negotiating objectives of the United States regarding foreign investment" that "foreign investors in the United States are not accorded greater substantive rights with respect to investment protections than United States investors in the United States, and to secure for investors rights comparable to those that would be available under the United States legal principles and practices" by among other things "seeking to establish standards for expropriation and compensation for expropriation, consistent with United States legal principles and practice. . . .").

28. See, e.g., Been & Beauvais, 78 *N.Y.U. L. Rev.* at 52 ("there is little agreement about what the preexisting customary international law had to say about the issue of regulatory takings").

29. See generally, Meltz, Robert. 2004. "Takings Law: Whence We Came, Where We Are Now." SJ052 *ALI-ABA* 1.

30. At least one U.S. government official involved in the drafting process maintains that the inclusion of the three *Penn Central* factors in U.S. investment treaties was meant to provide nothing more than "some guidance" and that the U.S. government "never had the ambition or thought . . . that it would be a definitive or near-definitive guidance on the subject." Discussion at the Fifth Biennial MIGA–Georgetown University Symposium on International Political Risk Management, Washington, DC, November 3, 2006. While that may have been the intent, there is nothing in the language of these treaties that explains such a limited role. Moreover, it is a canon of treaty interpretation that language specifically addressing a subject—here, regulatory takings contained in Annex B of the 2004 U.S. Model BIT, for example—takes precedence over more general language on expropriation—contained in Art. 6 of the 2004 U.S. Model BIT, for example.

31. 438 U.S. at 124. See *Eastern Enters. v. Apfel,* 524 U.S. 498, 523 (1998) (describing process by which court determines whether compensable taking has occurred as "ad hoc and fact intensive").

32. See CAFTA Annex 10-C(4) ("The determination of whether an action or series of actions by a Party, in a specific fact situation, constitutes an indirect expropriation, requires a case-by-case, fact-based inquiry. . . ."); 2004 U.S. Model BIT Annex B(4)(a) (same).

33. *Nollan v. California Coastal Comm'n,* 483 U.S. 825, 866 (1987) (Stevens, J., dissenting).

34. See, e.g., *Concrete Pipe & Prods. of Cal., Inc. v. Construction Laborers Pension Trust,* 508 U.S. 602, 645 (1993) (declining to treat an interest in a pension plan as the entire property and finding no taking

where the regulation allegedly resulted in a 46 percent diminution in shareholder equity overall); *DeBenedictis*, 480 U.S. at 498-500 (no taking where regulation allowed property owner to mine 50 percent of its coal).

35. See *Lucas v. South Carolina Coastal Council*, 505 U.S. 1003, 1015 (1992).

36. See, e.g., *Greystone Hotel Co. v. City of New York*, No. 98-9116, U.S. App. LEXIS 14960, at *5 (2d Cir. June 23, 1999) (unpublished decision) ("Regulations that do not render property valueless will effect [a regulatory] taking only if the regulations do not substantially advance legitimate state interests."); *Evac, LLC v. Pataki*, 89 F. Supp. 2d 250, 258 (N.D.N.Y. 2000) (rejecting takings claim where government action did not nullify all economically viable uses of plaintiff's property); *Burnette v. Carothers*, Nos. 3:94-CV-00420, 3:94-CV-00676, 1998 WL 136177, at *4 (D. Conn. March 11, 1998) (unpublished decision) ("For a successful claim under regulatory jurisprudence, a plaintiff must plead and prove that the regulation at issue does not advance a legitimate state interest or deprives a property owner of all economically viable use of his property"); *Sag Harbor Port Assocs., Inc. v. Village of Sag Harbor*, 21 F. Supp. 2d 179, 186 (E.D.N.Y. 1998) ("A demonstrated decrease in the value of one's property is insufficient to constitute a taking. Rather, a party must prove that the state has deprived it of 'all reasonable uses' of its land." [citation omitted], aff'd mem., 182 F.3d 901 [2d Cir. 1999]); *Hinesburg Sand & Gravel Co. v. Chittenden Solid Waste Dist.*, 959 F. Supp. 652, 657 (D. Vt. 1997) ("A regulatory taking exists if a government regulation of property 'goes too far,' such that its effect is a total or near-total deprivation of the owner's interest in the subject matter," citing *Mahon*, 260 U.S. at 415); *Elias v. Town of Brookhaven*, 783 F. Supp. 758, 761–762 (E.D.N.Y. 1992) (rejecting claim that change in zoning ordinance effected a regulatory taking on ground that regulation had not denied owner all economically viable use of his land, and noting that "[r]egulations causing diminution in value of land by large percentages have consistently been held not to be takings," citing *Ambler Realty Co.*, 272 U.S. at 384 (77 percent); *Hadacheck v. Sebastian*, 239 U.S. 394, 405 (1915) (87.5 percent); *Pompa Constr. Corp. v. City of Saratoga Springs*, 706 F.2d 418, 420 n.2, 424 (2d Cir. 1982) (77 percent)); *Dean Tarry Corp. v. Friedlander*, 650 F. Supp. 1544, 1550 (S.D.N.Y.) (stating that landowner must show that he has been deprived of "all reasonable use of his land" in order to show a regulatory taking, and noting that "substantial devaluations in property value have been held to not constitute constitutional takings," aff'd, 826 F.2d 210 (2d Cir. 1987), citing *Park Ave. Tower Assocs. v. City of New York*, 746 F.2d 135 (2d Cir. 1984) (holding that plaintiff's inability to earn a "reasonable return" on its investment does not amount to a constitutional taking).

37. See, e.g., *Florida Rock Industries, Inc. v. United States*, 18 F.3d 1560, 1567 (Fed. Cir. 1994) (implying that diminution of value of approximately 60 percent might be compensable). Compare *McCay v. United States*, 199 F.3d 1376, 1383 (Fed. Cir. 1999) (citing *Florida Rock* favorably for proposition that a regulatory taking may cross the line from a "noncompensable 'mere diminution' to a compensable 'partial taking'"); *Forest Props., Inc. v. United States*, 177 F.3d 1360, 1364 (Fed. Cir.) (same, although concluding that a denial of permit to fill 9.4 acre lake bottom was not regulatory taking of entire 62-acre plot), cert. denied, 528 U.S. 951 (1999); *Hendler v. United States*, 175 F.3d 1374, 1385 (Fed. Cir. 1999) (citing *Florida Rock* favorably and noting that there need not be a "total wipeout" before the Fifth Amendment requires compensation) with *Clajon Production Corp. v. Petera*, 70 F.3d 1566, 1577 (10th Cir. 1995) (rejecting "the *Florida Rock* approach" in favor of "the more traditional analysis outlined in *Penn Central*," and holding that a regulation must prohibit all economically beneficial use to effect a taking).

38. *Lucas*, 505 U.S. at 1016 n.7.

39. See, e.g., *Pennsylvania Coal Co. v. Mahon*, 260 U.S. 393, 415 (1922).

40. For one of the few examples of an international tribunal and then a U.S. district court wrestling with what denial of property rights can constitute an expropriation under international law, see *McKesson Corp. v. The Islamic Republic of Iran*, 1997 U.S. Dist. LEXIS 8903 * 30 (D.D.C. 1997).

41. See, e.g., MIGA Convention, art. 11(a)(ii), defining expropriation in relevant part: "any legislative action or administrative action or omission attributable to the host government which has the effect of depriving the holder of a guarantee of his ownership or control of, or a substantial benefit from, his investment, with the exception of non-discriminatory measures of general application which governments normally take for the purpose of regulating economic activity in their territories. . ."

42. See, e.g., *McKesson,* supra n. 40.

43. See, e.g., *Penn Central,* 438 U.S. at 130–31 ("'Taking' jurisprudence does not divide a single parcel into discrete segments and attempt to determine whether rights in a particular segment have been entirely abrogated. In deciding whether a particular government action has effected a taking, this Court focuses . . . on the nature and extent of the interference with rights in the parcel as a whole.").

44. However, as discussed above, even when evaluating takings claims with respect to real property, courts still must sometimes grapple with the "denominator problem," that is, identifying the specific property that allegedly lost value in order to determine whether the loss was near-total.

45. But see *Andrus v. Allard,* 444 U.S. 51 (1979). In that case, the owner of Native American artifacts challenged a ban on selling products containing eagle feathers. The Court rejected the takings claim, holding that "where an owner possesses a full 'bundle' of property rights, the destruction of one 'strand' of the bundle is not a taking, because the aggregate must be viewed in its entirety." Id. at 65–66. Of course, the particular facts of that case counsel caution about how broadly to apply that principle.

46. See Choharis, Peter Charles. 2006. "U.S. Courts and the International Law of Expropriation: Toward a New Model for Breach of Contract." 80 *Univ. So. Cal. L. Rev.* 101 at Part IV.B.3 (January 26, 2007).

47. See id.

48. See The Restatement (Third) of The Foreign Relations Law of the United States, § 712 & Reptr's n. 8 (1987).

49. See Choharis, supra n. 46, Part III.B.1 and 2.

50. See Choharis, supra n. 46, Part III.B.3; Christie, supra note 7, at 332; Weston, supra note 7, at 115–16 (questioning utility of trying to evaluate governmental motives or purposes of taking).

51. The term "*Lochner*" comes from *Lochner v. New York,* 198 U.S. 45 (1905), which struck down a state law to protect workers' health and welfare by capping the number of daily and weekly hours that bakers could be required to work by their employers. The term originally described a judicial approach that applied a strict and skeptical analysis of laws that interfered with private economic transactions. Eventually and more loosely, the term has become shorthand for nonelected judges substituting their own ideas about what constitutes good public policy in place of decisions made by elected legislatures. I use the term in this latter sense of courts (or arbitrators) improperly substituting their own public policy choices for those of elected officials.

52. For an example of how broadly such police powers can extend, see *MOL, Inc. v. Peoples Republic of Bangladesh,* 736 F.2d 1326, 1329 (9th Cir. 1984) (holding that breach of contract claim was barred by sovereign immunity since contract for sale of rhesus monkeys concerned "Bangladesh's right to regulate its natural resources . . . a uniquely sovereign function.").

53. See, e.g., *West v. Multibanco Comermex, S.A.,* 807 F.2d 820 (9th Cir. 1987) (holding that international law recognized Mexican government's authority to respond to a fiscal crisis, thereby rendering resulting breach of its obligations not an expropriation); *Braka v. Bancomer, S.A.,* 589 F. Supp. 1465, 1472, (S.D.N.Y. 1984) (similarly holding that "the mechanisms used by Mexico are conventional devices of civilized nations faced with severe monetary crises, rather than the crude and total confiscation by force of a private person's assets"); Choharis, supra n. 46, Part III.C.2; The Restatement (Second) of the Foreign Relations Laws of the United States, §§ 197–201.

54. Ironically, recent arbitral awards suggesting that a supposed violation of reasonable investment-backed expectations comprises a separate cause of action under international law may thwart such reform efforts. A future article on this subject will argue that express stabilization clauses are necessary in order to proceed under this theory.

55. Not many arbitral awards address the issue of systemic reforms generally or deregulation specifically. Nor are there many U.S. cases that have addressed constitutional challenges to "stranded costs" incurred by regulated industries as a result of deregulation—mainly in the power sector. However, those courts that have addressed such constitutional claims have uniformly upheld the deregulatory measures as constitutional and thus not meriting compensation. See, e.g., *Energy Ass'n of N.Y. State,* 653 N.Y.S.2d at 513–16 (rejecting utilities' claim that they are entitled to recover all losses resulting from deregulation); see also *In re Retail Wheeling Tariffs,* 575 N.W.2d 808, 815–16 (Mich. Ct. App. 1998) (rejecting utilities' takings claim that retail wheeling order effected physical occupation of their

systems and that such order "require[d] them to involuntarily devote their property to a new business and to expand their services"; court explained that "[b]ecause a public utility is a regulated entity and its property is used for a public purpose, such reasonable interference is constitutional"), *rev'd, on other grounds,* 596 N.W.2d 126 (Mich. 1999).

56. In the regulatory takings context, causation is a key consideration, since property rights may be diminished due to intervening causes such as hyperinflation, high interest rates, or other market forces. See *Methanex Corp. and United States of America,* Partial Award, at par. 147 (NAFTA's expropriation provision requires a "legally significant relation" between the government action and alleged injury); Restatement (Third) § 207, cmt. e ("When a state is responsible for a violation [of its obligations due to state action or inaction], there is generally a willingness to adopt a liberal view of causation and to enlarge the category of injuries resulting from that violation for which the state is to be held accountable and for which it is required to make reparation").

57. For one approach, see *Banco Nacional de Cuba v. Chemical Bank,* 658 F.2d 875, 239 (2d Cir. 1981) (quoting The Restatement (Second) § 192 for the proposition that "[c]onduct attributable to a state that is intended to, and does, effectively deprive an alien of *substantially all the benefits of his interest in property,* constitutes a taking of the property . . . even though the state does not deprive him of his entire legal interest in the property").

58. See Choharis, supra n. 46, Part III.C.

59. See Wesley, Roger C. "Establishing Minimum Compensation Criteria for Use in Expropriation Disputes." 25 *Vand. L. Rev.* 939, 945 (1972) (describing debate over standard of compensation among communist, developing, capitalist, and developed countries).

60. See id. at 262–63 (contrasting traditional Hull Doctrine of prompt, adequate, and effective compensation with "view derived from the extensive measures of socialization adopted after the Second World War").

61. See Haue, Inaamul, and Ruxandra Burdescu. 2004. "Monterrey Consensus on Financing for Development: Response Sought From International Economic Law." 27 *B.C. Int'l & Comp. L. Rev.* 219, 224 (contending that developing countries "want strong international institutions, a favorable external environment, and effective instruments with firm legal foundations. These elements will provide poor nations with the necessary protection and enabling means to ensure that the economic integration will reduce poverty and close gaps within and between nations. Developing countries are particularly concerned with issues of attracting private capital flows, gaining unrestricted access to markets, receiving adequate development assistance, benefiting from technology transfers, improving global economic governance, and enhancing the coherence and consistency of the international systems in support of development.").

62. For an early expression of this rule, see Factory at Chorzów (*Germany v. Poland*), 1928 PDIJ Rep Series A No. 13, at 47 (Sept. 13).

63. See Lauterpacht, Elihu. 1997. "International Law and Private Foreign Investment." 4 *Ind. J. Global Legal Stud.* 259, 263, 270–71 (citing as evidence the expansion of the BIT regime even among developing countries, the European Energy Charter Treaty of December 1994, the North American Free Trade Agreement, the draft MAI, and arbitral decisions).

64. See, e.g., Franck, Susan D. 2005. "The Legitimacy Crisis in Investment Treaty Arbitration: Privatizing Public International Law Through Inconsistent Decisions," 73 *Fordham L. Rev.* 1521, 1523) ("Rather than creating certainty for foreign investors and Sovereigns, the process of resolving investment disputes through arbitration is creating uncertainty about the meaning of those rights and public international law").

ARE YOU IN GOOD HANDS WITH YOUR INSURANCE COMPANY? REGULATORY EXPROPRIATION AND POLITICAL RISK INSURANCE POLICIES

Mark Kantor
Attorney, Washington, DC

The PRI community is a very practical arena. Public authorities, arbitral tribunals, litigators, and scholars debate the parameters of international expropriation law. Issuers and users of PRI instead ask a simple question about a claimed regulatory expropriation: "Is it covered by the policy?" In this article, I will review provisions of some current equity PRI policies to try to answer that question. As we will see, however, the answer is far from clear. Therefore, insured and insurer alike may benefit from candid upfront discussions about the scope of expropriation coverage in a PRI policy before that cover is issued.

Allegations of "indirect expropriation" by means of regulatory conduct have gained visibility as many countries have shifted from an economic model of state-owned enterprises toward a model of state regulation of private (or partially privatized) enterprises. A number of countries are only partway down the path toward a regulatory model, with state-controlled enterprises competing in a marketplace that now includes private actors as well as other state-controlled enterprises. The approach to price, rate of return, output, and competition regulation taken by host government regulators continues to shift, as countries experiment with different approaches. Moreover, in developing and transition economies, overlapping relationships among government officials, state-controlled enterprises, and state "champions" create additional challenges for private investors. The potential for protectionism, cronyism, and corruption further complicates the situation. Claims of "regulatory expropriation" arise out of this fertile ground.

There is disagreement between arbitral award language and commentators on those decisions about the extent to which customary international law protects a foreign investor from regulatory conduct of a host government that deprives the investor or investment of significant value.[1] The very definition of "regulatory expropriation" remains the subject of much discussion, as do such concepts as "creeping expropriation" and "indirect expropriation" that often encompass host government regulatory conduct.[2] For ease of discussion in this article, I will simply adopt the definition of "indirect expropriation" employed by the U.S. government in its recent free trade agreements and bilateral investment treaties,[3] without endorsing or rejecting that definition. The 2004 U.S. Model BIT, for example, provides in Annex B as follows:[4]

Expropriation

The Parties confirm their shared understanding that:

1. Article 6 [Expropriation and Compensation](1) is intended to reflect customary international law concerning the obligation of States with respect to expropriation.
2. An action or a series of actions by a Party cannot constitute an expropriation unless it interferes with a tangible or intangible property right or property interest in an investment.
3. Article 6 [Expropriation and Compensation](1) addresses two situations. The first is direct expropriation, where an investment is nationalized or otherwise directly expropriated through formal transfer of title or outright seizure.
4. The second situation addressed by Article 6 [Expropriation and Compensation](1) is indirect expropriation, where an action or a series of actions by a Party has effect equivalent to direct expropriation without formal transfer of title or outright seizure.

(a) The determination of whether an action or a series of actions by a Party, in a specific fact situation, constitutes an indirect expropriation, requires a case-by-case, fact-based inquiry that considers, among other factors:

(i) the economic impact of a government action, although the fact that an action or series of actions by a Party has an adverse effect on the economic value on an investment, standing alone, does not establish that an indirect expropriation has occurred;

(ii) the extent to which the government action interferes with distinct, reasonable investment-backed expectations; and

(iii) the character of the government action.

(b) Except in rare circumstances, non-discriminatory regulatory actions by a Party that are designed and applied to protect legitimate public welfare objectives, such as public health, safety, and the environment, do not constitute indirect expropriations.

That definition is taken almost word for word from U.S. Supreme Court precedents addressing "regulatory takings" under the Fifth Amendment to the U.S. Constitution, principally the *Penn Central*[5] decision. Consequently, it is unclear whether most other nations would adopt the same definition. However, a number of states have entered into international investment agreements with the United States adopting that definition,[6] and Canada has incorporated virtually the same definition into its own model bilateral Foreign Investment Protection and Promotion Agreement (FIPA)[7] and in its recent FIPA with Peru.

How is a claim of regulatory expropriation addressed in a standard PRI policy? Perhaps the most important provisions in the policy to consider for that question are the confidentiality and dispute resolution clauses found at the back, not the scope of cover or exclusion provisions. A typical policy issued by a private insurer will provide that "the Insured shall not disclose the existence of this insurance policy to any third party, with the exception of the Insured's bankers and other professional advisors on a confidential basis, without the prior written consent of the Underwriter."[8] Moreover, most policies provide for resolution of disputes in arbitration. Commonly used arbitration rules preserve the privacy of arbitral proceedings.[9] Among PRI insurers (whether public or private), only the U.S. agency, OPIC, makes publicly available its claims determinations and arbitration awards relating to disputes with its policy beneficiaries. There is no reason to believe that other insurers feel themselves bound to follow OPIC's practice as expressed in those claims determinations; indeed, other insurers have been known to argue in claims disputes that differences between OPIC's policy wording and the wording of their own policy demonstrate that a different meaning was intended.

The protections of privacy are also its perils. In an environment of confidential dispute resolution, little practical information exists to inform insured parties of prior claims practice with respect to a regulatory expropriation claim. In light of these confidentiality obligations, underwriters retain the ability to argue for a strict construction of policy provisions without adversely affecting their position in the marketplace. Underwriters may, of course, make such arguments because they believe the beneficiary has misled them or is inappropriately seeking compensation for uncovered events. Thus, the insurer may feel justified in employing an "all available defenses" litigation strategy in the circumstances. However, the protective screen of confidentiality may also encourage extremely strict interpretations of policy coverage and exclusions by insurers that would, if publicly disclosed, surprise many potential customers. Similarly, policy beneficiaries may offer exaggerated claims about a host state's conduct, confident that such allegations will not reach the ears of regulators, investors, or the media.

With the slippery-slope risks of confidentiality in mind, let us review a number of coverage provisions in policies to determine the kind of arguments a claim of regulatory expropriation may face. We will look at several areas; including scope of cover, exclusions from cover, and disclosure obligations.

I. Scope of Cover

One common private PRI policy (hereinafter referred to as the "sample private policy") defines "expropriation" as follows:

> A.1 Expropriation
> An Expropriation means an act or series of acts taken by the Host Government that:
> (a) effectively deprives the Insured of all or part of its Insured Interest in the Foreign Enterprise relating to the Project; or
> (b) Effectively prevents or restricts, through financial, regulatory or other measures, the operation of the Foreign Enterprises relating to the Project, causing the total cessation of the Foreign Enterprise's operations relating to the Project; or
> (c) Effectively deprives the Foreign Enterprise of all or part of its real or tangible property relating to the Project; or
> (d) Effectively prevents the Insured or the Foreign Enterprise from effectively controlling funds in the Host County which constitute dividends or profits on, or proceeds from disposal of, the Insured Investment;

Provided such act or acts (i) are violations of international law (without regard to the availability of local remedies), and (ii) continue for the duration of the Waiting Period."

If the insurer strictly construes this clause, an insured investor seeking compensation for a regulatory expropriation claim will face a number of difficulties.

Failure to Act First, Clause A.1 of the sample private policy covers only "an act or series of acts" taken by the host government. Often, an investor will argue that the regulatory misconduct of the host government lies in the *failure* of regulators to act on a timely basis. For instance, in *Azurix v. Argentina*,[10] an ICSID arbitral proceeding, the tribunal held that Argentine authorities engaged in delay or failed to take action, thus causing materially adverse consequences for the investor:

> 102. To conclude, the bidders were not provided with accurate information on the variations, and the Province seems to have engaged in a protracted dilatory process; first in identifying the construction variations and then in delaying the re-categorization. As in the case of the zone coefficients, the concern was on the political effect rather than with applying the terms of the Concession Agreement.
>
> 107. The Province proceeded to change the valuation system in the first quarter of 2000, shortly after the Concession was awarded. The bidders were not informed of the upcoming change. When the change occurred, no alternative methodology was provided. The complaint of Azurix seems to be more on the lack of a meaningful response by the Province than anything else. Even the arrangement proposed by ABA [Azurix Buenos Aires] in February 2000 was put forward at its own initiative, although it was the Province's responsibility to provide alternative methodologies as explained by the Respondent. Irrespective of the merits of ABA's proposal and whether it meant a raise on applicable tariffs to the properties affected by the valuations, this tariff conflict could have been avoided by simply instructing the Concessionaire on what to do at the time the new law was issued and as part of its implementation. It seems that the administration of the Province was not very pro-active in search of solutions to a problem that the Province itself had created.
>
> 143. However, the Concession Agreement was based on certain factual assumptions that did not turn out to be correct. It is not contested that the Algae Removal Works were not completed, notwithstanding that at the time of bidding for the Concession they were represented to be 98% complete and expected to be completed by April 1999, at least two months before the beginning of the Concession and a full year before the extraordinary algae bloom occurred. The reservoir was kept by the Province only 25% full to permit completion of the works. In turn the low water level contributed to the extraordinary nature of the algae bloom. The works undertaken by the Province had the objective to obtain treated water at the outlet of the Patagonia plant with "levels of the chlorophyll photosynthetic pigment below 1mg/m3, irrespective of the species or number of cells, pH, etc. present in the water." This objective was not achieved. The filters installed at the microfiltering plant were inadequate for filtering algae, a fact on which the ORAB [Organismo Regulador

> Bonaerenses] and the consultants of Azurix agreed. The Bahia Blanca Drinking Water Supply Monitoring Report prepared by the ORAB noted that it had not found domestic or international precedents where these microfiltering systems were used for the primary elimination of this type of plankton organisms. Similarly, the report prepared by the consulting firm JVP employed by ABA concluded that the direct filtration system at Paso de las Piedras was not fit for the treatment of water because of the high concentration of algae/chlorophyll reaching the Patagonia plant due to the properties of the water from the reservoir and the removal capacity of the microscreens system. Since August 1999, ABA had repeatedly advised the ORAB, to no avail, of the measures necessary for ABA to take possession of the Algae Removal Works. For instance, in a letter to the ORAB dated August 24, 1999 (less than two months into the Concession and eight months before the April 2000 incidents) ABA alerted the ORAB that there was an increase in "the algae problem" due to the unusual low level in the reservoir. In the same vein, ECODYMA, the contractor engaged by AGOSBA [Administración General de Obras Sanitarias] to carry out the Algae Removal Works, wrote to the General Administrator of Sanitary Works of the Province on July 19, 1999 to bring to her attention that the quality of the water of the reservoir did not meet the standards used as a base for its bid because of the high level of turbidity of the water, and the algae bloom in large number and variety.

An underwriter may argue that the policy language in Clause A.1 of the sample private policy above does not cover failures to act, especially if it is unclear under local law whether the host government regulators have a duty to act in a timely manner following receipt of the investor's request for regulatory action. The MIGA Contract of Guarantee for Equity Investments,[11] in contrast, specifies that expropriation cover encompasses a loss due to "any direct or indirect action *or inaction,* in one or a series of events" (emphasis added). Counsel for an underwriter may point to this contrast in policy wording to reinforce the underwriter's argument that policy language in the sample private policy does not cover a "failure to act," only affirmative conduct.

The question of whether the host government regulators had a duty to affirmatively act affects the proper interpretation of the phrase "act or series of acts." Local regulatory law may answer that question, but often the regulatory framework leaves that question unaddressed. Some international agreements speak to that issue, notably the WTO General Agreement on Trade in Services. The WTO General Agreement on Trade in Services Article VI[12] states:

> 2(a). Each Member shall maintain or institute as soon as practical judicial, arbitral or administrative tribunals or procedures which provide, at the request of an affected service supplier, for the prompt review of,

and where justified, appropriate remedies for, administrative decisions affecting trade in services. Where such procedures are not independent of the agency entrusted with the administrative decision concerned, the Member shall ensure that the procedures in fact provide for an objective and impartial review.

3. Where authorization is required for the supply of a service on which a specific commitment has been made, the competent authorities of a Member shall, within a reasonable period of time after the submission of an application considered complete under domestic laws and regulations, inform the applicant of the decision concerning the application. At the request of the applicant, the competent authorities of the Member shall provide, without undue delay, information concerning the status of the application.

Other international treaties establishing a limited duty to act in a prompt manner in certain circumstances include GATT 1947 (Art. 10.3(b), relating to customs duties) and the Agreement on Trade-Related Aspects of Intellectual Property Rights, Arts. 42 and 49, relating to notice of administrative and judicial proceedings relating to intellectual property.

Total Cessation A PRI policy may call for compensation if inter alia the host government conduct causes "total cessation" of the investment's operations. Thus, Clause A.1 of the sample private policy above defines "expropriation" to encompass conduct that causes "the total cessation of the Foreign Enterprise's operations relating to the Project." In contrast, the OPIC and MIGA PRI policies do not expressly contain such a "total cessation" requirement. MIGA's Contract of Guarantee defines "expropriation" to inter alia include conduct that "deprives or prevents the Guarantee Holder from exercising. . . effective control of all or a portion of the Guaranteed Investment." OPIC's policy also makes no reference to a "total cessation;" that policy instead defines "expropriation" to inter alia cover acts that "prevent, unreasonably interfere with, deprive, or unduly delay effective enjoyment of the Investor's fundamental rights in the insured investment (rights are 'fundamental' if without them the Investor is substantially deprived of the benefits of the investment)."

The distinction between "total cessation," on the one hand, and deprivation of "fundamental rights" or "effective control," on the other hand, may be especially significant in the context of a regulatory expropriation. For example, in the ICSID case of *CMS v. Argentina,* the claimant alleged that Argentina's conduct in requiring payments in pesos rather than U.S. dollars, breaching an obligation to adjust payments for inflation and preventing tariff adjustments, constituted expropriation under the U.S.-Argentina BIT. Nevertheless, the local gas transmission company at the heart of that dispute had continued its local operations, although with significant losses. In that case, the tribunal held that Argentina's conduct did not constitute expropriation.[13] If, instead of testing the impact of Argentina's conduct under international law, the tribunal had been testing that conduct against a PRI policy's "total cessation of operations" standard, then the tribunal may very well have reached the same result. What if, though, the PRI policy contained a "deprivation of fundamental rights" standard? In such a case, the inquiry might have been broader, possibly with a different result. Since a host government's regulatory misconduct may often leave the regulated enterprise operating but greatly injured, it only makes sense for the insured and underwriters to appreciate fully the applicable standard of impact under the PRI policy before issuance of the cover.

Violation of International Law The definition of "expropriation" found in PRI policies has evolved over the years. Today, neither OPIC nor MIGA expressly refers to "international law" in its definition of "expropriation." The OPIC policy does refer to acts that "constitute an outright taking" or "have the effect of taking the Investor's insured investment" language that may require application of customary international law to interpret the word "taking." A number of private PRI policies, though, do contain an express requirement that the conduct in question must constitute a breach of international law. Thus, Clause A.1 of the sample private policy not only requires, illustratively, a "total cessation of operations"; that policy further requires the host government's acts to have been "violations of international law." As the introduction to this article makes clear, the state of international expropriation law is in flux. Consequently, the inclusion of a "violation of international law" threshold into a PRI policy has the effect of introducing considerable uncertainty into the scope of the sample private policy's "expropriation" cover. It is also worth noting that the reference in the sample private policy is not limited to "international expropriation law." Counsel for the insured may therefore make the same arguments heard by the tribunals in *CMS* and *Azurix*, alleging breaches of the international "fair and equitable treatment" standard, in addition to expropriation. There is no information publicly available to help determine whether such an argument would be persuasive to the PRI insurer or an arbitral tribunal considering the claim.

Start-up Companies and Operations As quoted above, the sample private policy (like many other PRI policies) requires that the host government's regulatory conduct must result in the total cessation of the investment's "operations." The term "operations" is, unsurprisingly, open to interpretation. If the covered enterprise is in a start-up or development phase, it may only be engaging in activities related to contract negotiation, business planning, or the raising of finance. Arguably, that enterprise has not yet begun its "operations" for accounting and appraisal purposes, because it has not yet commenced income-generating activities.[14] Similarly, in limited recourse project financings, it is common terminology to divide the project's stages of activity into three phases: development, construction, and operations. The last of those time periods, the operations phase, only commences once construction of the facility has been completed and that facility is capable of generating revenue. If that interpretation of "operations" is applied to Clause A.1 of the sample private policy, then an "expropriation" arguably does not occur if the improper regulatory conduct arises in either the development or construction phases. Such an interpretation might be quite surprising to the insured and its counsel. Again, it may be worthwhile for the parties to clarify in advance how broadly or narrowly the term "operations" is to be understood.

Intent vs. Effect One of the most-discussed issues in the development of the international law of regulatory expropriation is whether the host government's conduct must have been *intended* to produce the expropriatory injury or merely to have had the *effect* of an expropriation, regardless of intent. That distinction has obvious importance for many claims of regulatory expropriation. The definition of "indirect expropriation" in Annex B to the U.S. Model BIT resolves this question in favor of an "effects" test, following in this regard the U.S. Supreme Court decisions in *Penn Central* and *Lingle v. Chevron USA*. As Kunoy notes:

> In spite of many inconsistencies in the case law relating to indirect expropriations, it is generally held that there need not be a *mens rea*—to borrow a term from criminal law—because indirect expropriation, by its very nature, arises out of its effects.[15]

Similarly, Newcombe argues:

> No matter how the expropriation is described, international expropriation law looks to the effect of the government measures on the investor's property. The form and intent of the government measure is not determinative, although it is often relevant.[16]

Notably, many PRI policies are unclear on this issue, even if the policy makes no reference to international law. Some PRI policies do employ terms that are more easily interpreted as incorporating an "effects" test. Illustratively, Clause A.1 of the sample private policy utilizes the phrases "effectively deprives" and "effectively prevents." Each of these terms lends itself to an "effects" approach toward determining if an expropriation has occurred. Other PRI policies, however, employ a different term, i.e., "expressly." That latter term is easier to construe as requiring an element of intent. The impact of the "effects" test, as distinct from the "intent" test, is most acute when the investor argues that the host government's failures to act, rather than affirmative actions, constituted a key aspect of the alleged regulatory misconduct. Situations of "creeping regulatory expropriation" also raise difficult issues. In such circumstances, no single act may constitute expropriation of the investment, but a number of acts attributable to the host government may cumulatively result in a total cessation of operations or deprivation of fundamental rights. Where a number of government authorities take the various acts, and evidence of coordinated conduct among those authorities is lacking, the difficulties of satisfying either an "intent" or "expressly" test are compounded.

Discrimination A "discrimination" requirement is another aspect of a PRI policy that may create interpretive problems. Dramatic regulatory changes often arise amid times of rapid economic, political, or social change. Some PRI policies define expropriation to, inter alia, include conduct by a host government that "*discriminatorily*" or "*selectively*" restricts operations so as to cause a total cessation or fundamental deprivation. Thus, in many regulatory circumstances it will be challenging to show that the host government's conduct discriminated against the insured.

Two obvious situations illustrate the difficulty of applying this language in a regulatory context. First, for some regulatory environments, the challenged host government conduct may apply to all market participants—for instance, an across-the-board change for all participants in a regulated industry like the changes in currency obligations and tariff adjustments addressed in *CMS v. Argentina* and *LG&E v. Argentina*.[17] While such conduct may have been sufficiently severe to bring about a total cessation of operations, it may not have discriminated between affected market participants.

Second, there are situations where the foreign investor is the only actor in the industry; the Azurix water project in Argentina was such a case. Situations of single-actor regulated activities often occur for water projects, pipelines, electricity transmission or distribution companies, and other regulated monopolies. Here, there may be no other investment against which to compare the treatment offered the insured's project. PRI policies do not define the class of entities to be compared and contrasted for determinations about selective or discriminatory treatment; they fail to identify the "comparator" or the analogous circumstances against which the allegedly offending conduct should be compared. Many bilateral investment treaties face a similar problem in their "national treatment" and "most-favored-nation treatment" protections. In that context, UNCTAD has recommended greater drafting clarity:

> The specification that "*no less favorable treatment*" shall apply only when foreign and domestic investments are "*in like circumstances*" provides greater guidance for the application of the national treatment standard. This wording makes it clear that providing different treatment to foreign investments and investors, which in fact are not in the same circumstances than domestic investments or investors, would not violate the national treatment standard.[18]

PRI policies in general fail to identify a comparator or to employ an "in like circumstances" measure of discriminatory or selective application. Consequently, parties to a PRI policy may not have a clear advance understanding of how to draw comparisons for the "discriminatorily" or "selectively" requirement for an expropriation claim. That problem will be especially hard to solve if the covered enterprise is a monopoly provider, with no direct competitors.

Multiple Sources of Causation Events like the Latin American debt crisis of the 1980s, the Asian financial collapse of the late 1990s, and the Argentine crisis will trigger widespread economic, political, and social change. Not surprisingly, large shifts in regulatory conduct often accompany such events. Privatizations and renationalizations, the introduction of a market economy or a command economy, and fundamental changes in the role of the state in the development of natural resources or public delivery of services—in each case, the crisis will be a source of a change in regulatory approach. Additionally, the transition from one model of economic management to another model (say, from a socialist model toward a market economy) may be in the middle of its course, with an uncertain final destination. The host government may be experimenting with different approaches, especially if a government following one approach falls and is replaced by a government espousing a different approach.

In all of these circumstances, if the insured alleges expropriation resulting from the regulatory changes by the host government, then the parties will have to confront the problems of multiple causes and ultimate causes. If a claim is made under a PRI policy, insurer and insured alike will consider the sources of causation for the complained-of injury. Illustratively, to what extent did the injury to foreign investors in Argentina result from the "pesification" enactments of the Argentine government? To what extent did that injury result instead from enormous macroeconomic pressure on Argentina? And if the latter, was that pressure the result of worldwide economic movements, or of Argentine central or provincial economic management policies?

OPIC has described its approach toward causation issues in the *Joseph Companies* claims determination.[19] In that claim, the investor (Josco) sought compensation for expropriation by Jamaica of an equity investment in the expansion of a vegetable oil processing facility (JSPI). OPIC stated that:

> To establish direct causation, Josco must demonstrate that the loss was not the result of exogenous factors, such as the failure to derive benefits from the marketplace. Relevant questions in establishing causation are (i) whether JSPI was financially sound prior to the government action, and (ii) whether the loss would have occurred even in the absence of the government action.[20]

But, how would such an argument have fared under a different PRI policy? Here too, the exact wording of the PRI policy will be important. The sample private policy above requires compensation for "the Insured's Loss caused . . . *principally* and directly" by an expropriation (emphasis added). Thus, under that policy the parties (or an arbitral tribunal) would search for the prime source of causation to determine if an expropriation had occurred. However, other private PRI policies require payment for "the Insured's Loss caused *solely* and directly" by an expropriatory act. The standard for causation under a policy containing a "solely" test appears much higher than the standard under a policy with a "principally" test. The distinction between conduct that is the principal cause of the injury and conduct that is the sole cause of the injury may be decisive when the alleged regulatory expropriation occurs in the middle of a national crisis, or as part of a shifting legal and business landscape.

The Host Government PRI policies also require that the improper conduct be attributable to the "host government." The definition of the term "host government" is thus crucial in a regulatory expropriation claim. In transition economies, for example, the dominant player in an industry may be a state-controlled enterprise. That state-controlled enterprise may own or have legal authority over assets that are central to the economic viability of private sector participants in the same industry. Thus, a dominant state telecommunications enterprise may control network and switching assets. If the state telecommunications enterprise does not afford a private competitor the right to interconnect with the network on commercially reasonable terms, then the result may indeed be a total cessation of operations by that private telecommunications provider. Similar issues may arise as well for state enterprises controlling electricity transmission and distribution services or pipelines.

When is that conduct by the state enterprise attributable to the host government? The definition of "host government" in the sample private policy provides as follows:

"Host Government" means:

(a) the present or any succeeding governing authority (without regard to the method of its succession or as to whether it is internationally recognized) in effective control of all or any part of territory of the Host Country or any political or territorial subdivision thereof (including any dependent territory); and
(b) any other *public authority* in or of the Host Country *on which regulatory powers are conferred by the laws of the Host Country* (emphasis added).

Subclause (b) of this definition treats "public authorities" as the "Host Government" if "regulatory powers are conferred [on that authority] by the laws of the Host Country." Difficult issues of proof arise where the dominant state enterprise has legal authority or practical control over access to crucial assets like a pipeline, but applicable law does not employ Western legal terms to describe that authority. Is the dominant state enterprise's authority regulatory, ministerial, administrative, commercial, or the like? If the state enterprise denies a private market participant interconnection to a network, to the economic benefit of that state enterprise, is that conduct regulatory in character or commercial? When do the terms offered by that enterprise for interconnection become so burdensome as to be legally inappropriate? Since the insured and insurer will normally not be able to compel the state enterprise to testify in claims proceedings or arbitrations related to the PRI claim, only limited evidence of the actual facts about the state's enterprise's authority may be available. Parties may be reduced to parsing poorly drafted laws and regulations, and articles written at a distance, when the actual conduct of the state enterprise is obscured by the lack of testimony.

The issue of how to properly characterize a state enterprise's monopoly control over assets that are essential to other market participants may be exacerbated in transition economies if there is a practice of state officials moving into corporate positions in the dominant enterprise (whether state-controlled or privatized). Similarly, state officials from other areas of the government often sit on the supervisory board of a state enterprise, again blurring efforts to characterize the powers of the state enterprise as regulatory, ministerial, or commercial. If the beneficiary of a PRI policy is a player in an industry with such characteristics, such as power, gas transportation, or telecommunications, then that beneficiary would be well advised to discuss in advance with its insurer the proper characterization of the state entity controlling the crucial interconnection assets.

II. Exclusions from Cover

Even if the challenged regulatory conduct falls within the policy's scope of coverage as an "expropriation," the coverage exclusions customarily found in a PRI policy may create unusual difficulties for a claim of regulatory expropriation. Those difficulties arise out of the regulatory process itself.

Multiple Causes Redux The issue of multiple and ultimate sources of causation arises again in the context of policy exclusions. Causation is important in determining if a policy exclusion is applicable. The MIGA Contract of Guarantee for Equity Investments, for example, states that "MIGA shall in no case be liable for any Loss *which is due to*" an excluded circumstance. If the covered investment's loss was only partially caused by the excluded circumstance, then the phrase "due to" leaves uncertain whether the loss is covered or excluded. OPIC's policy offers more clarity: "No compensation shall be payable if . . . the *preponderant cause* of the expropriation" (emphasis added) is the excluded circumstance. Even under the OPIC formulation, though, both insured and insurer will face the difficult factual task of weighing various causes in the effort to determine which one is preponderant. As described above, in the *Joseph Companies* claim, OPIC applied a direct causation standard, requiring the investor to show that the loss was "not the result of exogenous factors, such as the failure to derive benefits from the marketplace." To reach that conclusion, OPIC considered several questions to be relevant, such as whether the covered investment was financially sound prior to the government action and whether the loss would have occurred even in the absence of the government action. In *Joseph Companies*, OPIC applied that test to determine whether an expropriation had occurred, not whether that expropriation was excluded from cover by a policy exclusion. Nevertheless, the *Joseph Companies* claims determination is instructive as to OPIC's approach toward issues of causation.

Some private PRI policies are written far more favorably than OPIC's policy from the perspective of an insurer and correspondingly less favorably from the insured's perspective. The "exclusions" article of the sample private policy commences as follows:

> The underwriter shall not pay compensation for any loss in the event that the loss was *directly or indirectly caused or contributed to by, or arose from,* an excluded circumstance. (Emphasis added.)

On its face, that language is quite broad. It purports to exclude coverage whenever an excluded event "contributes" to a loss, regardless of whether that contribution was a preponderant cause of the loss, a material cause, or even an incidental cause. Other private PRI exclusions may not be so broadly drafted, but instead call for noncompensation of a loss "arising from" an excluded circumstance. The phrase "arising from," like MIGA's "due to" language quoted above, leaves the consequences of multiple sources of causation for further discussion.

Even if the policy specifies that the excluded circumstances must be the preponderant cause of the loss, a number of other common PRI policy exclusions give rise to challenging issues in regulatory expropriation cases. These exclusions often overlap in practice, if not in language.

Failure to Comply with Law and Failure to Maintain Permits PRI policies regularly exclude coverage if the loss was caused by the failure of the investor or the investment to "comply with the laws of the Host Government." Of course, in the context of a regulatory expropriation there may be a considerable element of circularity with respect to this policy exclusion. If the allegedly expropriatory conduct was itself a legal requirement, and the failure or refusal of the enterprise to comply was the basis for the alleged injury, did the failure of the enterprise to comply with the regulatory enactment constitute an exclusion vitiating cover under the policy? This exclusion may also pose problems for claims by an insured that a regulatory expropriation arose out of a "creeping expropriation." It is not unlikely that, at some point during the process of regulatory "creep," the covered enterprise will have fallen out of compliance with one or more of the host government's regulatory requirements. PRI policies are not often drafted with the "creeping expropriation" scenario in mind. Careful attention to the interrelationship between a regulatory environment and "creeping expropriation" during policy drafting may pay dividends in clarity at the time a loss occurs.

Another common policy exclusion is for losses caused by the failure of the investor or the investment to comply with the permitting requirements of local governments. Almost exactly the same questions occur with respect to policy exclusions for failure of the investment to obtain or maintain all necessary local permits, as occur in relation to the policy exclusion for failure to comply with local laws.

Breach of Contract PRI insurers often seek to divide coverage into "expropriation" and "breach of contract." A debate exists in international law as to whether breach of an investment agreement by a host government can constitute an expropriation and, if so, in what circumstances. Some PRI policies address this issue through interpretation of the general term "expropriation" once a claim arises. OPIC has, for example, regularly assured investors that a breach of contract by a state can, in some circumstances, rise to the level of an expropriation under international law.[21] Other PRI policies, however, expressly exclude breach of contract from "expropriation" cover. The sample private policy, thus, excludes from expropriation cover:

> the material breach by the Host Government of any contractual agreements with the Insured or the Foreign Enterprise;

Applying the "plain meaning" rule of contract interpretation, such a "contracts" exclusion would seem to exclude cover for any loss caused (or contributed to) by the host government's breach of contract—even if the host government's breach had in the circumstances caused a total cessation of operations and also constituted an expropriation under international law. The sample private policy also does not require that the breach by the host government occurr in a commercial capacity. Thus, a contract breach motivated by governmental objectives appears to be treated under this language in the same manner as a host government's contract breach motivated by commercial considerations. Notably, the similar exclusion in the MIGA policy is limited to circumstances where the host government was acting in a commercial capacity:

> A Loss due to breach by the Host Government of its obligations under any agreement between or among the Host Government and the Guarantee Holder, the Project Enterprise, or both, *where the Host Government is acting in a commercial capacity,* shall not constitute an Expropriation. (Emphasis added.)

As discussed in more detail below, expropriation coverage under PRI policies commonly distinguishes between covered conduct by a government entity acting in a government capacity, and uncovered conduct by a government entity acting in a commercial capacity. If a similar distinction is not employed in a "contracts" exclusion, however, then claims for regulatory expropriations involving host government concession agreements, stabilization clauses, contractual tax holidays, and other common investment agreements may be excluded from expropriation cover by the mere fact that the government's obligations were reduced to writing in the form of a contract.

Acting in a Commercial Capacity Both international expropriations law and PRI expropriation coverage treat acts by a host government in a commercial, rather than government, capacity, as outside the scope of compensable expropriations. Thus, the sample private policy excludes losses caused by "the host government acting in its capacity as a supplier, creditor, shareholder, director or manager of or purchaser from, the Foreign Enterprise." The difficulties of establishing when a state-controlled enterprise is acting in a commercial capacity, as distinct from a governmental capacity, are of course well known in international expropriation law, and are also regularly explored by courts considering the "commercial" exception to sovereign immunity under the U.S. Foreign Sovereign Immunities Act and the U.K. State Immunity Act of 1978.

OPIC claims determinations have also addressed this distinction under the OPIC PRI policy. In the course of rejecting a claim by Marine Shipping Corporation (MSC), based on alleged misconduct by the Egyptian Government (GOE), OPIC ruled that the conduct in question was commercial in character, not governmental.[22]

> First, with respect to the Insured's general harassment theory, this claim is based on fee and price disputes between the Insured and various Egyptian entities, including the Canal Company, the Port Authority, and MSC's various contract partners. The disputes with the Canal Company appear to have involved disagreements over the price offered to purchase MSC's assets. The fee disputes with the Port Authority involved fees assessed on MSC for dredging the quay and a berthing fee. The disputes with MSC's contract partners involved MSC's claim that it was being underpaid, under the terms of its agreements with these entities, and MSC's dissatisfaction with proposed new Contract terms. Even as alleged by MSC, each of these fee and price disputes was commercial in nature. The GOE entities involved were parastatal corporations acting for commercial reasons in a commercial capacity rather than from governmental motives. Nothing MSC has submitted demonstrates that these entities acted in bad faith or in violation of their contractual commitments to MSC. Even assuming that this had occurred, a

> state does not commit a violation of international law by engaging in commercial actions of this character. That is especially true when the state affords the foreign national a dispute settlement procedure. (See generally Restatement [Third] Foreign Relations Law §712 Comment h, Reporters' Note 8.) MSC filed actions, and later at least one appeal, in Egyptian courts regarding some of these matters, and it appears that judgments were found in favor of the GOE entities. There has been no claim that MSC suffered a denial of justice in the proceedings in Egyptian courts. Accordingly, there is no basis for concluding that the alleged instances of harassment constituted violations of international or local law.

Also, in its Memorandum of Determinations relating to the expropriation Claim of Bank of America, as Trustee, with respect to the Dabhol Power Project in India, OPIC interpreted a similar policy exclusion. OPIC held that the inquiry under the policy language centered on the capacity in which the host government entity acted, not the motives underlying its actions. Note that the particular OPIC policy exclusion in question excluded acts by a state authority "in its capacity *or through its powers*" as a commercial counterparty. That reference to "through its [commercial] powers," whether or not the conduct was "in its [commercial] capacity," played an important role in OPIC's application of the exclusion.[23]

> Section 4.02(b) of the Contract, as amended by Section 10.05, excludes from coverage any expropriatory action taken by a foreign government authority "in its capacity or through its powers" as, among other things, a purchaser from DPC [Dabhol Power Company] or as a guarantor of any payment obligation to DPC, absent satisfaction of certain additional requirements that all parties agree have not been met. It may be that, as the Insured argues, MSEB's [Maharashtra State Electricity Board's] motivation in defaulting in payments and in rescinding the PPA was governmental rather than commercial. The exclusion under Section 4.02(b) does not, however, depend on the motivation behind the MSEB's action. Rather, the exclusion is of actions taken by governmental actors through certain specifically cited relationships with the Project. The Insured's interpretation would have the phrase "in its capacity" read to mean, "motivated by." Thus, MSEB, if motivated by governmental rather than commercial objectives, is said by the Insured to be acting in its "capacity" as government, rather than in its "capacity" as a commercial actor.
>
> This reading is wrong for at least two reasons. First, it is wrong on its face. The obligations on which MSEB defaulted arose under its unique capacity as party to the PPA. Others may have contributed to the occurrence of those defaults, but only MSEB, which carried the obligations, could default. Likewise,

> only MSEB as party to the PPA could purport to rescind the contract. Regardless of the motivation, those actions could only be taken by the MSEB in its capacity as a party with DPC to the PPA. Second, even if doubt existed as to whether "capacity" might mean "motivation," the operative language states "in its capacity or through its powers." It is clear that the power to default and the power to rescind lay uniquely with MSEB as party to the PPA. Expropriatory actions taken through the powers bestowed by that relationship, or by any of the relationships to the project specified in Section 4.02(b), are excluded from the contract's coverage. There can be no doubt that MSEB's rescission of that PPA was taken in its "capacity or through its powers" as a purchaser from DPC. Consequently, such action is subject to the exclusion of OPIC's expropriation coverage provided for in Section 4.02(b) and, therefore, cannot form the basis of a claim for expropriation under the Contract, absent the Insured's satisfaction of the additional specific conditions provided in Section 4.02(b).
>
> The Claim Application alleges that political pressure from the GOM [Government of Maharashtra] is the real reason for MSEB's payment defaults under the PPA and the GOM's payment defaults under the GOM Guaranty and MSEB's rescission of the PPA. The Insured cites as evidence statements by the GOM's Financing and Planning Chief Minister indicating that these payment defaults were not driven by the GOM's finances, but rather were strategic decisions taken to determine whether to renegotiate or to "scrap" the PPA.
>
> It is not clear, however, that this statement demonstrates that MSEB's actions were not essentially commercial. Indeed, the minister's statement could be entirely consistent with GOM concurrence with a rational economic decision by MSEB to attempt to force, within the confines of Indian contract law, avoidance of a tariff that MSEB could not afford to pay. The failure to demand power in Maharashtra to meet the aggressive projections made at the time the PPA was signed and the subsequent failure of MSEB to improve its record in collecting payments for power delivered together posed a specter of inevitable payment default by MSEB.

OPIC also took issue with Bank of America's argument that "creeping expropriation" was an expropriation under international law that automatically fell outside the "commercial exclusion." Instead, OPIC asserted that the "commercial exclusion" only comes into play if the conduct in question has already been found to fall within the policy's definition of expropriation. As OPIC explained, its policy does not cover all expropriations, but rather only those expropriations that do not also fall within the "commercial exclusion":

> The opinion provided by Prof. W. Michael Reisman argues that, if government acts aggregate to a creeping expropriation, then "the §4.02(b) exclusion

for commercial action does not apply" because "[b]y nature, a creeping expropriation is *jure imperi* and therefore falls outside the commercial action exception in §4.02(b)." OPIC would disagree. The point of the exception is not to exclude commercially-motivated acts that do not constitute, or contribute to, expropriations—in which case, there would be no need for the exception—but rather expressly to exclude those that do. It is precisely because of the concern that such mixed commercial/governmental actions, alone or in aggregation, could contribute to an expropriation that leads to their explicit exclusion from coverage. As an underwriting matter, OPIC is not typically prepared to take the unfortunately high risk that governmental parties too might breach their contractual undertakings, unless that risk is specifically accepted. Here, for instance, OPIC was willing to be responsible for expropriation losses caused by governmental breaches of the PPA, or of the guaranties thereof, only if the special conditions set forth in the amendments to §4.02(b) were met. OPIC does not dispute, however, that an argument could be made outside the context of an OPIC insurance contract that the acts complained of violate international law. The contractual exclusion of Section 4.02(b) limits only the claims that the Insured can raise against OPIC as insurer. Other GOM authorities and politicians may not have objected to, and may well have encouraged, the actions that MSEB took, but one need not look further than MSEB's own financial straits to find adequate motivation for its payment defaults.

MSEB's actions—the payment defaults and the subsequent repudiation of the PPA, as well as the pursuit of an aggressive litigation strategy to avoid being held responsible for those defaults or that rescission—all appear to be in direct pursuit of MSEB's clear commercial interests. The disputes between MSEB and DPC largely pertain to the PPA, which the Insured described in the Response Letter (exhibit E) as "plainly commercial" and "an ordinary contract, commercial by its very nature."

The insured also asserts that MSEB's actions were taken at the direction of the GOM. The GOM may be able to affect the behavior of MSEB (through its power to appoint MSEB's board of directors or otherwise), but this does not necessarily make each act of MSEB attributable to the GOM. The inference would be more tempting if we were trying to explain actions taken by MSEB against its own commercial interests, but this is clearly not the case. As the Godbole Committee's Report makes clear, MSEB was on the verge of being bankrupted by its payment obligations under the PPA. While it is certainly possible that actions of the GOM may have motivated the MSEB's actions, the facts presented by the Insured or otherwise available to OPIC do not show that MSEB's actions were the result of intervention by the GOM or, for that matter, any

> GOM or GOI authority. It is clear, however, that MSEB's obligations to DPC were putting it into a financially untenable situation. MSEB's own financial straits may have provided a sufficient motive for the actions it took. Finally, and of most importance for application of the Contract, the Contract does not, in any event, exclude the listed acts only if undertaken for commercial reasons. Rather, it strictly excludes them, unless the stated conditions are met, which they undeniably were not. Thus, even if MSEB's rescission of the PPA was in response to political pressure, it was nonetheless an action by MSEB in its capacity, or through its power, as a purchaser from DPC and, therefore, is subject to the exclusion in Section 4.02(b).

OPIC thus concluded that MSEB's conduct was commercial in character and that the injury was effected through MSEB's commercial powers. Consequently, that particular alleged misconduct was excluded from expropriation cover, MSEB's motivations notwithstanding. With state enterprises often serving intertwined regulatory and commercial functions, the OPIC holding in *Bank of America as Trustee* has significant implications for many regulatory expropriation claims. However, in *Bechtel Enterprises International (Bermuda) Ltd. et al. v. Overseas Private Investment Corporation,* an American Arbitration Association (AAA) tribunal reached the opposite conclusion based on the same facts involved in the Dabhol dispute, upholding a PRI claim against OPIC by GE and Bechtel affiliates for expropriation and overruling a contrary determination by OPIC. The arbitrators ruled that the political motivations of MSEB and the GOM were decisive:[24]

> 48. MSEB's motivations for failing to pay for power, repudiating the PPA and petitioning MERC [Maharashtra State Electricity Regulatory Commission] for an injunction were political. To the extent MSEB was experiencing financial hardship, it was caused solely and directly by political choices. In particular, the GOM and MSEB engaged in a program of politically motivated subsidies, handouts and favors to large power-consuming constituencies, and failed to check rampant power theft and other transmission and distribution losses. . . .
> 52. The GOM's decision not to pay DPC was a political choice: GOM politicians wanted to "scrap" the politically unpopular PPA. The decision was not due to the GOM's lack of financial resources. . . .
> 75. None of the actions taken by MERC, the GOM, the GOI and the Indian courts were taken as "a supplier, creditor, lessor, shareholder, director, or manager of or purchaser from, DPC, or as a guarantor of any payment obligation to MERC."
> 76. The acts of all the Indian government entities which constituted total expropriation of DPC as set forth above, were politically motivated.

Since OPIC granted the claimants in *Bank of America as Trustee* compensation on other bases put forward in their PRI claim, the apparent conflict in the approaches taken by OPIC in *Bank of America as Trustee* and by the AAA tribunal in *Bechtel Enterprises* on the same facts remains to be resolved.

For purposes of deciding if a creeping regulatory expropriation has occurred, these interpretive difficulties are exacerbated when the covered investment operates pursuant to arrangements where crucial inputs are supplied by the host government, or the output of the enterprise is purchased by the host government. Take, for instance, an IPP that purchases its fuel under a long-term gas supply agreement from the state's oil and gas monopoly and sells its electricity to the state's monopoly national power company under a long-term power purchase agreement for resale to the ultimate users. If, as occurred in the late 1990s, gas prices are rising and electricity demand is falling, both state entities may be sustaining large losses under their contracts. If the host government effects an expropriation by encouraging the host government fuel supplier to cease providing gas at a now-below market price, is that otherwise expropriatory conduct excluded because the state entity was acting in a commercial capacity as fuel supplier?

OPIC's ruling in the *Ponderosa* claim offers some additional guidance for answering these questions. In that determination, OPIC considered again the relationship between a contractual arrangement with a host government entity and the motivations underlying the government's conduct. OPIC expressly held that the License granted by the Argentine Government to TGS (the covered investment) for gas transportation operations was a "contract." Applying the distinction between governmental and commercial acts, OPIC ruled that the motivation of Argentine government actors in causing the breach of that license was relevant in determining whether an expropriation existed under international law, and decided that an expropriation had occurred.[25] However, unlike the situation in *Bank of America as Trustee,* OPIC then determined that the conduct of Argentina in causing the breach of the license was not excluded from cover by operation of the "commercial" exclusion. OPIC decided that the "commercial" exclusion did not apply to acts of the Government of Argentina (GOA) in its legislative capacity, notwithstanding the fact that Argentina was at the same time the contracting party. OPIC ruled as follows:

> When the License was originally granted, GOA retained a 30% interest in TGS, but this interest was subsequently sold to TGS employees and the general public; therefore, GOA is not a shareholder of the TGS. Furthermore, GOA entered into the License as a regulator and not as a purchaser or supplier of natural gas. GOA is not a purchaser, supplier, creditor, shareholder, director or manager of TGS.
>
> We have already found that the repudiation was motivated by noncommercial reasons. While the original request by GOA to defer the PPI-indexed

> tariff was made in its capacity as a contracting party, the same cannot be said for enactment of the Emergency Law. The Emergency Law was undertaken by the GOA acting in its sovereign capacity, as it was a legislative act. The Emergency Law was passed by the Senate and House of representatives of Argentina, pursuant to the Argentine Constitution. Article 8 of the Emergency Law in particular notes that it relates solely to contracts "subject to public law." Thus, since the law was passed for reasons related to the public interest and not in GOA's capacity as a contracting party, and was the underlying cause of, and the channel for, the GOA's repudiation of the License, OPIC finds that the government exclusion does not apply.[26]

By focusing on the legislative enactment of the Emergency Law, rather than the earlier breach of concession obligations related to indexing the tariff for inflation (PPI) increases, OPIC thus concluded that the conduct of the host government was governmental rather than commercial. The distinction may have been that, in *Bank of America as Trustee,* the contract counterparty (MSEB) was also in OPIC's view the host government "acting party" for purposes of the expropriation. In contrast, in *Ponderosa,* the acting party for purposes of the expropriatory action was in OPIC's view the Argentine legislature (when it enacted the Emergency Law).

Similarly, in its *SAIC* claims determination, OPIC held that evidence of a plan by República Bolivariana de Venezuela to expropriate SAIC's investment (INTESA) was sufficient to trigger the expropriation coverage notwithstanding the use of the Venezuelan state oil company's (PDVSA's) contractual relations with INTESA as one of the means to effect that expropriation. PDVSA was the 40 percent joint venture partner in INTESA with SAIC, provided 95 percent of INTESA's revenues, and supplied certain necessary telephone and utility services to INTESA.[27] However, the "commercial" exclusion in the SAIC policy had been modified (by §10.03 of the SAIC policy) to make the "commercial" exclusion inapplicable if "the Insured has demonstrated to OPIC's satisfaction that such action or inaction could not have been justified under the terms of any underlying commercial arrangement."[28]

> The direct evidence of a governmental plan to expropriate INTESA, including through acts initially ordered by PDVSA President Ali Rodriguez, renders the exclusion under Article 4.03(b) (as amended by Article 10.03) inapplicable.[29]

Even though PDVSA was clearly a commercial contract counterparty of INTESA and the expropriatory conduct was effected in part "through" its commercial powers, OPIC determined that PDVSA's actions "could not have been justified under the terms of any underlying commercial arrangement" within the meaning of Article 10.03 of the OPIC policy. Thus, the "commercial" exclusion did not apply.

The *Joseph Companies* (Josco) claims determination also addressed the "commercial" exclusion, with OPIC again holding that the existence of a contractual obligation did not prevent coverage under the policy if the Government of Jamaica (GOJ) was acting in its sovereign capacity:

> There is no question that the changes in Jamaica's tariff regime were undertaken by the GOJ acting in its sovereign capacity. However, the expropriatory action determined to have been taken is not the change in tariffs, but the breach by the GOJ of its continuing contractual obligation to protect JSPI [Jamaica Soy Product Industries] from external competition and to ensure the maintenance of certain pricing margins through tariffs or some other mechanism. In this context, the issue is whether this contractual undertaking was an obligation of the GOJ in its capacity as a shareholder of the foreign enterprise or in its capacity as a sovereign government.
>
> The GOJ's obligation to maintain pricing margins is pursuant to the Heads of Agreement, which was executed by JNH [Jamaica Nutrition Holdings] in its capacity as a shareholder of JSPI, and established other purchasing, marketing and other relationships that the GOJ would have with JSPI. The GOJ's acknowledgement of its obligations was evidenced through the Letter of Assurances which was provided as a condition subsequent under the Heads of Agreement. The Heads of Agreement expressly provides that the GOJ's obligations thereunder will continue as long as Josco has an interest in JSPI. After the privatization, the GOJ was no longer a shareholder of JSPI, and due to import liberalization and pursuant to agreement with JSPI, the GOJ's responsibilities as a supplier of beans and marketer of JSPI's products were also terminated. Therefore, any continuing obligations that the GOJ was required to fulfill under the Heads of Agreement were in its capacity as a sovereign government, and this exclusion is not applicable.[30]

As these rulings demonstrate, finding the line between "commercial" and "governmental" conduct is difficult under OPIC's policy language. That process is far more difficult under other PRI policies, with different exclusionary language and no publicly available claims determinations or arbitral awards to provide guidance to policy parties.

Provocative Acts by the Insured When does an aggressive and determined investor response to the intermediate stages of a "creeping regulatory expropriation" fall outside the ordinary course of business? Once again, common policy exclusions are not easy to apply in the context of a claim for regulatory expropriation.

The OPIC policy excludes losses if the preponderant cause is:

> actions, other than actions taken in the ordinary course of business attributable to the Investor, the foreign enterprise, or the controlling equity of the foreign enterprises, provided such actions are in any way related to the project

> or (ii) violation of any . . . applicable law relating to bribery, kickbacks or similar covert business practices by the Investor, the foreign enterprise, or such controlling equity investor.

OPIC has considered the application of its "provocation" exclusion in connection with a claim by an Enron subsidiary arising out of the Argentine crisis. In *Ponderosa,* OPIC concluded that the exclusion did not apply:

> In this case, the cause of the Investor's Loss is GOA's enactment of the Emergency Law. Although Ponderosa did agree to defer the PPI-indexed increase in 2000, thereby arguably allowing for the loss for this period, the action was reasonable under the circumstance, and the subsequent enactment of the Emergency Law cannot be attributed to this concession. According to Ponderosa, TGS has at all times complied with all of its obligations under the License, and continues to operate the pipeline despite the losses incurred due to the limitation on its revenue stream. Furthermore, although Enron was allegedly involved in unorthodox accounting practices, these allegations are unrelated to the expropriation and to the Investor's Loss in Argentina, and all of the financial records relating to this transaction have been fully reviewed by OPIC's accountant RNCO. Therefore, OPIC finds that the provocation exclusion does not apply.[31]

In contrast, OPIC concluded in *Marine Shipping Corporation* that its conduct did trigger the exclusion.

> Specifically, any blockage of MSC's funds or attachment of its assets by the GOE [Government of Egypt] taxation authorities were the result of MSC's failure to pay taxes indisputably due for the years 1992–1993. This non-payment of outstanding taxes was unreasonable action attributable to the Insured. Furthermore, MSC's decisions to cease negotiating with the Port Authority with respect to the rental fee issue, to cease seeking to obtain a License, to reject proffered assistance from the American Embassy, and to leave Egypt (abandoning its assets) were also unreasonable.
>
> Upon deciding in June 1993 that it was no longer going to continue in business in Egypt, a reasonable course of conduct on the part of MSC would have been payment of the outstanding taxes, payment of the disputed berthing fees as determined by the Egyptian court, removal of the Project from Port Said, and sale of MSC's assets. Even assuming that Mr. Kell genuinely feared for his personal safety on different occasions, MSC could have continued to protect its interests through the use of local or other representatives.
>
> The available information supports the conclusion that MSC wished to abandon the Project for business reasons and attempted to use the Insurance Contract as an exit vehicle. MSC was performing services under a series of

> contracts with Egyptian government entities. MSC was not entitled to renewal of these contracts on MSC's own terms. MSC's decision to abandon the Project rather than continue under less attractive terms was a business decision within MSC's discretion and not the basis for a valid claim under the Insurance Contract.[32]

Similar "provocation" exclusions are found in private PRI policies. One reads as follows:

> Situations where the preponderant cause of loss is unreasonable action attributable to the Insured or the Foreign Enterprise; including corrupt practices . . .

Under such a private policy, the ejusdem generis principle of contract interpretation might be argued by counsel to limit the scope of the phrase "unreasonable actions" to conduct similar to "corrupt practices." In contrast, the drafting of the "acts of the Insured outside the ordinary course" exclusion in the OPIC policy makes clear that such "outside the ordinary course" conduct may be a "provocation" excluded separately from OPIC's "corrupt practices" exclusion.

Perhaps the sample private policy illustrates the problem most succinctly. That policy excludes compensation for losses caused directly or indirectly by "the Insured, the Foreign Enterprise or their representatives . . . *provoking* the Host Government in some manner." (Emphasis added.) As we all know, foreign investors are quite provoking in defending their economic position, particularly when they insist on compliance with the literal terms of a contract or demand equitable treatment from a regulatory authority unaccustomed to Western notions of due process. Such an exclusion, construed in accordance with ordinary principles of contract interpretation, may eliminate many circumstances of regulatory expropriation. Prudent investors may wish to seek clarity about the scope of the "provocation" exclusion before accepting that exclusion in a policy covering a regulated entity.

Financial Default of the Covered Investment No claim under a PRI policy would ever be made unless the insured suffered a loss resulting from the expropriation. Naturally, that Loss may create severe economic difficulties for the covered enterprise, producing financial defaults by that enterprise under financings and other commercial contracts alike. That effect may be particularly obvious in the intermediate stages of a "creeping regulatory expropriation," as each individual regulatory step creates additional economic pressure on the investment's financial viability. Often, though, a PRI policy will exclude compensation for Losses resulting from the financial default of the covered enterprise. The sample private policy, for example, contains an exclusion for losses caused by "the insolvency, bankruptcy or financial default of the Insured or the Foreign Enterprise, or from the repossession of property by a title holder."

Here too, causation becomes a crucial area of inquiry. Did the host government's conduct cause the financial default? The difficulty of understanding the impact of these policy exclusion increases where, as in the case for the sample private policy, the policy's coverage is excluded if the exclusionary circumstance is merely a contributing factor to the Loss, not the preponderant cause of the Loss. Counsel for lenders to projects covered by PRI often face this issue, since the exercise of common lender remedies such as termination of commitments, acceleration of outstanding loans, or recovery of collateral may be the event that crystallizes cessation by the covered enterprise of its operations. For lenders seeking PRI coverage, we strongly recommend advance discussion of the "financial default" exclusion with the underwriter to fully understand the scope of that exclusion.

Bona Fide Host Government Acts It is not uncommon for a PRI policy to exclude regulatory conduct that constitutes a bona fide nondiscriminatory act. Thus, the sample private policy states:

> An act or series of acts taken by the Host Government which constitutes a *bona fide* nondiscriminatory measure of general application of a kind that governments normally take in the public interest shall not be the basis for a Claim of Expropriation.

The MIGA policy contains a similar, but not identical, exclusion:

> 4.2 No Measure shall constitute an Expropriation under Section 4.1 above, if it constitutes a *bona fide,* nondiscriminatory measure of general application that governments normally take for the purpose of regulating economic activity, ensuring public safety, raising revenues or protecting the environment, unless the measure is designed by the Host Government to have a confiscatory effect.

Unlike the sample private policy, the MIGA policy limits the bona fide acts exclusion if the host government designed the measure to have a confiscatory effect. Thus, the MIGA policy excludes from expropriation cover a bona fide nondiscriminatory regulatory measure unless the host government has designed the measure to have a confiscatory effect. That formulation, of course, blurs the line between "expropriatory effect" and "expropriatory intent" that was mentioned earlier in this article. The sample private policy, though, does not contain a similar override for measures "designed" to have a confiscatory affect. Accordingly, as a matter of basic contract interpretation the sample private policy arguably sets a higher barrier for regulatory expropriation claims to overcome.

Interestingly, the definition of "indirect expropriation" in the U.S. Model BIT contains a slightly different formulation of the exclusion for bona fide nondiscriminatory measures of general application. Paragraph 4(b) of Annex B provides:

> (b) *Except in rare circumstances*, nondiscriminatory regulatory actions by a Party that are designed and applied to protect legitimate public welfare objectives, such as public health, safety, and the environment, do not constitute indirect expropriations. (Emphasis added.)

The "indirect expropriation" definition in the U.S. Model BIT, as previously discussed, follows U.S. Supreme Court "takings" precedents under the Fifth Amendment to the U.S. Constitution. The introductory words to the "bona fide" exclusion ("Except in rare circumstances") also arguably derive from U.S. Supreme Court practice. Illustratively, the Supreme Court has held a South Carolina land use regulation covering seaside property to constitute a "taking" under the Fifth Amendment.[33] The landowner had purchased two residential lots on which he intended to build homes. South Carolina thereafter enacted a Beachfront Management Act, which barred the landowner from erecting any permanent habitable structures on his two parcels. When the Act was challenged, the trial concluded that the Act deprived the land of all economically beneficial use. South Carolina clearly passed the enactment for bona fide purposes, including environmental concerns. The effect was sufficiently severe, however, that the bona fide purposes behind the legislation did not, in the Supreme Court's view, override the expropriatory effect.

The Court identified "at least two discrete categories of regulatory action as compensable without case-specific inquiry into the public interest advanced in support of the restraint":[34]

> The first encompasses regulations that compel the property owner to suffer a physical "invasion" of his property. In general (at least with regard to permanent invasions), no matter how minute the intrusion, and no matter how weighty the public purpose behind it, we have required compensation. For example, in *Loretto v. Teleprompter Manhattan CATV Corp.*, 458 U.S. 419, 73 L. Ed. 2d 868, 102 S. Ct. 3164 (1982), we determined that New York's law requiring landlords to allow television cable companies to emplace cable facilities in their apartment buildings constituted a taking, id., at 435–440, even though the facilities occupied at most only 1 1/2 cubic feet of the landlords' property, see id., at 438, n.16. See also *United States v. Causby*, 328 U.S. 256, 265, 90 L. Ed. 1206, 66 S. Ct. 1062, and n.10 (1946) (physical invasions of airspace); cf. *Kaiser Aetna v. United States*, 444 U.S. 164, 62 L. Ed. 2d 332, 100 S. Ct. 383 (1979) (imposition of navigational servitude upon private marina).
>
> The second situation in which we have found categorical treatment appropriate is where regulation denies all economically beneficial or productive use of land. See *Agins*, 447 U.S. at 260; see also *Nollan v. California Coastal Comm'n*, 483 U.S. 825, 834, 97 L. Ed. 2d 677, 107 S. Ct. 3141 (1987); *Keystone Bituminous Coal Assn. v. DeBenedictis*, 480 U.S. 470, 495, 94 L. Ed.

> 2d 472, 107 S. Ct. 1232 (1987); *Hodel v. Virginia Surface Mining & Reclamation Assn., Inc.*, 452 U.S. 264, 295-296, 69 L. Ed. 2d 1, 101 S. Ct. 2352 (1981). As we have said on numerous occasions, the Fifth Amendment is violated when land-use regulation "does not substantially advance legitimate state interests *or denies an owner economically viable use of his land.*" *Agins, supra,* at 260 (citations omitted) (emphasis added).[35]

Thus, if a PRI policy follows the U.S. Supreme Court and current U.S. treaty practice in this regard, then an expropriation may be effected even by a bona fide nondiscriminatory public welfare enactment, if the regulation requires the investor to accept a "physical invasion" or deprives the investment of "all economically beneficial use" (at least if the investment comprises real property). If the PRI policy does not track the approach taken by the U.S. Supreme Court, then instead those circumstances might not limit the bona fide exclusion. And if the PRI policy incorporates customary international law, then only future arbitral awards will help us understand the scope of the bona fide exclusion.

III. Continuing Obligations

PRI policies impose as well a number of continuing obligations on covered parties. Failure by the insured to comply with these obligations entitles the insurer to terminate the policy. Here too, the circumstances of a regulatory expropriation may create special interpretive difficulties.

Duty to Disclose Either by covenant or by exclusion, PRI policies appropriately require the insured to disclose relevant information to the underwriter on a continuing basis. For example, the sample private policy contains the following obligations on the part of the insured party:

> B.1 The Insured represents, warrants and/or covenants that:
>
> (a) as of the date of its execution of this Insurance Policy, it had no knowledge of any circumstances which could give rise to a loss under this Insurance Policy;
>
> (b) all information that the Insured has provided in the Application for Insurance, and that the Insured will provide to the Underwriter, whether in written or verbal from, is true and correct and that no material information has been or will be withheld;

Breach of either of those obligations will entitle the underwriter to void the policy.

The sample private policy also contains a general condition entitled "False or Fraudulent Statement, Reports or Claims; Concealment." That provision also relates to the Insured's duty to disclose material information:

> This Insurance Policy shall become void, and all claims hereunder shall be forfeited, if the Insured makes any material Statement, report, application, or claim, where the Insured knew or should have known that the Statement, report, application or claim was false or fraudulent, or the Insured knowingly conceals any material fact, including but not limited to, a material change in the Project agreements or in implementation of the Project.

These disclosure obligations on the part of the insured of course make sense generally. Unlike commercial lenders to an enterprise, an insurer does not undertake a significant investigation of the covered investment before binding the policy. Instead, the insurer will rely on the information provided by the insured prebinding, and on the duty of the insured under the PRI policy to make continuing disclosure of material information thereafter.

However, the parameters of the insured's disclosure duties with respect to an investment in a regulated industry are unclear. Prior to making an investment in a highly regulated environment, a thoughtful investor will typically undertake an extensive examination of the regulatory framework and market participants, in addition to the other underlying financial and commercial circumstances surrounding the investment. That investigation may be encapsulated in a single final report, or it may be incorporated in numerous small memos, e-mails, reports of conversation, reports from advisors, gossip, meetings and brainstorming sessions, and the other substrata out of which a final report might be prepared. Inevitably, given the types of countries for which PRI is necessary, that diligence effort will unearth regulatory uncertainties and ambiguities having a direct impact on the covered investment. Does the insured have to open the entirety of its files about that regulatory investigation to the insurer? Is the standard of disclosure the same as the document production requirements in a court or arbitral proceedings, like the broad rules in the Federal Rules of Civil Procedure[36] or the narrower International Bar Association Rules for the Taking of Evidence in International Commercial Arbitration?[37] If a higher threshold than judicial/arbitral discovery applies, as would seem sensible, what is that standard? The "materiality" standards of SEC Rule 10b-5 also do not seem appropriate—but what is? PRI policies simply do not provide guidance on the extent of the insured's disclosure responsibilities for information about host government regulatory risks.

This same ambiguity also affects the duty of the insured to make continuing disclosure. Regulatory authorities routinely consider changes to their regulatory framework, even in the most stable of countries. In countries with unreliable and erratic governments (i.e., countries where PRI makes sense), information about such changes is often not available transparently; it arrives through gossip, informal contacts with government officials, and conversations with local professionals, business, and interest groups. Here again, the extent of an insured's disclosure responsibilities under a PRI policy is unclear. PRI policies routinely require the insured to "notify the Underwriter immediately, and in no event later than XX days, following the occurrence of any event that *could* give rise to a Claim" (emphasis added). With 20–20 hindsight, of course, one of those earlier conversations may have identified the regulatory conduct that later gave rise to the alleged regulatory expropriation. The insured is surely not obligated to "do a daily document dump" on the underwriter to satisfy its continuing duties. But if not, then what standard does a PRI policy establish to help the insured decide which bits and pieces of information about the regulatory conduct of the host government must be disclosed? This area, too, is an appropriate topic for discussion between underwriter and insured before the PRI policy is finalized.

Duty to Minimize Losses Like the continuing obligation to disclose material information, it is customary for a PRI policy to obligate the insured to take reasonable steps to minimize losses and enhance recoveries.[38] Thus, OPIC's Contract of Insurance provides:

> 9. Preservation, Transfer and Continuing Cooperation. . . . Prior to the assignment of rights required by §8.02, the Investor shall, in consultation with OPIC, take all reasonable measures to preserve property, to pursue available administrative and judicial remedies, and to negotiate in good faith with the governing authority of the country in which the project is located and other sources of compensation. After a transfer of rights or delivery of local currency, in exchange for reimbursement of reasonable out of pocket expenses, the Investor shall take all actions reasonably requested by OPIC to assist OPIC in preserving the property and rights transferred to OPIC and in prosecuting related claims.

The comparable provision is the sample private policy that is simultaneously more detailed and more unclear.

> It and the Foreign Enterprise will take all reasonable steps to avoid or minimize any Loss. The Insured and the Foreign Enterprise shall cooperate fully with the Underwriter in the investigation of any Claim, the resolution of any potential claim situation and the pursuant of any Claim salvage. The Insured will not enter into any agreement concerning a Loss or potential Loss without the Underwriter's prior written consent. Prior to any Compensation payment, the Insured will pursue all reasonable diplomatic, legal, administrative, judicial and informal means which may be reasonably available to minimize or recover any Loss. The Insured will also preserve any legal, judicial and administrative remedies applicable to any Claim and furnish reasonable assistance in maintaining any rights or property transferred to the Underwriter.

More than just drafting ambiguities are at issue here. The duty to take reasonable steps to mitigate losses may, in a regulatory context, create tensions with other obligations of the insured under the PRI policy. If, illustratively, a strong and continuing defense by the foreign investor of its regulatory position "provokes" the host government, has compliance with the obligation to "pursue all reasonable diplomatic, administrative, judicial and informal means" triggered the "provocation" exclusion under the policy? When does acceptance of controversial regulatory enactments (perhaps an intermediate step in a "creeping regulatory expropriation") constitute prohibited entry into an "agreement concerning a Loss without the Underwriter's consent?" To comply with this requirement, must the insured involve the underwriter in discussions of regulatory tactics and strategy long before a claim under the PRI policy is presented? Here as well, the ambiguities of a standard PRI policy are magnified in an active regulatory environment.

Addressing a similar issue in the *Ponderosa* claim, OPIC ruled that Ponderosa's agreement in 2000 to the Argentine request for deferral of Argentina's 2000 PPI-indexing obligation "constituted a waiver of a project agreement, not a modification or amendment *per se*."[39] OPIC also held in that Determination that a modification must have a material adverse effect on the risks borne by OPIC to trigger application of the exclusion for modifications without OPIC's consent. According to OPIC:

> The only effect was to limit the revenues TGS was allowed to receive. Such limitation, absent the Emergency Law, would not be sufficient to constitute an expropriatory event. Therefore, OPIC finds that the Investor has satisfactorily complied with the requirements of this provision.[40]

Accordingly, OPIC construed the obligation in its policy to mean that the prohibited agreement must have had a material adverse effect on the risks borne by OPIC. While such an interpretation seems reasonable, the text of the OPIC policy does not contain any statement of that principle. Moreover, it would not be prudent for an investor to rely on OPIC's interpretations of the OPIC PRI policy to govern the conduct of other underwriters construing their own policies.

IV. Conclusion

As the foregoing illustrates, the circumstances of a regulatory expropriation claim may give rise to more questions than answers under a PRI policy. The issues identified above by no means exhaust the potential for ambiguity under PRI policies. Insured and underwriter alike are well advised to discuss these issues in advance, rather than asking an arbitrator to settle the question once the loss has crystallized.

Notes

1. See, generally, Rubins & Kinsella. 2005. *International Investment, Political Risk and Dispute Resolution: A Practitioner's Guide,* Chapter 5, 174–188. Oceana Publications, Inc.

2. Id., at pps. 182–184.

3. To date, 14 countries have signed agreements with the U.S. incorporating this approach, although not all of those States have yet completed ratification of the treaty to which they are signatory. Canada as well has incorporated a virtually identical formulation in its 2004 Model Treaty for the Promotion and Protection of Investments and in its 2006 FIPA with Peru. In addition to extant agreements, the United States has announced that it is negotiating further free trade agreements (FTAs) and BITs with numerous other countries. The U.S. government is actively engaged in investment or FTA negotiations with numerous countries, including the Republic of Korea, Pakistan, Thailand, Malaysia, Panama (agreed but not yet signed), and the United Arab Emirates.

4. Available at www.state.gov/documents/organization/38710.pdf.

5. *Penn Central Transportation Co. v. New York City,* 438 U.S. 104 (1978). See also *Lingle v. Chevron USA, Inc.,* 544 U.S. 528 (2005). In following U.S. Supreme Court precedents for its definition of "indirect expropriation," the U.S. government has been true to the congressional mandate set out in the 2002 Trade Promotion Act: "the principal negotiating objectives of the United States regarding foreign investment are to reduce or eliminate artificial or trade-distorting barriers to foreign investment, while ensuring that foreign investors in the United States are not accorded greater substantive rights with respect to investment protections than United States investors in the United States, and to secure for investors rights comparable to those that would be available under United States legal principles and practices. . . ." An alternative test considered in the U.S. courts was the "substantially advances legitimate government goals" test drawn from *Agins v. City of Tiburon,* 447 U.S. 255 (1980). That test was a so-called "means-ends" test permitting a court to inquire more deeply into the substance of the challenged measure. If the regulatory conduct did not substantially advance the interests specified by the government, then the measure constituted a regulatory taking. However, that approach was unanimously rejected by the U.S. Supreme Court in *Lingle* as not an appropriate test for determining whether a regulation effects a Fifth Amendment taking. The *Lingle* decision reaffirmed the general standards in *Penn Central* for determining under the Fifth and Fourteenth Amendments to the U.S. Constitution whether a regulatory taking has been effected. According to the *Lingle* decision, a plaintiff seeking to challenge a government regulation as an uncompensated taking of private property may proceed by alleging: (1) a *Penn Central* taking of the type adopted into Annex B of the 2004 U.S. Model BIT; (2) a "physical" taking (see *Loretto v. Teleprompter Manhattan CATV Corp.,* 458 U.S. 419 [1982]); (3) that the regulatory action completely deprived an owner of all economically beneficial use of her property (see *Lucas v. South Carolina Coastal Council,* 505 U.S. 1003 [1992]); or (4) that the government had required the property owner to give up the constitutional right to receive just compensation in exchange for a discretionary benefit that has little or no relationship to the property (see *Nollan v. California Coastal Commission,* 483 U.S. 825 [1987] and *Dolan v. City of Tigard,* 512 U.S. 374 [1994]).

6. As of February 2007, those states are Costa Rica (not yet ratified), Colombia, the Dominican Republic, El Salvador, Guatemala, Honduras, Nicaragua, Morocco, Uruguay, Chile, Singapore, Australia, and Oman. In addition, Panama has initialed a text but not yet signed. The similar annex in the U.S.-Peru Free Trade Agreement (awaiting ratification) does not contain the reference to customary international law found in Paragraph 1 of the DR-CAFTA Annex, but does contain the *Penn Central* factors from Paragraph 4.

7. See Annex B. 13(1), available at www.dfait-maeci.gc.ca.

8. Quotations of policy language in this article are based on policy forms in the author's personal files. The identity of the underwriter or insurer is omitted to observe confidentiality obligations when required. Naturally, wording may vary from policy to policy.

9. See AAA Commercial Rules Rule R-23, AAA International Arbitration Rules Article 20.4, LCIA Rules Articles 19.4 & 30, ICC Arbitration Rules Article 21.3, and MIGA Rules of Arbitration Article 39.2.

10. *Azurix Corp. v. The Argentine Republic,* ICSID Case No. ARB/CAF/01/12, Award dispatched July 14, 2006.

11. See Rubins & Kinsella, supra n. 1, Appendix VII.

12. Available at www.wto.org/English/docs_A/legal_A/26-gats_01_A.htm.

13. *CMS Gas Transmission Company v. The Argentine Republic,* ICSID Case No. ARB/01/8, Award, May 12, 2005. The tribunal did, however, hold that Argentina's conduct breached the separate international law obligation of "fair and equitable treatment." The tribunal awarded damages based on the adverse impact of Argentina's regulatory conduct on the investment's market value.

14. See www.bvappraisers.org/glossary/glossary.pdf. For example, the International Glossary of Business, Valuation Terms, jointly adapted by inter alia the American Society of Appraisers and the American Institute of Certified Public Accountants, defines an "Operating Company" as "a business that conducts an economic activity by generating and selling or trading in a product or service." Also, there is a line of international investment arbitration awards concluding that, for purposes of calculating compensation for an expropriation, lost profits or future earnings losses are only appropriate if the expropriated enterprise had an extended period of operations prior to the expropriation. See, e.g., *Sola Tiles v. Islamic Republic of Iran,* Award No. 298-317-1, 14 Iran-U.S. C.T.R. 223 (1987). In *Sola Tiles,* the Tribunal concluded that the business in question (Simat) was not a "going concern" because inter alia "Simat had the briefest past record of profitability, having shown a loss in 1976, its first year of trading, and a small profit the next year." Id., Para. 64. The expropriation date was November 1978, and thus Simat had been operating for almost three years before the expropriation date.

15. Kunoy. 2006. "The Notion of Time in ICSID's Case Law on Indirect Expropriation." 23 *J. Int. Arb.* 337, 337–38.

16. Newcombe. 2005. "The Boundaries of Regulatory Expropriation in International Law." 20 *ICSID Rev.-F.I.L.J.* 1, 8.

17. *LG&E Energy Corp. et al. v. The Argentine Republic,* ICSID Case No. ARB/02/01, Decision on Liability, paras. 146-148, 3 October 2006 (Argentine conduct not discriminatory because it applied across the board to all investments in gas distribution industry).

18. UNCTAD. 2006. *Bilateral Investment Treaties 1995–2005: Trends in Investment Rulemaking.* (April).

19. OPIC Memorandum of Determinations, Expropriation Claim of Joseph Companies Incorporated of Minneapolis, Jamaica–Contract of Insurance No. E197 (June 27, 1999).

20. Id., at 11.

21. See, e.g., OPIC Memorandum of Determinations, Expropriation Claim of Ponderosa Assets, L.P., Argentina–Contract of Insurance No. D733, at 7 (August 2, 2005), available at www.opic.gov/insurance/claims/report/index.asp.

22. OPIC Memorandum of Determinations, Confiscation Claim of Marine Shipping Corporation, Contract of Insurance No. CO15 (July 2, 1999), at 2–3.

23. OPIC Memorandum of Determinations, Expropriation Claim of Bank of America, as Trustee, India, Contract of Insurance No. F041 (September 30, 2003), available at www.opic.gov/insurance/claims/report/index.asp.

24. *Bechtel Enterprises International (Bermuda) Ltd. et al. v. Overseas Private Investment Corporation,* AAA Case No. 50 T195 00509 02 (September 3, 2003), at 16, 17 & 23, available at http://www.opic. gov/insurance/claims/awards/documents/2294171_1.pdf.

25. OPIC Memorandum of Determinations, Expropriation Claim of Ponderosa Assets, L.P., supra n. 21 at 10–12.

26. Id., at 15.

27. OPIC Memorandum of Determinations, Expropriation Claim of Science Applications International Corporation, OPIC Contract of Insurance No. E833 (July 12, 2004), at 21.

28. Id., at 21. See also OPIC Memorandum of Determinations, Expropriation Claim of MidAmerican Energy Holdings Company (formerly CalEnergy Company, Inc.), Contracts of Insurance Nos. E374, E453, E527, and E759 (November 1999), at 5 (policies contain similar Sec. 10.03).

29. OPIC Memorandum of Determinations, Expropriation Claim of Science Applications International Corporation, supra n. 27 at 21–24.

30. OPIC Memorandum of Determinations, Expropriation Claim of Joseph Companies Incorporated of Minneapolis, supra n. 19 at 13–14.

31. OPIC Memorandum of Determinations, Expropriation Claim of Ponderosa Assets, L.P., supra n. 21 at 14–15. See also OPIC Memorandum of Determinations, Expropriation Claim of Science Applications International Corporation, supra n. 27 at 20 (rejecting Venezuelan corruption allegations as fabricated).

32. OPIC Memorandum of Determinations, Confiscation Claim of Marine Shipping Corporation, supra n. 22 at 3.

33. *Lucas v. South Carolina Coastal Council,* 505 U.S. 1003 (1992).

34. Id., at 1015.

35. Id., at 1015–16 (footnotes omitted).

36. "Parties may obtain discovery regarding any matter, not privileged, that is relevant to the claim or defense of any party. . . . Relevant information need not be admissible at the trial if the discovery appears reasonably calculated to lead to the discovery of admissible evidence." F.R.C.P. Rule 26(b)(1).

37. Article 3 of the IBA Rules permits a party in arbitral proceedings to request production of documents if the request contains: "(a) (*i*) a description of a requested document sufficient to identify it, or (*ii*) a description in sufficient detail (including subject matter) of a narrow and specific requested category of documents that are reasonably believed to exist; (b) a description of how the documents requested are relevant and material to the outcome of the case; and (c) a statement that the documents requested are not in the possession, custody or control of the requesting Party, and of the reason why that Party assumes the documents requested to be in the possession, custody or control of the other Party."

38. The insurance market often refers to this as a "due diligence" obligation. Commercial and financing parties in investment transactions, however, use that same phrase instead to refer to preclosing investigations. The confusion about the meaning of this term can complicate discussions between insurer and insured.

39. OPIC Memorandum of Determinations, Expropriation Claim of Ponderosa Assets, L.P., supra n. 21 at 19.

40. Id.

A SWORD IN A STONE: PROBLEMS (AND A FEW PROPOSED SOLUTIONS) REGARDING POLITICAL RISK INSURANCE COVERAGE OF REGULATORY TAKINGS

Frederick E. Jenney
Morrison & Foerster LLP, Washington, DC

Introduction

Investors in developing countries face the constant threat of regulatory change. In extreme cases, regulatory action can constitute a type of expropriation known as a "regulatory taking." To an investor, a regulatory action that causes significant economic harm to its investment often seems like such a taking.

Political risk insurers, on the other hand, intend that expropriation coverage does not protect against the effects of most regulatory actions of the host government. The reason is simple: when a political risk insurer pays an expropriation claim to an insured investor, the insurer needs to be in a position to make a claim back against the host government for its action. A host government, however, is only liable for the consequences of its actions that are wrongful, as opposed to legitimate.

Which actions are "legitimate" is a complex question. Investors must turn to international law, where the standards for regulatory takings are murky. In general, there is agreement only that international law requires that a taking be: (i) for a public purpose, (ii) nondiscriminatory, and (iii) accompanied by just compensation.

Traditional expropriation insurance excludes coverage of ordinary regulation, typically described as a "*bona fide* non-discriminatory measure of general application of a kind that governments normally take in the public interest. . . ." This language is helpful and reflects the basic international law standard, but does not answer the hard questions:

- Can the line be drawn between legitimate regulation and wrongful regulatory taking?
- If so, who is in the best position to draw that line, and at what point in the process?
- Most importantly, is there a satisfactory way for PRI to cover wrongful regulatory takings?

Expropriation Standards Under International Law

Classic Expropriation

Traditional PRI expropriation coverage protects against confiscation, expropriation, nationalization, and other acts by the host government that prevent the return to a foreign investor of its investment. The coverage squarely addresses "classic" expropriation, which is outright acts of nationalization and confiscation, and generally falls into two categories: (i) expropriation of assets—typically done with tanks and soldiers; and (ii) expropriation of an investor's rights—typically done by executive or legislative action (e.g., publication of a decree or change in law), Cuba in 1959 being one clear example. Even though it was achieved by formal governmental action, there was no doubt as to the discriminatory intent, or the effect, of Fidel Castro's actions against U.S. investors. Those were the good old days . . . at least for clarity.

Regulatory Takings Present a Different Problem

However, as too many investors have learned the hard way, many government actions that fall well short of classic expropriation can also significantly diminish the value of an overseas investment. These include discriminatory regulations targeted at a particular investor or industry, typically one dominated by foreign investors, which are designed to transfer wealth from the investor to the government (or to consumers) or otherwise curtail the economic rights of the investor.

On the other hand, legitimate regulation in the public interest—such as taxation, environmental laws, and even price measures in a regulated industry—also has the effect of transferring wealth from the investor to the government (or to consumers) and curtailing the investor's economic rights. Almost by definition, every change in regulation: (i) changes someone's expected revenue or cost structure, and therefore their expected profit; and (ii) changes someone's expectations or understanding of the market.

If every regulatory change were treated as an expropriation in violation of international law, no government could afford to make any changes at all—defeating the very purpose of legitimate regulation. Yet governments clearly have the power, and often the purpose and intent, to achieve wrongful ends through regulation. Unfortunately for the PRI industry, it is extremely difficult to find an appropriate legal standard that distinguishes between "wrongful" and "legitimate" government regulatory actions.

The first obvious problem is that host country law is generally of no help. The same executive that enacted and enforced the regulation can assert that it is legal. Legislators may well be focused more on addressing problems than on maintaining fundamental principles. Host country courts, especially in developing countries with a less independent judiciary, will be inclined to interpret the law to find that the suspect regulation is legal.

The second obvious problem is that existing foreign investors are often politically disfavored by local governments, and may even lack standing to pursue a claim under the local legal system.

Overview of International Law

Given these problems with local law standards, international law has emerged as the only practical mechanism for protection of foreign investors.

International law is the law of the international community of states. It consists of specific rules, as well as principles of general application dealing with the conduct of nation-states and their relations with other states. Although originally conceived as a mechanism for resolving disputes between nation-states, in the last 50 years the international law of takings has evolved into a set of principles for settling disputes between the host state and individual foreign investors, including individuals, business organizations, and other legal entities.

Of course, at the international level there is neither a "world government" (in the sense of an executive), nor a central legislature with general law-making authority—and there certainly is no World Supreme Court.

A rule of international law is one that has been accepted as such by the international community of states: (i) in the form of *customary law,* (ii) by *international agreement* (i.e., bilateral and multilateral treaties), or (iii) by derivation from *general principles* common to the major legal systems of the world.

Although the sources of international law distinguish it from domestic or national law, nation-states treat international law as law, consider themselves bound by it, and attend to it with a sense of legal obligation and with concern for the consequences of violation. Having said that, however, international law has some serious limitations, as discussed below.

International Law Standards for Regulatory Takings

Commentators have long debated the definition of a wrongful taking. The most often-cited recitation of the standard for wrongful takings under international law is in the Restatement of Foreign Relations Law of the United States:

> A state is responsible under international law for injury resulting from . . . a taking by the state of the property of a national of another state that (a) is not for a public purpose, or (b) is discriminatory, or (c) is not accompanied by provision for just compensation . . . .

Multilateral and bilateral treaties have followed the Restatement approach. For example, the NAFTA treaty provides that:

> [n]o Party may directly or indirectly nationalize or expropriate an investment of an investor of another Party in its territory or take a measure tantamount to nationalization or expropriation of such an investment, unless the government's action is (1) for a public purpose; (2) is non-discriminatory; (3) meets due process of law and minimum treatment accorded to the government's own nationals; and (4) pays compensation fully, promptly, in convertible currency.[1]

However, the international law of expropriation allows a government broad discretion to adopt bona fide regulations that do not discriminate against foreign investors. For example, a NAFTA case in 2000 set out a restrictive standard of regulatory takings, holding that government regulation, while not immune from liability, enjoyed a presumption in favor of legality:

> The general body of precedent usually does not treat regulatory action as amounting to expropriation. Regulatory conduct by public authorities is unlikely to be the subject of legitimate complaint under Article 1110 of the NAFTA, although the tribunal does not rule out that possibility.[2]

As Mark Kantor notes in his accompanying paper, the definition of "indirect expropriation" in the U.S. Model BIT contains a slightly different formulation, but supports the same proposition:

> *Except in rare circumstance,* nondiscriminatory regulatory actions by a Party that are designed and applied to protect legitimate public welfare objectives, such as public health, safety, and the environment, do not constitute indirect expropriations.[3] (Emphasis added.)

Applying Basic International Law Standards

Basic Challenges

Applying these international law standards has proven to be challenging. Not surprisingly, in practice it is difficult to draw the line between normal regulation and a regulatory taking.

On the spectrum of host government regulatory action, most observers can readily identify cases at the extremes. A moderate, general increase in income taxes would not be expropriatory; a 100 percent tax levied on an individual investor would be. If the host government passes a regulation that nationalizes a private party's copper mine, perhaps on the pretext of worker safety or environmental protection, few would doubt that the government's action fits within the classic definition of expropriation.

Most cases are harder. If a state changes its regulatory framework so that 90 percent of profits of venture are "lost" (i.e., passed on to the state or its citizens), is it still an expropriation? Does this hold even if the government did not take control and the investor still owns the business? Or even if the business is turning a nominal profit?

The Restatement commentary acknowledges much of the line drawing is difficult:

> As under United States constitutional law, the line between 'taking' and regulation is sometimes uncertain.[4]

Basic concepts such as "discrimination" are also elusive. The Restatement provides:

> Discrimination implies unreasonable distinction. . . . Discrimination may be difficult to determine where there is no comparable enterprise owned by local nationals or by nationals of other countries, or where nationals of the taking state are treated equally with aliens but by discrete actions separated in time.[5]

The Restatement also notes that different sources may be consulted for guidance, yet the variety alone of these sources suggests that one clear standard is unlikely to emerge.

> A challenged regulation might be compared with the practice of major legal systems; . . . the fact that a given regulation is supported by guidelines adopted by an international agency to guide the behavior of multinationals may be seen as evidence of its legitimacy.[6]

Thus the question of what constitutes a taking for which compensation should be paid can be determined only on a case-by-case basis.

New Theories Emerge

Because regulatory actions rarely involve clear takings of property, but are more likely to involve subtler detriment to the investor's interests, the case-by-case approach has led to new theories. In order to describe investor interests and government actions against them, arbitral tribunals and commentators have developed international law concepts such as "economic benefit" and "meaningful return."

In one of the better-known cases regarding regulatory takings, the tribunal in the 2000 *Metalclad* case affirmed that NAFTA recognized a regulatory taking as an expropriation under NAFTA's Article 1110:

> Expropriation . . . includes not only open, deliberate and acknowledged takings of property, such as outright seizure or formal obligatory transfer of title in favor of the host state, but also covert or incidental interference with the use of property which has the effect of depriving the owner, in whole or in significant part, of the use of reasonably-to-be-*expected economic benefit* of a property even if not necessarily to the obvious benefit of the host State.[7]

The *Metalclad* tribunal held the Mexican government liable for $17 million, in part:

> [b]ecause the actions of the Mexican authorities resulted in the "complete frustration" of the claimant's operation of the landfill and "negate[d] the possibility of *any meaningful return* of Metalclad's investment.[8]

It is safe to say that the discussion of expectations in the *Metalclad* case raised hopes among international investors aggrieved by host country regulation.

A whole series of NAFTA cases have followed, as have claims under BITs against the Government of Argentina. As outlined in the accompanying papers by Mark Kantor and Peter Choharis, these cases have developed new theories of regulatory takings under international law, based on such concepts as inducement and breach of representation by the host country, investor legitimate expectations, and breach of the duty of "fair and equitable treatment."[9]

Resulting Lack of Clarity

Based on a review of these arbitral awards (and of the papers presented at the 2006 MIGA-Georgetown Symposium), it is safe to say that the international law of regulatory takings is unclear at best. A catalog of the more specific shortcomings of the international law standard includes:

- It is hopelessly *vague:* Any standard based on principles such as "public policy," "discrimination" and even "taking" (much less "fair and equitable treatment") will be interpreted differently by people from different cultures with differing expectations about international investment protection.

- It is *inconsistent:* The international law of regulatory takings is being developed mostly through ad hoc and administered arbitrations under bilateral and multilateral treaties throughout the world. Results are inconsistent; there is no stare decisis principle in international arbitration (i.e., that decisions must be consistent with previous decisions), and no World Supreme Court to sort out inconsistent results.
- It is *evolving:* The law of regulatory takings is not going in circles, but rather evolving toward new principles, many of which are more protective of investors, but some of which have caused a backlash. What was a legal regulatory action in 1950 may be an illegal regulatory taking today.
- It is *political:* The issues are complex, not only legally but because they are susceptible to different interpretations depending on policy goals and political philosophy. Principles of state regulatory autonomy in emerging economies often clash with protection of investors from wealthier developed countries.

Indeed, the one thing on which all commentators agree—whatever their respective views on the appropriate standards and application of those standards to individual cases—is that the international law of regulatory takings is unclear.

Managing Regulatory Risks

Change of Law Risk

To better understand illegal regulatory takings, it helps to start with an understanding of regulatory risk. Regulatory risk, also known as "change of law risk," is present in every domestic or international transaction.

Government regulation is a fact of life in the business world. Nevertheless, overseas investors are highly suspicious of foreign regulation when making investments. Although they freely choose to invest in developing countries in regulated industries, some foreign investors have an aversion to development in the regulation of those industries. For some, it is tempting to view a regulatory change that causes economic harm to an enterprise as a wrongful regulatory taking.

Is Changing the Rules Unfair?

Investors sometimes argue that changing the rules in the middle of the game is unfair. One response would be that changing the rules is exactly what regulators are supposed to do, for example when the game is being played unfairly, and that that change always comes "in the middle" to the players who joined the "game" earlier. In other words, regulators are supposed to change the rules to effect good public policy, and it's always in the middle of the game because the game goes on forever.

This is the myth of the "stable regulatory environment." A regulatory environment is stable only so long as there is no need for regulators to intervene. When the existing regulations prove inadequate, either as written or as applied, good public policy suggests that it is time for a change. Not only is a host government entitled to change laws, but in a real sense it is the government's job to do so in response to changing conditions.

Use of Stabilization Clauses

However legitimate, regulation can certainly disrupt the activities of an enterprise, including one owned by foreign investors. Over the years, investors have developed various methods for ensuring (or at least encouraging) a stable regulatory environment. These come in a variety of forms, from outright guarantees to mere comfort letters, but the most common is the investment agreement.[10]

Such an agreement, whether in the form of a concession, a contract, or other binding commitment from the host government, defines specific undertakings of the host government to support the investment, including limiting the impact on the investor of future regulatory changes.

For specifically addressing regulatory risk, the preferred mechanism is the stabilization clause, which is a commitment from the host government to insulate the investor from the consequences of change to aspects of the legal and regulatory environment, often inserted as a section or clause in a longer investment agreement (hence the term).

A stabilization clause, while not a promise by the government to refrain from making changes to the law, is an agreement to compensate the investor for the consequences to it of those changes, for example by exempting the enterprise from tax increases, whether legitimate or not. The scope of a stabilization clause may be limited as to time, type of regulation, or overall amount of compensation.

Problems in Insuring Regulatory Risks

Change of Law Risk Is Not Insurable

While change of law risk is present in every transaction, it is perceived to be greater for investments in developing countries—which are the investments most likely to have PRI. So perhaps not surprisingly, investors sometimes assume that PRI is designed to address change of law risk. It is not.

Normal change of law is not an insurable event, because it is not a wrongful action under international law. As noted above, legitimate regulatory actions do not give rise to a right of recovery against the government; if they did, no government could afford to make changes to a regulatory regime. Consequently, no insurer would be in business long if it offered coverage against the impact on a company's revenues of legitimate regulatory changes, for which the insurer would have no right of recovery.

Stated differently, PRI protects the rights under international law that an investor actually *has* (to be free from wrongful regulatory takings), not what it *wishes it had* (to be free from all regulatory change). Political risk insurers can insure only valuable existing rights; they are not alchemists.

No Coverage of Legitimate Regulatory Action

Therefore, for a political risk insurer to cover a regulatory taking it is crucial that the host government regulatory action be a violation of international law.

Political risk insurance policies reflect this crucial requirement. As Mark Kantor notes in his accompanying paper, policies typically contain either (i) an express requirement that an expropriatory action be a violation of international law, or (ii) language closely tracking the consensus standard for what is required for a taking to be in violation of international law.[11]

To further emphasize that point, PRI policies often contain a regulatory action exclusion such as the following:

> This policy does not cover any loss or damage resulting from *bona fide* non-discriminatory measures of general application of a kind that governments normally take in the public interest for such purposes as ensuring public safety, raising revenues, protecting the environment, or regulating economic activities.[12]

This language, although it reflects the international law standard, has all the same shortcomings. In a PRI claim situation, as in international law cases regarding the definition of regulatory taking, lawyers can (and do) have a field day.

- What does "bona fide" mean? Is it a test of the government's *intent* or the *effect* of a regulation?
- How general is "general application"? If all the power producers in the country are owned by foreigners, does regulation of the power industry therefore target foreign investors?[13]
- Does "of a kind that governments normally take in the public interest" mean that some government in the past has to have taken the measure for it to be legitimate?
- Does "for such purposes as" allow for purposes other than the ones listed?
- Does "regulating economic activities" have any practical limit? Could a government completely ban an industry (such as casino gambling)?

- Finally, how much of a causal link is required by "resulting from"? If a government campaign regarding the health effects of cigarette smoking leads to a decline in smoking, but there is at the same time a discriminatory government action against foreign tobacco companies, what proportion of a tobacco company's loss or damage can be said to result from the bona fide nondiscriminatory health campaign?

The answers to these questions are no more clear in the PRI context than in the context of the international law of regulatory takings.

Problems with Recent Political Risk Insurance Claims

Political risk insurers have in recent years seen a spike in the number of claims for regulatory takings. Regulatory action is clearly governmental action, government actions can have unclear motives and unintended effects, and most regulatory effect is of some detriment to foreign investors, so there is often a colorable claim that a regulation wrongfully caused a loss.

For an insured investor, the benefits of a successful expropriation claim, even when discounted by a low probability of success, may outweigh even hundreds of thousands (or millions) of dollars spent assembling the requisite international law arguments to demonstrate a wrongful regulatory taking.

Faced with unclear international law on regulatory takings, and not being obligated to pay a claim where there has been no clear violation of international law, political risk insurers have denied a large proportion of these regulatory taking claims. Claim denials have led to disputes with insured investors, accusations that insurers have acted in bad faith, and expensive arbitrations under PRI policies.

These claims and arbitrations have put political risk insurers on the front lines in the battle to clearly delineate illegal regulatory takings from legitimate regulation. Many insurers have attempted to clarify the regulation exclusion in their policies, but have run up against the inherent lack of clarity in the legal standard.

Cases also tend to be very fact-specific, and therefore difficult to analyze based on general principles. As Mark Kantor notes in his accompanying paper, the particular facts and circumstances of a regulatory expropriation claim may give rise to more questions than answers under a PRI policy.

For insurers, covering regulatory risk has become an exercise in high-stakes line drawing. Although expropriation coverage was not expressly designed for regulatory takings, it has allowed for coverage of them. Faced with a claim, the political risk insurer must draw the line correctly: if it pays a claim that later proves to have been not an illegal regulatory taking, the insurer has no recourse.

Some insurers are changing their coverages. Finding that it is too difficult to draw a line between legitimate and illegal regulatory actions, some insurers are excluding from coverage *all* regulatory action. The following is a typical exclusion:

> This policy does not cover Regulatory Action, which means any claim or dispute relating to any action taken by the Host Government . . . for the regulation of the [describe] industry or the Project, including without limitation any claim with respect thereto against [name of regulator] . . .[14]

Other insurers have gone farther and stopped writing expropriation coverage altogether for projects in regulated industries, such as power and water.

Limitations of Existing Political Risk Insurance

In summary, the challenge for political risk insurers is as follows:

- For a regulatory action to be insurable, it must be compensable by the host government
- For it to be compensable it must be wrongful, as opposed to legitimate
- The only workable definition of "wrongful" is that it be a violation of international law
- International law on the subject is hopelessly inconsistent, evolving, political, and (ultimately) unclear.

Principles for Coverage of Regulatory Takings

There are a few principles that can be set out before political risk insurers consider the challenge of covering regulatory takings. There are at least five such relevant principles:

1. To be insurable, a regulatory action must be a violation of international law. For the reasons noted above, the international law standard must apply to regulatory takings. It is fundamental to expropriation insurance that an insurer writes coverage on the basis that the amount it pays as a claim gives rise to an equal right of recovery against the host government.

2. Political risk insurers should not be put in a position of having to determine whether a regulatory action is a violation of international law. If arbitral tribunals cannot draw a clear line, it is unreasonable to expect political risk insurers to do so. The solution also cannot be expected to come in the form of improved PRI policy language, so insurers and insureds should stop trying to refine PRI language with respect to regulatory takings. There are no magic words. Ultimately a PRI policy can be no clearer than the law it aims to reflect.

3. *Investors should get no more than what they bargained for at the beginning.* It is a basic tenet of PRI (and indeed of all insurance) that insurance coverage will not put the insured in a better position than it would have been absent the alleged loss.[15] In other words, the purpose of PRI is to assure a bargained-for result, not improve upon it. Investors who fail to structure their arrangements with the host government to protect against the possibility (indeed probability) of regulatory change in a highly regulated industry should not expect to turn to their insurers to compensate them for a normal business risk that they could have reasonably anticipated.

4. *For investor rights to be protected by insurers, they must be protected by the host government.* Investment agreements and stabilization clauses have existed in the international investment world for years. Investors concerned with regulatory risk and regulatory takings must seek such a clause. Most investors, however, have nothing that rises to the level of an agreement with the host government. Much foreign investment is done on the basis of a concession granted by the host government to the investor, or even a bare foreign investment license. A concession or license is unlikely to address any rights of an investor to a stable regulatory environment.

Investors sometimes argue that they had reasonable expectations of a stable regulatory environment, and in relying on those expectations were induced by the host government into making an investment.[16] While the international law of regulatory takings may some day fully protect investor expectations, for PRI protection today, investors must have a more solid basis for a claim against the host government.

5. *Where a host government has made an agreement in a concession or a contract, arbitral award default coverage is available to backstop enforcement of that agreement.* Arbitral award default coverage has long been available for failure of a sovereign entity to honor an arbitration award issued against it. It is separate from expropriation coverage, and is designed to preserve for the insured the benefits of an agreement containing international arbitration as the dispute resolution mechanism.

Under arbitral award default coverage, the idea is that commercial disputes between the parties must go through arbitration first. The dispute resolution mechanism, not a political risk insurer, is best able to distinguish between (i) a commercial, factual, or contractual dispute, where the host government has a legitimate reason for not making a payment; and (ii) a political action by the host government, where the host government has lost the arbitration, has a clear obligation to pay, and is just making excuses.[17]

An arbitral award is much more easily insurable than a contractual promise to pay, or even a court judgment for payment, because an international arbitral award is more dependably enforceable against the host government. International arbitral awards have the force of law and are enforceable without judicial review, by virtue of the U.N. Convention on Recognition and Enforcement of Arbitral Awards (known as the "New York Convention") and similar international treaties, both in the host country and in other countries party to the same treaty. In other words, failure to pay is a violation of international law.

There are a few requirements for arbitral award default coverage. The biggest is that the investor must obtain an arbitral award that is final and nonappealable under the rules of the dispute resolution procedure.

Happily, most dispute resolution procedures provide for only limited rights of appeal, and normally an arbitral award can be treated as being final and nonappealable notwithstanding that it is subject to challenge or contest by the host government in the courts of the host country or otherwise outside the dispute resolution procedure.

Arbitral award default coverage can cover only defaults that would result in a monetary award to the investor. This means that actions to compel performance and other nonmonetary remedies are not covered.

The arbitral award must meet the customary standard for enforceability of legal obligations. It must be valid, binding, and legally enforceable against the host government. Note that this does not require that the award be "practically enforceable," in the sense that there is a likelihood of being able to successfully enforce it and get paid, but instead only that the award is in proper legal form for enforcement. In this sense insurers are taking a collection risk on the arbitral award.

A Few Possible Solutions

Based on these principles, there are a few approaches that political risk insurers might offer as protection against regulatory takings.

Provide Arbitral Award Default Coverage of a Stabilization Clause

The surest approach is to use arbitral award default coverage to insure an express stabilization clause in an investment agreement that is subject to international arbitration. Breach of that clause, together with international arbitration to demonstrate the wrongfulness of that breach, can define an insurable political risk, and has a number of advantages.

To begin with, although it may be difficult for investors to obtain awards from a government in many cases, because a stabilization clause is an agreement by the host government to limit its own flexibility in adopting future regulatory changes, it demonstrates a clear choice by a host government with respect to regulatory risk.

No legal right has value without a meaningful remedy, which the contractual choice of international arbitration provides for a foreign investor. For political risk insurers, international arbitration also serves to sort out the political actions of the host government from its legitimate contractual claims. Arbitral panels can sort out fact-specific questions with respect to regulation, including in connection with investment agreements containing stabilization clauses protecting against the effects of regulatory changes. In essence, it is the arbitral panel, not the political risk insurer, which determines that the host government has wrongfully breached a stabilization clause in an investment agreement and what the damages are.

Provide Arbitral Award Default Coverage for Other International Arbitral Awards

A somewhat more challenging possibility for political risk insurers would be to use arbitral award default coverage more broadly to cover awards resulting from international arbitrations arising from treaties, rather than from direct agreements with the host government.

Investors may have standing and rights to compensation under international agreements such as BITs or multilateral treaties such as NAFTA. The responsibilities of a state under international agreements to which it is party are in addition to, and therefore may be broader than, its obligations under general principles of international law.[18] As noted above, international arbitral awards, including those arising from treaty-based disputes, have the force of law and are enforceable without judicial review, and so are generally insurable. An investor concerned about the possibility of a wrongful regulatory change could purchase arbitral award default coverage to protect its treaty-based rights, even if it could not obtain an investment agreement with the host government.

One key issue for this sort of PRI coverage is the timing of its availability for purchase. Although some investors would want to purchase coverage against regulatory risk when they make their initial investment, certainly more investors would be interested in purchasing coverage later, if concerns about regulatory risk arise.

This creates obvious problems of adverse selection (i.e., buying coverage after a risk arises), which means that many insurers may not be interested in offering this coverage in the "aftermarket," so to speak. However, as noted above, the default that arbitral award default coverage addresses is the failure by the host government to pay the arbitral award. In insurance terms, the "date of loss" is the date the host government defaults on payment, not the date that the dispute arises. In other words, the risk is not the possibility of a dispute, or even the initiation of arbitration, but the possibility that the host government would not honor an arbitral award were it to lose the arbitration.

A related question is how far along in the sequence of events leading to a regulatory taking could an investor still represent, as required in all PRI policies, that there had not yet occurred "an event which could give rise to a loss." Consider the following possibilities:

- A pledge by a presidential candidate to change a given law or regulation if elected
- Election of that presidential candidate, who then repeats such a pledge
- Legislative passage of a change to the law or regulation
- Enforcement of law or regulation against foreign investors in general
- Enforcement of law or regulation against the particular insured company or investor
- Initiation of an arbitration proceeding challenging the law or regulation.

Establish a Standing Pool of Arbitrators to Address International Law Issues with Respect to Political Risk Insurance Policies

Certainly one of the most vexing aspects of determining whether a regulatory taking has occurred is to understand and apply the myriad principles, theories, and cases that together constitute the body of relevant international law. An insurer and its insured investor are each naturally suspicious of the other's analysis of the issue as being result-oriented—that is, to prove or deny a claim.

To address this, political risk insurers and insured investors could collectively organize a standing pool of regulatory takings experts who would be available to address international law issues.

The pool could be drawn from the large (and growing) group of international arbitrators and other experts specializing in the area. Concerns about bias in the pool could be addressed up front, before the battle lines are drawn in connection with a claim.

Political risk insurance policies would then provide for referral to one or more experts from this pool who are chosen at random at the time a dispute arises, perhaps subject to limited veto rights by the parties to reduce the size of the pool. Such an international law expert should be in the best position to draw the line between legitimate regulation and wrongful regulatory taking. In that way, some of the steep learning curve (and expense) in analyzing regulatory takings issues can be avoided.

The chosen expert would be charged specifically with identifying whether a particular act was a violation of then-current international law. All other aspects of the PRI claim would be left to resolution by the parties, including ultimately by arbitration under the PRI policy.

A key issue would be the amount of weight to give to the expert's findings in any such future arbitration under the policy. The findings could be deemed to be absolutely binding on the issues addressed, or alternatively not binding, but admissible as evidence. Reinsurance policies could provide that reinsurers be similarly bound by the result.

An important feature would be that the PRI policy would provide that the expert's findings be made public. This would enhance the understanding of insurers and insureds in future claims situations.

Making the decision public would also have a salutary effect on the insurer, the insured investor, and the expert. The insurer would not lightly reject a contrary decision if it were public. The insured investor would be hard-pressed to pursue a claim if the expert's decision was adverse to its position. Experts in this area, who care strongly about their reputations for analytical accuracy, would decide cases judiciously.

Such a system could be structured to provide other key benefits for insurers. It is much more practical to refer a specific technical legal issue to one of a known pool of qualified experts than to try to define coverage of a regulatory taking in advance and in the abstract.

Because insurers are concerned about their ability to make a claim against the host government, the time when the dispute arises is the best point in the process to make an international law determination. This minimizes the possibility that the law will change between the determination under the policy and the determination of the insurer's claim against the host government.

The burden of proof would remain on the insured investor, so uncertain or close cases should yield a finding of no regulatory taking. This would allay insurers' concerns that the expert could decide a close case in favor of the insured, and then that the insurer could meet the opposite result in an action against the host government.

Notes

1. Article 1110, The North American Free Trade Agreement ("NAFTA"), January 1, 1994, NAFTA Secretariat, available at http://www.nafta-sec-alena.org/DefaultSite/legal/index.

2. *S. D. Myers and Canada,* Partial Award, November 13, 2000, at Par. 281. Available at http://www.dfait-maeci.gc.ca/tna-nac/documents/myersvcanadapartialaward_final_13-11-000.pdf. The tribunal

did, however, find violations of Article 1102 (National Treatment) and Article 1105 (minimum standards of treatment, interpreted as fair and equitable treatment).

3. Mark Kantor. 2006. "Are You in Good Hands with Your Insurance Company?: Regulatory Expropriation and Political Risk Insurance Policies." Presented at 2006 MIGA-Georgetown Symposium, at Paragraph 4(b) of Annex B.

4. Restatement, Commentary (*g*) to §712.

5. Restatement, Commentary (*f*) to §712.

6. Restatement, Reporter's Note 6 to §712.

7. Par. 103, at 195 of *Metalclad Corporation and United Mexican States,* I.C.S.I.D. Case No. ARB(AF)/97/1, Award (Aug. 30, 2000) (emphasis added), available at http://www.worldbank.org/icsid/cases/mm-award-e.pdf.

8. *Metalclad Corporation v. United Mexican States* (2), Par. 113, at 197 (emphasis added).

9. For example, in *Waste Management v. Mexico,* the tribunal stated, with respect to the "minimum standard of fair and equitable treatment," that "in applying this standard it is relevant that the treatment is in breach of representations made by the host State which were reasonably relied upon the claimant."

10. Guarantees of the payment obligations or of the performance of key government counterparties to the project company (such as an offtaker) are certainly the strongest form of government support. However, guarantees have fallen into disfavor because governments are generally unwilling to give them, and in recent years have been discouraged from doing so by policies imposed by the International Monetary Fund and others.

11. Some political risk insurance policies enumerate "expropriation, confiscation, nationalization, requisition or sequestration" as specific elements of expropriation coverage, implying but not stating that the action must be wrongful at some level. A specific reference to international law is normally clearer. In fact, OPIC's expropriation coverage for years required *only* that a claim be based on a host government action that was a violation of international law, whether or not it fit into the subset comprising expropriation, confiscation, nationalization, requisition, or sequestration.

12. This quote is from a standard PRI contract, but the provider has not been identified.

13. This problem is recognized in the Restatement: "One test suggested for determining whether regulation and taxation programs are intended to achieve expropriation is whether they are applied only to alien enterprises. In many instances, however, particularly in developing countries, there may be no comparable locally-owned enterprise." Restatement, Reporter's Note 6 to §712.

14. This quote is from a standard PRI contract, but the provider has not been identified.

15. This is sometimes expressed as "political risk insurance will not make a bad deal better," but it would be more accurate to say that political risk insurance will not make *any* deal better.

16. This is clearly turning the concept of inducement on its head. The sequence of events starts not with government action, but with the investor's expectation, so that the alleged government action is the failure to meet expectations!

17. Note also that the "default" in question is not the breach by the host government of a contractual or treaty-based promise, or the initiation of arbitration as the dispute resolution mechanism, but rather the failure by the host government to pay the arbitral award.

18. See Restatement, Commentary (*a*) to §712.

DISCUSSION OF THE CHALLENGE OF MANAGING REGULATORY RISK

Symposium Panelists and Participants

There was a provocative discussion about whether U.S. political risk insurers refuse to pay claims more frequently than their counterparts in London. Most of the commentary was focused, however, on the U.S. government definition of expropriation, offering rather sharp observations about where U.S. attempts to define expropriation have led the political risk community.

Question: Much of the reference in these papers has been claims experience in the United States. Might it be said that when arbitrating disputes between insurer and insured the London market offers a more fair and balanced approach to resolving disputed claims? In 20 years of underwriting, the only two times litigation has been required in the questioner's experience have been with U.S. insurers—AIG and Chubb. This leads to the question of whether U.S. insurers have a tendency of avoiding claims payments more than London insurers?

Kantor: I do not believe that there is any distinction in responsiveness of insurers based in London, or in Zurich, or in Bermuda, or in the United States. I do believe there is a growing sensitivity to complex facts. As a result, insurers are digging deeper into what is presented to them by parties. But I do not think that you will find a market-based distinction.

Choharis: In Europe there may be more skepticism of government action and more willingness to assume that a property right has been interfered with in violation of international law, which may be reflected in insurers concluding "well, we do have to pay that claim." At the same time, however, the United States has a very robust bad faith jurisprudence against insurers who deny claims without good reason. So in terms of ultimate legal protections, I do not see that the European market would be more attractive.

Jenney: I would add that the process is different. It may be that in London there is a more of a "clubby" environment in which the community, including the claims adjustors, has been using the same terms to mean the same thing for hundreds of years. This is distinct from the United States, where not only is the community not as small, but there is more of an adversarial approach to resolving issues.

Participant Comment: Trying to craft the definition of expropriation in the [U.S. government's] expropriation annex was a very contentious, politically difficult exercise. There were at least 100, and the other 99 are in garbage cans throughout the U.S. government. It was never intended to suggest that this was a definition that should be applied by itself; and certainly in the context of investment insurance, it was never thought that this would be appropriate as a definition. Furthermore, the U.S. government representatives never thought and never said that this was customary international law. The intent was to provide some guidance in what is the inchoate nature of international jurisprudence on regulatory expropriation, not to provide a definitive interpretation of the issue.

Kantor: I respectfully disagree about how the reader might understand the first paragraph of the expropriation annex, which says that Article 6 is intended to reflect customary international law. Most individuals who read the treaties do not have the benefit of the history of the drafting that has just been presented. Instead they will conclude "the drafters are trying to explain what they think customary international law is." The history offered here today is quite useful because it helps practitioners understand that the nature of what the United States government is trying to do is perhaps different from what ordinary readers may think about the annex.

My view is that even if the U.S. government is not trying to define customary international law, it is trying to create a standard that a growing community of countries bind themselves to at the time when they sign a treaty with the United States. From the perspective of a political risk insurer, it seems to me that it is important precisely because an insurer needs a legal standard to determine when conduct was unlawful.

Choharis: I appreciate that the U.S. government interagency processes can be very contentious and inconclusive, but let me respectfully submit that we do not need the current 100 drafts, but one more, a 101st draft—because the current 100th draft is very unsatisfactory. In CAFTA, in Article 10.7.1 there is the NAFTA definition of "direct" and "indirect." The annex, however, includes the three *Penn Central* factors (economic impact, owner's reasonable investment-back expectations, and character of regulatory action). Then it says, in Annex 10 (c), the parties confirm that 10.7.1 is intended to reflect customary international law concerning the obligation of states. So, there are the three *Penn Central* factors, and there is customary international law. Which should be applied?

From the perspective of someone who's litigated this, here is what happens. First, the jurisdiction of the arbitral panel is challenged. Then, the arbitrators are challenged. Further, the choice of law is challenged. Which choice of law? Is it customary international law, or the *Penn Central* factors? If the U.S. government never really intended *Penn Central* to be customary international law, then what is it doing in that annex? And if *Penn Central* is meant to be customary international law, the annex makes no sense.

Under normal principles of statutory construction, one does not simply say that something makes no sense and then discard it. Instead, one asks what these three factors mean, for which one goes to U.S. jurisprudence, and finds that Justice Stevens, on the left, and Justice Scalia, on the right, all admit that *Penn Central* is ad hoc and provides very little guidance. This is what the U.S. government has bequeathed to 16 nations, and counting.

And it gets worse. The U.S. government ignores the fact that *Penn Central* is not American law, that there have been subsequent cases that look at the substance of regulatory expropriation. In *Agins,* and in *Nolan*, regulation has to substantially advance legitimate government goals.[1] So now arbitrators have to ask themselves, should one look to customary international law, whatever that is? Should one look to *Penn Central?* Should one look only to *Penn Central*, or to other U.S. jurisprudence? Should one look at the Washington, DC Circuit Court, or at the Court of Claims? Why, if the reference is international law, should one look only at U.S. cases? And the answer is, who knows? This is just a gift to litigators. It is a tremendous disservice to the investment community.

Note

1. See note 6 in Peter Choharis's paper, "Regulatory Takings Under International Law," in this volume, for a fuller explanation.

Part Four

THE INTERNATIONAL POLITICAL RISK INSURANCE INDUSTRY IN 2010

OVERVIEW

Theodore H. Moran and Gerald T. West
Editors

In this final section, five experienced practitioners from different parts of the industry offer appraisals of the current state of the PRI industry and hazard predictions about the future.

At one time, recalls John J. Salinger, President of AIG Global Trade & Political Risk Insurance, it was popular to predict that private sector underwriting would not survive in the face of government-backed political risk insurers. But the opposite has come to pass, and the private sector is now dominant in short-term export credit insurance. In the area of political risk insurance for direct investments, public and private sectors enjoy approximate equality. At first, private political risk insurers would not write policies with a tenor longer than three years, a practice driven by the three-year accounting and reinsurance cycle in London. In 1996, AIG broke through this barrier with seven-year coverage, and now private underwriters can write policies for up to 15 years.

The longer coverage enhanced the ability of private and public insurers to cooperate more fully. According to Salinger, the U.S. public insurer, OPIC, was at first not interested in cooperation, essentially wanting to compete as aggressively as possible for business in the marketplace. But this changed in 2000–2001, he asserts, under the direction of OPIC's then-President, Peter Watson. Coinsurance and some forms of reinsurance have become more common.

Salinger's first prediction is that the future will see greater and deeper public-private sector cooperation, exemplified in the Berne Union's growth in both size and importance.

His second prediction is less sanguine. The Argentine crisis highlighted—once again—the risk associated with currency devaluation for investors and lenders. Protection against devaluation risk will remain largely the business of commercial banks and capital market participants. Political risk insurers may perhaps offer coverage for local currency loans, but not for full devaluation risk. They will continue to insist on exclusion of losses due to devaluation.

Salinger's third prediction is that political risk insurers may find new ways to address regulatory risk in emerging markets, with BITs playing a central role. Regulatory risk raises particularly thorny issues, since insurance policies acknowledge the government's right to take actions to regulate in the public interest to protect the country's well-being, as long as such actions are not discriminatory.

The use of BITs to deal with regulatory risk is not without difficulties, notes Salinger, but there is value in the ability—under a BIT—to bring an investment dispute to international arbitration. Political risk insurers might want therefore to split existing expropriation coverage into two parts—the first would apply to an outright appropriation of assets, while the second would protect the investor against unfair and inequitable treatment as determined by an arbitration panel. This removes the insurer from having to litigate with his client, and results in a judgment that places the burden of compensation on the offending government directly, if the arbitral panel so rules.

To be sure, acknowledges Christina Westholm-Schröder, Chief Underwriting Officer of Sovereign Risk Insurance Ltd. of Bermuda, the way in which the PRI industry will evolve depends in the first instance on what happens in the external environment, in the international economy and emerging markets.

But new issues that the PRI industry will have to address, she points out, are emerging from Basel II. The Basel II accord establishes capital adequacy standards with the goal of strengthening risk management practices and reporting procedures among financial institutions and banks. To respond to the needs of the latter, political risk insurers will have to design insurance contracts that remove some current exclusions, use language with less room for argument over what is covered, and shorten waiting periods. The political risk policies will be "unconditional" in the sense that most, if not all, events that are outside the control of the insureds will be covered, not excluded. The principal new product offered by the industry, she predicts, will be coverage that qualifies as a risk mitigator under Basel II.

What about future prices for PRI policies? Insurance prices are driven by risk and capacity, Westholm-Schröder observes, and for countries where demand is the highest, capacity tends to be used up rapidly, putting upward pressure on prices. Such pressure is magnified by the desire of insurers to diversify their portfolio of exposures, and not become overconcentrated in particular high-risk countries, no matter what the demand. High commodity prices are leading to renewed requirements for traditional coverages for mines and petroleum facilities. Investment in infrastructure projects is stimulating interest in coverage for regulatory risks, but both insurers and investors are coming to recognize how difficult it is to write policies in those sectors.

In the area of devaluation coverage, political risk insurers will simply not be able to offer much, Westholm-Schröder asserts, with the exception of local currency obligations in some of the larger and more stable emerging markets.

Finally, in the area of public-private cooperation, more national agencies are likely to buy reinsurance cover from private providers. At the same time, however, the reverse may be true as well, Westholm-Schröder concludes, with national agencies offering to reinsure private political risk insurers.

Looking first at the supply side, Joanne Palmer, Director of Political Risk Insurance at Export Development Canada, observes that PRI capacity has recovered in robust fashion in the aftermath of September 11, the Argentine crisis, and other upheavals, with the entrance of new market participants, increases in project coverage limits, and expansion of reinsurance, even while prices have been weak. On the demand side, flows of investment into emerging markets—especially in extractive industries—have resulted in strong business volumes, especially in the face of the resurgence of nationalistic forces in Latin America and elsewhere. At the same time, both insurers and insureds remember the losses and the disputes they have had to endure in volatile areas like Latin America.

Of particular note is the expansion of PRI coverage against the failure of host governments or government agencies to honor arbitral awards—arbitral award default coverage. But, Palmer points out, many concerns remain, such as how can investors deal with the amount of time arbitration may require? Will insurers offer coverage for frustration of the arbitration process? Will insurers compensate investors for partial losses incurred because arbitrating against the government harms the longer-term prospect for the investment?

There is continuing interest in coverage for multicountry portfolios of investments or assets, Palmer affirms. Portfolio coverage can be far less expensive than paying for insurance on every individual exposure. It also appears to give reassurance to shareholders and creditors that risk is being adequately managed. But the prospect of offering full devaluation coverage is not on the horizon. Political risk insurers are willing to cover losses, however, that arise when there is political interference with sales contracts in an environment of steeply fluctuating prices.

There may be new products that protect against failure of the host government to enforce intellectual property rights, predicts Palmer. More problematic is coverage to insure against being forced to pay bribes when such payments appear to have official backing.

As for banks, the aftermath of the disputes surrounding coverage during the Argentine crisis is that many financial market actors have stopped purchasing political risk insurance altogether. But demand for comprehensive sovereign nonpayment cover has grown. Also, in response to the provisioning requirements of Basel II, banks are buying political risk coverage with very narrow conditionality so as to be as close as possible to a guarantee. Coverage for local currency exposure may emerge, and so, too, may PRI for mezzanine financing, for both junior and senior debt.

Public sector insurers continue to have a role to play in political risk coverage, comments Palmer, without in any way replacing private sector insurers. Public sector participants can provide stability of capacity for difficult markets, and may be able to reinsure or coinsure with private insurers for some projects where the private sector will not take on exposure on its own. Public sector insurers may be more effective in seeking salvage, she asserts. They are required to provide insurance to smaller clients. Their corporate social responsibility mandates—although often considered burdensome—may sometimes appeal to investors or lenders who are concerned about the public profile of their activities. Finally, freedom from the strict confines of maximizing profits may allow public sector providers to be innovators in meeting new needs in the market.

Drawing on his experience as Director of Project Finance at Standard Bank of South Africa, Greg Ansermino observes that public sector political risk insurers are becoming more efficient and private sector political risk insurers are becoming more aggressive. In the past, the former considered themselves as "insurers of last resort," providing cover where the private sector was unwilling or unable to do so. In the contemporary period, public sector political risk insurers emphasize that their official backing gives them "deterrent" value. The willingness of public sector insurers to engage difficult governments directly to correct the conditions that led to a dispute, he asserts, is a clear mitigant to the risks borne by both lenders and borrowers. But the target market for both public and private insurers increasingly overlaps, creating the possibility of "crowding out."

Another factor on the supply side, notes Ansermino, is the growth of export credit agencies and political risk insurers from developing countries, like Sinosure of China. Thus far they are less competitive, he judges, because of their inflexibility, but they often offer submarket pricing.

On the demand side, the need for minerals and energy focuses attention on regions where risk is quite high, whether in Africa, Latin America, Russia-Central Asia, or the Middle East, and where nationalistic leaders are tempted to flex their muscles. Bilateral relationships with China reinforce their capability for independent action. This expands the demand for PRI; at the same time, it diminishes the appetite for exposure on the part of insurance providers.

For the banking sector, the new Basel II regulations will have important implications for the use of PRI, agrees Ansermino. Historically, banks priced political risk in an unsophisticated and largely subjective fashion, he asserts. The requirements from Basel II initially led banks to wonder whether project finance might die out. But they came to the conclusion that they might be able to continue if they adopted more sophisticated, statistical modeling assessments of risk. This will enable them to choose between self-insuring and purchasing political risk insurance, as they provision to meet the capital requirements.

Project finance has always tended to be costly, both in terms of finance and in terms of time and flexibility. With increased liquidity, corporate investors have become reluctant to bear the costs associated with project finance when they have the capability to finance projects from their own balance sheets. However, they continue to find the deterrence benefit from public sector insurance coverage appealing to deal with their exposure to political risk.

Looking to the future, argues Julie Martin, Senior Vice President, Political Risk, at Marsh, the PRI industry would be served by making information about their history of paying claims—and about the rationale for paying or not paying claims—public. Many large political risk insurers have been moving slowly in this direction, with the notable exception of Lloyd's syndicates. OPIC stands head and shoulders above others, she notes, not only providing information about claims paid, claims denied, and claims arbitrated, but in making its Memoranda of Determinations public. Brokers, investors, public officials, and NGOs can thereby subject OPIC performance to critical scrutiny. The Berne Union, in contrast, still keeps most claims information confidential.

Private insurers fear moral hazard if they publish which projects they insure, Martin acknowledges, with host governments possibly singling out covered projects for expropriation (knowing that the investor will be compensated). Private insurers also fear that those insured might use past claims determinations as precedents in future claims disputes. Public insurers may wish to preserve larger foreign policy relationships with problematic governments. But political violence or inconvertibility claims should not trigger moral hazard outcomes, and expropriation disputes could be made public after the claims have been disposed of.

Making claims information public would allow those who are considering purchase of insurance to know better what kind of coverage they are buying, and under what circumstances payment might be rejected. Investors should not be taken by surprise at how they will be treated when their projects are in crisis. Therefore, more transparency would have an overall impact on improving the marketplace for PRI providers and users alike.

PAST AND FUTURE PREDICTIONS FOR THE POLITICAL RISK INSURANCE INDUSTRY

John J. Salinger
AIG Global Trade & Political Risk Insurance Company

The observations and predictions in this paper are rooted in more than 20 years' experience as a practitioner in the trade credit and political risk underwriting industry.

One old prediction has certainly come to pass. The private sector underwriting industry, whose viability was doubted by many in the 1980s, has matured and established itself firmly in the market—and not merely as a secondary alternative to the government underwriters. The private sector is now the dominant player in the short-term export credit insurance market, and has moved to a position of rough equality with national and multilateral agencies in the area of investment insurance. Some underwriters have taken steps to provide medium and long-term export credit insurance, although the government export credit agencies (ECAs) will almost certainly remain the dominant providers of this cover.

I will hazard three predictions about the future:

1. Collaboration between government and private underwriters will continue to deepen and will be manifest in the rising influence of the Berne Union.
2. The insurance industry will not solve the problem of devaluation risk. The solution, if there is one, will come from commercial banks or the capital markets.
3. Insurers will take steps to partially solve the problem of regulatory risk in emerging markets and the solution will be based on bilateral investment treaties.

Since the origin of the private sector underwriting industry almost 30 years ago, its role and relationship with the government underwriters has been the subject of much discussion. In the mid-1980s, the two were completely separate, rarely cooperated, and regularly competed.

Export Credit Insurance

Twenty years ago, I argued that government-supported agencies should not compete with private sector underwriters like AIG. In one discussion, a senior official at U.S. Ex-Im Bank asserted that Ex-Im Bank needed to compete, through its underwriting agency, the Foreign Credit Insurance Association (FCIA), or AIG would be left with a monopoly. My rejoinder was that he did not understand free markets. I thought the taxpayers in most Organization for Economic Co-Operation and Development (OECD) countries would not care to continue to bear risk that the private sector was prepared to shoulder.

My prediction, not his, turned out to be right. Ex-Im Bank privatized FCIA in 1992. The market responded and today U.S. exporters can access 10 export credit insurers (Ace, AIG, Atradius, Coface, Euler-Hermes, Exporters, FCIA, HCC, QBE, and Zurich). The market has never been more competitive or more vibrant.

Even before Ex-Im Bank privatized FCIA, ECGD in the United Kingdom decided to leave insurance of short-term exports to the strong private sector that operates in the London market. When first proposed, U.K. exporters protested. So ECGD established an emergency fund to underwrite short-term export risks, if the private sector failed to respond. The reserve was never used.

Historically, the industry in Europe was neat and tidy. The Treaty of Rome of 1956 established the European Economic Community. While it determined that the state should not interfere in matters of trade, it did not prohibit each European country from supporting a national ECA. Most countries at that time also had a single domestic credit insurance company. Each operated as a virtual monopoly and did not trespass on the other's turf.

The rules in Europe changed dramatically in 1997 with a directive from the European Union that governments should no longer underwrite "marketable risks," i.e., short-term export commercial risks in high-income countries. The directive had less impact on the "Big Three" credit insurers than on other government-owned ECAs. Coface of France, Atradius of the Netherlands-U.K., and Germany's Hermes (later Euler-Hermes) were privately owned companies that also enjoyed monopoly access to a government reinsurance window to support "national interest" exports. They continued to underwrite marketable risks, both domestic and export, against their private capital and commercial reinsurance.

The impact, however, on government-owned ECAs was profound. Short-term export credit covering buyers in Europe and North America constituted a substantial part of their portfolios. Constraints to underwrite only export credit to emerging markets and medium or long-term credits promised to sharply reduce revenue and leave the ECA with a high-risk residual portfolio.

ONDD, the Belgian ECA, dropped the equivalent of an ECA bombshell at a 2003 meeting of the Berne Union in Mérida, Mexico. It announced a plan to form a new subsidiary that would seek private sector reinsurance, and would write marketable risks. When no legal challenges were mounted against ONDD, other European ECAs followed similar paths to "commercialize" themselves.

Today, there are only a handful of pure government ECAs, including U.S. Ex-Im Bank and ECGD, in the United Kingdom. Philosophically, both are committed to avoid direct competition with the private sector and neither is likely to follow the European trend. Both are at risk of being marginalized as their countries lose manufacturing jobs, their revenue shrinks, and expenses and risk increase. This is unfortunate since the private sector is unlikely to meet the medium and long-term export credit needs of U.S. and U.K. capital goods exporters.

These remaining ECAs would be well served if they became more active collaborators with the private sector by selling medium-term facultative reinsurance. Properly structured, such a program would combine the deep risk-taking capacity of the ECA with the more nimble, user-friendly market face of the private sector.

While less dramatic, change has also come in Asia. The Chinese regulatory authority granted three export credit licenses to AIG in 2004. Japan, which had doggedly maintained a government monopoly in export credit insurance, began granting export credit insurance licenses to domestic and foreign insurers in 2005.

Investment Insurance

As the short-term export credit business moved toward the private sector and the commercialized ECAs, private sector underwriters moved to make themselves more compatible with the investment insurance coverage offered by OPIC.

Historically, the most glaring weakness in the private sector was the three-year limitation on policy tenors. This did not meet customer needs and was an inferior product to that offered by OPIC and MIGA.

The root of the problem bore no relationship to foreign direct investment risk in emerging markets. Until the mid-1990s, Lloyd's of London was the primary source of political risk reinsurance. Lloyd's followed a unique three-year accounting cycle and the reinsurance syndicates would not support policies longer than three years. Hence, the three-year limit. In 1996 AIG decided to find an alternative method to manage the risk and began offering seven-year policies. Eventually, commercial reinsurers offered longer-term support and today private underwriters can issue policies with a tenor of up to 15 years.

This enhanced capacity opened the way for private insurers to collaborate more effectively with agencies like OPIC. Legislation authorizing OPIC prohibits it from competing with the private sector and encourages cooperation through coinsurance and reinsurance. In 1996, OPIC was not interested; the legislative directive was effectively ignored. OPIC management paid lip service to the idea and then evaluated underwriters based on the volume of business they produced. OPIC was an aggressive competitor in the market. That changed from 2001, with the new OPIC administration led by Dr. Peter Watson. He believed OPIC should return to its roots as a development agency. He thought a government agency should focus on risks that served public policy objectives and were not of interest to private sector underwriters, e.g., small business, or transactions in very high-risk countries.

OPIC also started to cooperate with the private sector in order to "crowd in" private sector risk-taking capacity. Coinsurance has become more common. Depending on the nature of the transaction, OPIC now shares risk by buying facultative reinsurance from the private sector. They also sell facultative reinsurance to private sector underwriters. Prior to Peter Watson's administration, this would have been unimaginable. Today, the U.S. market is served by seven investment insurance underwriters (Ace, AIG, Chubb, MIGA, OPIC, Sovereign, and Zurich) and has never been more innovative or competitive.

OPIC is the model for effective collaboration with the private sector and everyone has benefited.

Future Prediction #1: More Collaboration and Rise of the Berne Union

The International Union of Credit and Investment Insurers, popularly known as the Berne Union, was founded in 1934 and maintains a secretariat in London. It now has 52 members based in 43 countries. The primary purpose of the organization is to promote sound underwriting practices. From its founding until 1999, no strictly private sector underwriter was admitted for membership, which probably reflected its view of underwriting standards in the private sector. However, after a long process, AIG was admitted to the Berne Union in 1999. Since then, three other private companies have joined. The admission of private companies and the commercialization of the large European underwriters have revitalized the organization.

One prediction that will certainly come to pass is that the profile and effectiveness of the Berne Union as the authoritative repository of professional expertise in the trade and investment (political risk) insurance industry will rise. More underwriters will seek to meet the standards required for admission. The Berne Union will grow. It will tackle difficult underwriting issues like regulatory risk. And it will enhance its collective risk mitigation clout for the benefit of its members and their clients.

Future Prediction #2: Devaluation Risk

The devaluation of the Argentine peso resulted in significant losses and highlighted demands from investors and lenders for protection against devaluation risk.

The best mitigant to exchange-rate risk is local currency finance. At present, in many countries, local markets are not sufficiently deep or long term to meet project needs. However, this will change over time and will be a partial solution. Commercial banks and capital market participants will work to expand the market for options in exotic currencies as another partial, if expensive, solution.

Political risk insurers will play a role, probably by insuring local currency loans, but private insurers are not likely to find a comprehensive solution to devaluation risk, especially at rates significantly lower than those in the currency futures markets.

AIG has significant exposure to devaluation risk in our export credit insurance program. In fact, it is the largest systemic risk in the portfolio. Companies with devalued assets and nondevalued liabilities often do not have a sufficient equity cushion to survive a major devaluation. If they cannot raise additional capital they go bankrupt, resulting in losses for export credit underwriters that insured their off-shore suppliers.

On the other hand, PRI policies carry a short, simple clause that excludes loss due to currency fluctuation or devaluation. After Argentina broke the peso/U.S. dollar peg, some argued that the devaluation exclusion was intended to cover only currency fluctuation from the time a deposit for remittance was made until the time it was actually transferred.

This is simply not the case. The purpose of the devaluation exclusion is to draw a line between political risk that the insurer intends to cover, and commercial risk that the insurer does not. It is relevant to ask if, save for devaluation, would there have been a loss? If the answer is negative, the insurance should not respond. That does not completely negate the policy, however. One consequence of a devaluation event might be an outbreak of civil disorder that causes damage to property. If that property is insured against political violence, the insurer would pay a claim.

Insurers will continue to insist on a full devaluation exclusion to help draw the line between covered political risk and uncovered commercial risk.

Future Prediction #3: Regulatory Risk

During the 1990s, emerging market governments, many of them recovering from the international debt crisis of the 1980s, recognized they needed substantial new investment in power, telecommunications, water, and transportation. With limited ability to borrow, governments opened the doors to private sector investment to provide needed infrastructure development. With the exception of wireless communications, these sectors are subject to price regulation.

Many investors in these regulated industries sought coverage in the political risk market. If a government could privatize an industry, it could just as easily renationalize it. Expropriation and nationalization coverage was available. Investors and banks also sought protection against certain contractual risks, including default on PPAs, or arbitrary changes in concession agreements. Underwriters saw this as higher risk business since PPAs are routinely renegotiated in developed as well as developing countries. This cover was more difficult to place.

The wave of infrastructure privatization was followed by several external shocks, including the East Asia crisis, pesification and devaluation in Argentina, and the election of populist governments in Argentina, Bolivia, Brazil, Ecuador, India, Indonesia, and República Bolivariana de Venezuela, among others.

Many projects then encountered problems. Had renationalization taken place, political risk expropriation policies would have responded. Where coverage had been obtained specifically covering contractual default, coverage would also have been triggered. However, situations arose where contractual, concession, or regulatory changes were imposed and the only coverage in place was the traditional protection against confiscation, expropriation, and nationalization.

These cases raised difficult questions. Insurance policies specifically recognize a government's right to act to protect and regulate their country's health, welfare, environment, and economic interests. As long as the regulatory actions are not discriminatory, political risk insurance policies will not respond. Policies also give insurers rights of subrogation after a claim is paid. Political risk policies are written, structured, and priced with the idea that the underwriter has a chance of recovering paid claims from the government that caused the loss.

Can an investor successfully claim under an expropriation policy if the government does not take the assets of company? Can an investor that has suffered a significant loss due to a regulatory change claim on a political risk insurance policy and continue to operate in the country? If so, what rights of subrogation does the insurer assume? Does the insurer now own the operation? If the foreign investment returns to profitability, who benefits?

At what point does a regulatory act that causes a loss in value become tantamount to expropriation? At what point should insurance policies respond? If there is a modest increase in taxes, does this constitute a taking, or is it a business risk that is expected to be absorbed by the foreign enterprise and the investor?

At what point does a regulatory change become tantamount to expropriation? Each individual case was (or will be) eventually sorted out. However, it is much easier to ask these questions than to find satisfactory answers.

Regulatory risk has become the most difficult problem for the market to address. Without a resolution, those seeking protection in the future will not find it. The initial solution proposed by brokers in the London market was insurance that would protect against acts, regulatory or otherwise, that rendered the investment "economically unviable." Apparently some underwriters at Lloyd's have accepted this. The Berne Union underwriters have not.

Where is the line between economically viable and unviable? Can underwriters clearly discern that the cause of economic unviability is the direct result of the regulatory action, a general weakening of the economy, mismanagement by the company, or devaluation? It is safe to predict this will not be the model of the future.

What might be? There is increasing interest in BITs as a way forward. BITs permit an individual investor to bring a sovereign country to a forum of international arbitration. They are designed to protect against confiscation without compensation. They generally also guarantee that foreign investors will be given "fair and equitable" treatment. Importantly, an arbitration award under a BIT has the legal standing of an international treaty obligation.

While promising, BITs have a number of limitations and problems. There may not be an in-force BIT between the country of the investor and the host country. Even if there is a BIT, the industry segment of the investment may be excluded from full protection in the BIT. The process is long. The sovereign can challenge the jurisdiction of the arbitration panel. The outcome may be uncertain as different panels in different fora have reached different conclusions on what constitutes "expropriation" and what is the standard of "fair and equitable" treatment. While subrogation to a defaulted award provides an avenue to recovery, there are pitfalls to execution of the award if the country does not pay. There can be appeals. BITs do not require the country to waive sovereign immunity. There is no indication that international financial institutions like the IMF and World Bank will apply pressure to countries that default on BIT awards.

Nevertheless, there is clearly something here that might be the key, at least in some situations, for insurers to provide investors a more satisfactory way to address regulatory risk. One solution would require a change in the language of the policies. The basic language, still used today, was formulated in the 1970s. At that time, only a handful of BITs had been signed; today over 2,200 are in existence.

A "BIT policy" would offer two forms of protection. The first would cover outright expropriation, which would be clearly defined in the policy. It would require an appropriation of assets or a legal nationalization, or both. Claims involving such an outright taking would be paid at the end of the waiting period and the insurer would be subrogated to the insured's rights. The insured would be required to cooperate fully with any effort by the insurer to pursue legal action against the government.

The second cover would protect the investor against unfair and inequitable treatment by the host government *as determined by an arbitration panel.* If the investor won an award and the government did not pay, as is currently the case with Argentina, insurers would. This protection against unfair treatment is probably broader coverage than insurers currently provide.

A shortcoming of this approach is the time required to get an award. Some of the Argentine cases will take three to five years to reach a conclusion. Most companies will not buy an insurance policy that takes that long to respond. A simple solution to that problem is for the insurer to make partial payments, *on account,* at various stages of the process. A partial payment could be made when the insured files the action; more could be paid when the panel rules it has jurisdiction over the case, and so forth. If the award is not granted, the insured owes the money back. It would therefore be wise for an insurer to deal only with creditworthy customers. That is a limitation, but it is also good underwriting practice.

The principal advantage of this approach is that the heart of the process is an arbitration that involves the alleged wrongdoer, which is also the party that can provide the compensation required for a satisfactory final resolution. This is a far superior process to arbitration between an insured and an insurer, which does neither.

The principal advantage to the investor is a PRI policy that is clear and unambiguous in an area, regulatory taking, that is inherently unclear and ambiguous. The principal advantages to the insurer are that the insurer has a drastically simplified claims process, will not face the prospect of litigating with his customer, and, in the end, will have a clearer, cleaner path to achieve recoveries.

This is not a panacea. But there is enough substance here to become a meaningful solution in a meaningful number of situations that are virtually uninsurable today.

HOW WILL THE POLITICAL RISK INSURANCE INDUSTRY EVOLVE IN THE NEXT THREE TO FIVE YEARS?

Christina Westholm-Schröder
Sovereign Risk Insurance Ltd.

The answer to this question depends upon many factors that may not be on the horizon at the present time. It is interesting and educational to look back over the last few years, when we have seen significant and unanticipated developments that have altered the course of the industry. Good examples would be the economic meltdown in Argentina and the global impact of September 11, as well as the current market environment, where extremely high liquidity has spilled over to many emerging markets around the world.

How the industry will evolve really depends on what happens in the global economy and in emerging markets; whether oil and commodity prices remain at a high level; which other countries might adopt Chavez's policies; whether Russia will respect contractual rights; whether there will be an economic or political event significant enough for hedge funds to get out of the emerging markets. Whether new market participants, such as banks and investors from China and India will choose to continue to lend or invest uninsured will have a big impact, as will developments in the general insurance market. Since PRI providers, like providers of other types of insurance, typically reinsure a substantial portion of the transactions they underwrite, the PRI providers essentially compete for reinsurance capacity with other lines of insurance. Hence, the number of hurricanes hitting the U.S. East Coast driving up insurance premiums in the catastrophe lines, will also affect the availability and pricing of reinsurance in the PRI market.

So, trying to predict the future for the PRI industry is not at all a straightforward kind of projection. This is not a very reassuring answer. What buyers of insurance would like to hear is that the PRI insurers will all convert themselves to become guarantors and offer unconditional guaranties. And, in some respects, we will. The following are some key areas to watch.

Regulatory Environment/Basel II

Aside from what is happening on a global scale, and more specifically in the emerging markets, and the industry in general, one of the major challenges—or opportunities—that the PRI industry is facing over the next few years is the implementation of the Basel II framework. As a consequence, in order to remain relevant, PRI insurers will have to start to offer "unconditional guaranties" (as defined in the Basel II framework). By 2010, we will all be doing that.

In the simplest characterization, the Basel II framework, which aims at improving risk management and reporting standards among financial institutions and banks, is a set of revised capital adequacy standards. The underlying principles of Basel II are to make sure that capital requirements imposed on financial institutions reflect the risks borne by that institution as appropriately and adequately as possible. It does so through three distinct instruments, or "pillars": Minimum Capital Requirements, Regulatory Overview, and Market Discipline. Compared to the Basel I framework, Basel II increases banks' risk sensitivity, penalizing banks for unmitigated risks by increasing capital requirements. Basel II also aims at improving banks' internal risk management capabilities, and providing greater flexibility to the more "advanced" banks. Perhaps the most important difference between Basel I and Basel II in the context of PRI insurance, is the fact that the framework explicitly recognizes a number of risk mitigation instruments.

PRI providers will offer "guarantees," but this is not quite as good as it sounds. The "unconditional guaranties" that PRI insurers will be offering will still, in effect, be conditional insurance contracts. But such conditional contracts may still qualify as a "guarantee" within the Basel II framework. Under these policies the insured party will still have to fulfill a number of obligations, but it's to be hoped the policy will be written in such a way that there will be less scope for argument over what is covered. Nonetheless, the policies will be "unconditional" from the perspective that most, if not all, events that are outside the control of the insureds will not be exclusions under the policies or reasons for a policy not to respond. Perhaps even more importantly, policies will be "unconditional" in the meaning ascribed to the word under the Basel II framework.

Despite earlier speculations that Basel II would be the doom of the industry, at least for the private players, it appears instead that Basel II will make their product more valuable to banks. Basel II, different from its predecessor, Basel I, will explicitly recognize policies that meet the framework requirements as risk mitigants and it will thereby allow for provisioning relief.

Cost of Coverage

What buyers of insurance also would like to hear is that the cost of the coverage will come down. Indeed it might for some countries, but not across the board—not in those markets where capacity is scarce. PRI pricing is based on a number of factors, but the two most fundamental are risk and available capacity. The issue with the PRI market today—which is not likely to change by 2010, or even by 2020—is that insurers are often close to their country limits in those markets where the demand is the greatest. That is arguably not due to too little supply, but rather that the capacity available (e.g., in Russia, Turkey, and Nigeria) is already being more or less fully deployed. In these cases, pricing is capacity-driven rather than risk-driven. That is why it is cheaper today, even after having adjusted for perceived or real risk levels, relatively speaking, to get coverage in Brazil than in Russia.

In fact, there will never be enough insurance capacity at a "reasonable" price (i.e., fitting under a diminishing margin) in the high-demand countries. Why? There are two reasons: First, competition among banks forces the spreads to come down in a hot market. This results in less room to pay for insurance and lenders therefore seek rate premium reduction from insurers. While rates do adjust, there is a level at which insurers can no longer justify coming down further in price, particularly since high demand puts upward pressure on the insurance premiums (the "Law of Supply and Demand" at work). There is also little chance that new capacity will be added in these markets unless pricing increases. At that point, when risk mitigation becomes more expensive, in theory, the bank margins should also increase. However, today, this theory does not seem to apply; we are in a cycle where the markets are so liquid that banks continue to lend even at very low spreads, with or without insurance. Will this continue? Probably yes, unless there is an emerging market event significant enough that the more volatile liquidity providers, such as hedge funds, decide to get out of the market.

The second reason why low-cost PRI insurance is unavailable for markets that most banks consider attractive, reverts to the fundamental principle of insurance—diversification. This means that PRI at "bargain rates" is available in markets such as Croatia because insurers want to add risk there, but not in Russia, where insurers already have a lot of exposure.

In a scenario where there are capacity constraints, what would happen in the case of a crisis pushing lending margins up? Would that mean that because banks now could pay higher prices for insurance, they would be able to get capacity? The answer is "no"—unless, of course, new capacity would be created. The insurance market would also react to the "crisis" that led to higher margins, and already having substantial exposure to a market that is now perceived as more risky, would make available less, rather than more, capacity. Reinsurers of PRI providers would obviously also follow the countries where they provide reinsurance, and would also be unwilling to provide more capacity should a country be perceived as more risky, and would indeed look to increase reinsurance rates. Furthermore, banks and investors that previously were happy to invest and lend uninsured would now be seeking coverage, thereby adding further to the supply-demand imbalance. Five years ago, this situation was true if you looked at Brazil. In 2010, perhaps it will be true in Georgia or Gabon.

Demand and Supply

What, then, are the driving forces on the demand side for PRI insurance in a particular country? A few come to mind immediately: risk and risk appetite (or lack thereof), cost of coverage, aggregation, and relationship with borrowers (to whom, despite lack of internal country limits, banks may feel "forced" to lend). At the "insurer" level, creditworthiness, claims payment ability, and the insurer's willingness to pay claims are all essential considerations. Another very important factor on the demand side, which will become perhaps the most important one in the future, is regulatory requirements. This reinforces the large impact Basel II will have on the industry in the next few years.

On the supply side, what are the driving forces? In some respects, they are the same factors as on the demand side: risk, price-premium level, availability of reinsurance at an acceptable level, and aggregation in the country or region in question and overall. At a client level, relationship and perhaps marketing aspects come into play.

Products

What implications do the global environment, with high oil and commodity prices, and the new regulatory environment for banks have on the products being offered and consumed over the next few years? These two factors actually serve to counterbalance each other, and it is my view that the product mix will remain similar to that seen in the industry today. Basel II requires that risk mitigants qualify as "unconditional guarantees." This will mean that banks, to the extent possible, will want to secure comprehensive, nonpayment coverage that qualifies as a risk mitigant under Basel II. On the other hand, high commodity prices will continue to encourage new investments in extractive industries, which have been at a very low level for the last few years. Limited recourse project financings for mines and similar projects have picked up and we have seen a renewed interest in the "traditional" products such as expropriation, war and political violence, currency inconvertibility, and nontransfer. As long as the global economy (read China and India) continue to grow, this trend is likely to continue. Given recent events and policy changes in República Bolivariana de Venezuela, Bolivia, and Russia, demand for expropriation coverage is likely to increase further, particularly for extractive industries.

Another likely consequence of the increased demand for project financings and "traditional" insurance coverage is further development and refinement of the banks' use of PRI for regulatory capital. The traditional coverages will not qualify as an unconditional guarantee, specifically because they are not designed to cover all risks, notably not the credit risk. However, as risk management techniques and familiarity with the application of Basel II increases, the banks using the advanced framework are likely to develop a methodology that will give regulatory relief even for the noncomprehensive products. That relief will not be to the same extent as the nonpayment coverage, but likely enough to be worth the banks' time to analyze and assess the coverage for this purpose. By 2010, banks might also view traditional PRI coverages as providing capital relief.

In writing about new products, I am sure many insureds would enjoy reading that devaluation coverage will be available by 2010. Unfortunately, it is not very likely that insurers will be offering this coverage, at least not on a significant scale. A product that may have more success would be coverage of local currency obligations. Sovereign and some of our colleagues in the industry are looking at the opportunities, and the risks, involved with such products. While not all countries will qualify for such coverage, the larger and more stable emerging markets might. This coverage would also lessen the need for devaluation coverage.

Cooperation among Public and Private Providers

Finally, before concluding, I also wanted to touch on my favorite subject, cooperation among private and public PRI providers. There is not much new to say here, except that over the next few years, more agencies will buy reinsurance coverage from private insurers. Budgetary restrictions in OECD countries will not ease, and the newer agencies will also run up against internal limits. ECAs often have country aggregations in markets different from private insurers, and increased cooperation will certainly assist in portfolio management on both sides. Over time, "reverse" reinsurance (i.e., ECAs reinsuring private market insurers) may also become more common. The reason why this has not been utilized more relates to the fact that agencies have restrictions with respect to "national interest," etc., which makes it more difficult to find transactions that qualify.

Conclusion

To summarize, there are a multitude of factors that impact on the PRI industry and our crystal ball is not flawless. Past prognostications are consistent in only one aspect; very few are exactly correct. Therefore, in order to succeed in the long run, an insurer will need to spend less time guessing what might happen and instead creating an organization that is flexible and creative enough to respond when the unexpected does happen. The PRI industry needs to be there for the long run and have the ability and willingness to not only pay claims in a timely fashion, but to also meet clients' evolving demands for products and support that satisfy internal and external requirements of risk protection.

LOOKING AHEAD: WILL POLITICAL RISK INSURANCE CONTINUE TO PLAY A MEANINGFUL ROLE IN THE GLOBAL INVESTMENT AND TRADE ENVIRONMENT?

Joanne Palmer
Director of Political Risk Insurance
Export Development Canada

As providers of PRI, we must continually ask ourselves: what is the future of the product? Is PRI a product that still has an important place in the toolkit of investors in emerging markets and their lenders? What is the most effective way for private and public sector institutions to contribute?

This paper attempts to briefly examine these questions from the viewpoint of a public sector insurer. First, I will take a look at recent trends in supply and demand in political risk insurance, and then at the products currently used by investors and international banks. Along the way, I will provide my own predictions with a medium-term outlook. I will then close by turning to the role of public sector insurers in this environment.

Recent Trends and the Current Environment

To ascertain the future of PRI over the next few years, it is helpful to look back over some of the recent trends in the international finance and PRI markets.

1. Industry Capacity—the Supply Side

Over the last five years, major events that we have experienced—such as September 11, the meltdown in Argentina, various hurricanes, and other natural disasters—have had, at most, only relatively temporary impacts on the growth in capacity of international finance and the PRI industry.

On the financing side, after some consolidation, especially of project finance expertise, we have seen the strengthening of traditional bank sources of financing, along with the emergence of new players such as institutional lenders and domestic financial institutions in certain markets. This continued increase in options and capacity has resulted in an extreme thinning of interest spreads on loans.

The insurance world has also experienced a very significant general softening of the market. Overall political risk insurance capacity has not only rebounded since the events of September 11, but has continued to grow steadily with the entrance of still more new players, increases in project limits, and strengthening of the reinsurance market. This competitive situation has shrunk premium levels to historical lows, making it close to impossible for insurers to price to risk. Barring some catastrophic disaster that would result in widespread claims on political risk insurers or an event that would result in a more permanent decrease in their reinsurance capacity, there is no reason to think this trend will be reversed any time soon.

As a result, both the bank and insurance markets will remain very competitive and on each side, banks and political risk insurers will continue to trip over each other to solicit low-revenue business in the arena of international investment and trade.

2. Investment and Trade Climate—the Demand Side

Although moderating somewhat, the general picture of global economic growth and investment, particularly in emerging markets, remains fairly strong, with annual rates of growth projected to exceed 6 percent for both 2006 and 2007. FDI flows into developing markets have increased dramatically in recent years and are expected to reach and stay in excess of US$360 billion in 2006. Led by China, Asia remains a top destination of investment into emerging markets; however, the amount is leveling off and we are seeing more investment into India and the Middle East, in particular in the areas of energy, real estate, and infrastructure. Investment flows into Africa are strengthening, especially in mining and energy, and Latin America is mixed, with investment decreasing somewhat in República Bolivariana de Venezuela and Brazil, but picking up in Argentina and Chile. Given the current boom in oil and metal prices, it is not surprising that a good part of this activity is in the natural resources sector, with some show of recovery in both power and telecommunications.

Overall, then, investments are continuing to take place in great quantity in markets and in the type of projects where there are political risks; there is the potential for political risk insurers to play a role. But are investors and their lenders continuing to seek PRI for this activity?

The year 2006 has seen a number of recent developments that could be positive for the political risk insurance industry. Overt actions by Presidents Chavez, Palacio, and Morales against investors in the Latin American resource industries have reinforced awareness of the concept of expropriation. In 2006, Lebanon was bombed and the Democratic People's Republic of Korea started nuclear testing, both recent reminders that there are always new challenges to relative states of political stability around the globe. Such actions should result in an increased desire for insurance coverage against traditional perils such as expropriation and political violence. While it is true that most political risk insurers are very busy writing business this year, I do not believe these events have caused a dramatic resurgence of demand for PRI.

An important contrary influence has been the experience of investors and lenders through the Argentine crisis, where many became aware of the limitations of traditional political risk insurance. Even though that was several years ago, policyholders have not forgotten the losses that were not covered by their PRI policies, and quite a number of these issues are still in the process of arbitration. A further limitation on the demand for PRI is the emerging importance of Chinese and other investors who are content to self-insure.

The conclusion then is mixed—demand is strengthened due to a reconfirmation of risks associated with traditional perils covered by the industry but, at the same time, there are residual concerns regarding the relevance of the product that are still keeping some segments of the market away.

Let us look at what investors who are buying PRI are seeking from the market.

3. *The Investor Viewpoint*

As they have for a number of years, investors are continuing to examine their political risk insurance coverage more closely, and increasing pressure on insurers to broaden the coverage to fit their needs. In the area of political violence coverage, for example, we have seen demand for coverage of losses due to the threat of political violence versus actual political violence, for losses due to violence that is not politically motivated, and for temporary loss of income rather than asset damage. Under expropriation coverage, we are being pressed to cover regulatory risks or at least lighten up on the standard "government acting for the good of the nation" (or equivalent) exclusion. I would put these demands in the category of tweaking traditional risk coverage parameters rather than new product development. With a soft market and some indications of increasing reliance on self-insurance, it would appear that at a minimum, insurance providers will have to be willing to be flexible regarding such demands in order to maintain investor interest in the product.

One of the more recent expansions of PRI coverage for investors has been insurance against the failure of a sovereign or quasi-sovereign entity to honor an arbitral award: i.e., arbitral award default coverage (AAD). This coverage is often referred to as the "fourth" point, beyond the traditional "three-point" coverage against perils of expropriation, political violence, and transfer and inconvertibility. While AAD coverage appears to address some of the quasi-commercial actions of government or other state entities, and to give comfort to investors that they are protected against partial losses due to contractual breaches, investors remain worried about the length of time that an arbitral process can take. There are a number of other questions that have arisen as well. To what extent are insurers willing to cover the frustration of that arbitral process? To what degree are insurers willing to compensate clients for partial losses in cases where arbitrating against the host government for a partial loss is perceived to be detrimental to the longer-term outlook of the project? Looking forward, it appears that arbitral process award cover will continue to be useful for certain investors and lenders, especially when trying to cover contracted obligations of state entities, but that insurers will be pressed to expand the coverage to properly accommodate frustration of the arbitral process and other issues facing investors and lenders in this regard. The willingness and ability of insurers to deal with these will likely have a great impact on the success of this product.

A long-standing interest of investors has been the protection of multicountry portfolios of investments or assets. Again, due to a generally soft market, investors are not willing to pay substantial premiums for this coverage, but do seem attracted by a "tick-the-box" mentality to keep purchasing this type of insurance on a standard basis. The portfolio coverage is a far more economical approach than paying for insurance on each individual investment, and the widespread use of options for reinstatement of liability gives investors a cheap proxy for traditional standby coverage. Having a global PRI policy in place allows an investor to tell shareholders and bankers that pertinent political risks have been covered at a relatively cheap price. This is not a demand that will likely go away. However, I would predict that there will be even more downward pressure on pricing of such portfolio coverage, and that demand will be most sustained where investors have investments in at least one or two very risky markets.

There are a number of investor concerns that are not yet being met, and may never be met, by political risk insurers. An investor's currency devaluation risk and commodity risk have long been considered purely commercial risks that are outside the framework of PRI. An exception to this was a narrowly focused currency devaluation product developed by OPIC, and then Sovereign. That product more or less protected the policyholder against a currency movement within a narrow band, and was available only for currencies with a stable history of movement. It did not meet investor needs very successfully and there has been little demand for it.

While the industry is still not willing to cover significant devaluation risk on its own, there has been some appetite where political events intertwine with commercial ones, such as when government actions or inactions interfere with companies being able to meet obligations on sales contracts. One example would be a mining company in an environment of rising prices where the company suffers losses because it has to buy higher-priced minerals on the spot market to meet its gold supply obligations. Insurers are currently covering these losses. I would expect this trend of covering this type of loss, and certain other currency and hedge arrangements, to not only continue, but to expand and potentially yield a number of new PRI products.

Protection of intellectual property rights is an area of concern to investors. Insurers are aware of this concern and agree that the failure of the host government to adequately protect investors rights in this area could be considered a political risk, but have yet to come up with an insurance product that adequately addresses the mutual requirements of investors (protection) and insurers (somewhat quantifiable risk and potential for recovery). A certain amount of discussion has taken place on this subject, so it is quite possible a product will emerge in the medium term.

Another unmet need that is even more problematic for insurers is the area of bribery and corruption. Most insurers, especially public sector ones, have specific exclusions denying liability for such risks rather than covering them. Many investors, however, want protection against being forced to pay bribes to unscrupulous official staff in cases where such actions appear to be officially sanctioned by the governments. It is very doubtful that the insurance market will touch this risk any time soon.

The overall picture in the investor segment of the market, then, is one where investors are continuing to buy traditional PRI against the three traditional perils of expropriation, political violence, and transfer and inconvertibility, especially for multicountry portfolios of investments, but they are demanding broader coverage from insurers. There has been some use of the fourth point of coverage, AAD, but there, too, we see pressure for expansions to the coverage. Finally, there are some new areas being developed that help somewhat with issues around currency and commodity price fluctuations, and some scope for future coverage of intellectual property rights.

4. *The Lender Viewpoint*

Now turning to the bank market, the most immediate effect of the high degree of competition in the bank market and low interest rate spreads is that there is no room in the bank's pricing in many markets for PRI premiums, even if the bank would like to buy that risk mitigation. So we are seeing banks lending uncovered in many markets (e.g., most recently in Vietnam) where they would have been insured a short time ago.

Another negative effect for insurers is that like investors, banks are looking much more closely and critically at their insurance contracts. Long gone are the days when PRI was standard coverage for banks and considered to address a significant portion of their political risks. One area of contention is the waiting period. A number of banks experienced difficulties claiming transfer risk losses under policies that covered loans to Argentina because the borrower was unable to generate a sufficient amount of sharply depreciated local currency at the end of the waiting period. Unfortunately, in many cases, rather than push for shortened waiting periods or other changes to the coverage, long-time bank users of traditional PRI have elected to stop purchasing it completely.

Where we have seen continued use of traditional PRI by banks has been on a much more selective, and often short-lived, basis. For a brief time, for example, such insurance was important in the Argentine market. EDC provided project financing and PRI (the latter in combination with several private sector insurers, i.e., Sovereign, Zurich, and Chubb) for the Veladero mining project in 2003. This was the first project financing in Argentina following that country's economic crisis, and was necessary to attract commercial lenders back to the market, but by 2005 banks were willing to finance resource sector projects at much lower rates and uncovered by insurance. Currently banks are being very restrained in their acceptance of three- or four-risk cover, with their appetite for traditional PRI limited to very difficult markets such as República Bolivariana de Venezuela and the Democratic Republic of Congo, or for complex financing structures such as those with extremely long tenors.

In contrast, one area of growth is in response to a long-standing push by banks for comprehensive cover. The resulting nonhonoring sovereign obligation cover (sometimes simply called sovereign nonpayment cover) has become a prevalent form of bank cover in the PRI industry and an important component of most providers' book of business. This form of insurance, which covers comprehensive payment risk, started in support of trade or investment transactions that were essentially sovereign risk, and has grown to cover many financial obligations of governments, state-owned enterprises, and subsovereign entities. The "political" risk is the sovereign nature of the payment risk, and is quite different in form and complexity from traditional three- or four-point cover. My expectation is that this form of PRI, long provided by export credit agencies, will remain an important product for both the public and private political risk insurer industry, and that banks will continue to stretch, with success, parameters such as length of tenor, type of loan structure, and more importantly, the definition of "sovereign." We will also see banks, from a Basel II provisioning perspective, continue to successfully push insurers to narrow the conditionality of their insurance policies so that the very minimum of events remains outside of bank control and the insurance is as close as possible to a guarantee.

Local currency financing has been a recent focus of much discussion in the project finance market, but so far it has not played a big role in actual project financings. That is not to say that this will not grow in the future when there is more investment in projects, such as in the telecommunications and power sectors, which are not foreign currency earners. And it is possible for the political risk insurer to play a role in these. True local currency financing, with no eventual conversion or crystallization of the liability into hard currency, removes the need for protection against transfer and conversion. If the local currency lender is—or is owned by—an outside party, such as an international bank, then there would still be an element of conversion risk. There can also still be expropriation and political violence risks associated with such transactions.

Another structure growing in popularity is mezzanine financing. PRI providers can assist in these structures; most likely to be acceptable is coverage of both the junior and senior debt rather than just one of them.

My expectation is that both these trends will continue. Banks will obtain comprehensive cover for "political" or quasi-political risks wherever possible. With respect to three- or four-risk cover PRI, only in high-risk markets or to support challenging financing structures will banks be willing to give up a portion of their limited margins. A little harder to predict is the potential growth in demand for political risk insurers to play a meaningful role in local currency financing or other new structures, and the ability of insurers to respond to those needs. As noted, one area where we should see product development is the same as those noted above for investors; banks will also push for insurers to share more of the commodity and currency pricing risks associated with projects.

Role of Public Sector Insurers

Next, there is the question of where (and where should) official public sector providers fit into this evolving PRI market. Most are of the view that the public sector operator should exist on a last-resort basis only. EDC and some of the others believe that a healthy portfolio of risks is necessary for a model to be sustainable without a high degree of government subsidies. Whichever the case, it is not the wish of the public sector institution to displace the private sector insurer. The current overflowing of private sector capacity then gives rise to an extra challenge for public sector providers to find meaningful roles for themselves in the industry.

For the most part, public sector insurers are sources of much greater individual capacity than the private sector insurers, whose project limits are usually less than US$100 million. That said, the brokerage industry can put together hundreds of millions of dollars of capacity for a single project on a coinsurance basis, which works well unless an investor or bank prefers a single insurer. The real differentiator here is the stability in the public sector capacity, which seems to be available for difficult markets on a more sustained basis due to high country limits, and is not subject to the same volatility of pricing if capacity does become at all limited.

Through reinsurance arrangements with private sector insurers, which are becoming increasingly prevalent in the industry, public sector providers have also been key to leveraging capacity from the private market. For example, a private sector insurer may be willing to reinsure or coinsure with MIGA on a project in the Democratic Republic of Congo, but may not be willing to take that country's political risk on its own. In such cases the public sector provider's multilateral or government status is viewed as an important reduction to the political risk of the transaction.

There are other cases where policyholders prefer a public sector insurer to be the primary or sole issuer of the policy. Two primary reasons for this are a common perception that public sector entities are more willing to pay claims, and that single policies can result in ease of administration (e.g., claims determination). In most banks' perspective, a policy providing banks with coverage against the nonhonoring of sovereign obligation is better fronted by a public sector insurer, as that entity's usually more positive rating governs Basel II provisioning requirements.

A unique mandate role assumed by many public sector entities is the provision of insurance to smaller clients that are not usually profitable, and thus often overlooked by brokers and private sector insurers. Most government and multilateral insurers have programs to increase the number of smaller clients served. The challenge is usually to streamline intimidating processes and documentation.

Cumbersome processes are also the basis of a major differentiator between public and private sector insurers. While the private sector also assesses environmental and other risks that fall into the realm of corporate social responsibility frameworks, public sector insurers embrace these principles as a necessity, regardless of the risk aspect. Avoidance of public sector information and analysis requirements that can significantly delay or hamper the finalization of an insurance policy often drives clients to the private sector, even if they feel involvement of a public sector entity would be a substantial mitigating factor in the risk of the transaction. That can also work in reverse. Investors or lenders will at times want a public sector entity involved precisely because such entities are well-known champions of environmental progressiveness, and their involvement will counter actions by NGOs or other potential opponents to the project.

These roles for multilateral and government insurers will likely continue over the coming years. Public sector insurers may play a pivotal role in the area of innovation. It very well may be the public sector insurers, who are less subject to the pressures of a profit model, who will respond to investor needs and push the boundaries of traditional PRI coverage.

Conclusion

There is not much to indicate that there are any revolutionary changes to the PRI market likely in the medium term.

Traditional insurance coverage such as multicountry policies will still be sought by investors. Banks will continue to subscribe to the nonhonoring of sovereign obligation coverage and will push the definition of "sovereign." Earnings on both investment and lender insurance policies will remain constrained. There are signs that insurers will have to understand and find a way to be more receptive to investor and bank concerns in the arena of political risk, which also puts a responsibility on investors and banks to articulate such concerns clearly. Insurers will continue to track and modify coverage to accommodate developments in financing structures.

Public sector insurers will continue to fill gaps, often by leveraging capacity from the private sector through reinsurance and coinsurance relationships, and will continue to support small investors. Their policies on environment, corruption, and other corporate social responsibility will sometimes be a deterrent and sometimes an attraction to those buying coverage. It is possible that some of the momentum for changing coverage in response to investor and lender needs will come from public sector entities.

Accordingly, it is my view that PRI will continue to play an important part in facilitating investments and trade into emerging markets, and that public sector insurers will continue to participate meaningfully in these efforts.

THE NEW SCRAMBLE FOR COMMODITIES: MEDIUM-TERM TRENDS IN POLITICAL RISK INSURANCE

Greg Ansermino
Director, Standard Bank of South Africa

Introduction

In 2002, Sasol Ltd, the South African synthetic fuels producer, finally secured the rights to develop the Pande/Temane gas fields in central Mozambique. In the context of industry norms, the gas fields are relatively small to justify the development, but Sasol had strategic reasons for pursuing the development. Sasol is a leader in the production of synthetic fuel and historically had been the only significant producer of liquid products from coal. Off this platform, Sasol had developed technology to use a similar process to produce liquid products from natural gas. In the context of the looming energy crisis, this technology would be a key opportunity for Sasol to expand its global business. Sasol's challenge would be to prove the technology on an industrial scale in order to pursue joint ventures to unlock opportunities where countries were long on gas and short on oil. With a new gas-to-liquid facility costing billions of dollars, potential partners would need persuasive evidence of the viability of the technology before they would commit to such a level of investment.

The project in Mozambique presented a number of strategic challenges to Sasol:

- Sasol's balance sheet was relatively undergeared and Sasol was reluctant go through the hassle and cost of a full project financing.

- Sasol had never made a major investment in Mozambique previously, and had no experience dealing with the Mozambican government.
- While the investment in the gas field, dewatering facility, and pipeline would cost around US$1 billion, this was not a true reflection of the impact that this investment would have on Sasol. In addition to investing in the gas supply, Sasol would convert part of its existing coal-to-liquid complex to the new gas-to-liquid technology. The replacement value of the new gas-to-liquid plant would be a multiple of the investment in the gas supply.
- Sasol was in the process of listing on the New York Stock Exchange and was concerned about investor perceptions of Sasol carrying a large exposure to Mozambique. Its price already reflected its South African base, but the Mozambican investment would introduce a whole new aspect to its political risk profile. Sasol had similar concerns relating to its credit rating.
- All the products would be sold in the South African market so the project would have a large exposure to the South African rand.

What became clear was that the management of Mozambican political risk would be critical to Sasol. Its preference was to find a solution that would be corporate from a commercial risk point of view, but which transferred the political risk to the funders or their insurers. In addition, the political risk-takers would need to take an active role with government if a political risk event occurred. Ideally, the facility should be rand-denominated. The result Sasol was seeking was achieved in two ways:

- A rand-denominated commercial bank facility was arranged that was covered by a diverse selection of public sector insurers. These included the World Bank through its partial risk guarantee program, South Africa's ECICSA, and MIGA, for its own account and as insurer of record for Italy's SACE and EFIC of Australia.
- A second tranche was arranged among a group of development finance institutions (DFIs), which included the European Investment Bank, the Development Bank of Southern Africa, the African Development Bank, FMO, DEG, and Proparco.

All these facilities were guaranteed by Sasol in every respect except for political risk events.

The structure was attractive to Sasol for the following reasons:

- There would be no full project finance-type due diligence, covenanting, or costs.
- The lenders had managed the political risk exposure effectively.
- In the event of threatened interference from the Mozambican government, the structure would act as a strong deterrent because such acts would have

consequences for Mozambique's relationships at many different levels in the international community.

- If the Mozambican government did take action despite the deterrent, Sasol would be able to engage the government with the active support of some of the most powerful public sector institutions in the industry, starting with the World Bank itself.

The Sasol Temane transaction is a good example of trends that we are seeing in the use of PRI in the financing of large projects in challenging jurisdictions. Corporates seem to be shying away from full project financing, particularly in an environment where there are high levels of liquidity, both in the corporate and financial markets. Despite the appetite to be aggressive commercially, political risk is seen as something that should be insured and there are concerns about currency mismatch. This is particularly important when corporates are listed on the main international exchanges, or rely on the bond markets in developed countries for the bulk of their long-term funding.

In looking for insurance partners, the public sector is seen as a deterrent and this reflects a more sophisticated approach to mitigating political risk. It was interesting that the DFIs were prepared to act as both commercial lenders and political risk-takers to create the capacity required by the project.

Finally, the project itself would never have happened had it not been for the looming energy crisis and rising oil prices.

In this paper, I will describe a number of the trends highlighted by the Sasol Temane transaction. The products traditionally used in our target markets have been relatively basic, due to the danger of overcomplicating already complicated markets. Consequently, the comments will follow trends in a general sense without presuming to have answers on the details of the product offering required.

Supply Side Drivers

As a consumer of PRI, we are not directly involved in the supply side of the industry; however, we do see trends in the industry through our interaction with the purveyors of PRI. By way of a loose categorization, we would include MIGA, ECAs, and special insurance programs with state or multilateral sponsors as the public sector, and privately owned commercial insurers as the private sector. The reinsurance market does create a little confusion as the public sector insurers are increasingly placing risk with the private reinsurance market. The trend of public insurers acting as insurers of record, then placing the risk with the private market is a trend that reflects the increasing sophistication of public insurers. While it might seem obvious that public insurers should increase their capacity to provide insurance through reinsurance, this is not necessarily standard practice across all public insurers.

The trend to reinsure by public sector insurers is a reflection of a trend across development finance to move away from an "aid" nature to being economically sustainable. In the developed world, development finance is coming under increasing pressure to wash its own face without additional support from its shareholders. This has given the impetus to these institutions to reform their product offerings and procedures to bring them in line with their private sector colleagues. This commercialization is positive and likely to become the norm across the whole of the public sector insurance market.

One of the less constructive consequences that has emerged is the "crowding out." This results from the target market for private and public sector insurers becoming increasingly similar. The question arises whether this trend is sustainable if the object of the public sector insurers is to provide a platform for development in countries where arguably higher levels of development will influence the environment, and consequently lead to higher levels of political stability. In the past, the public sector was focused on providing cover where the private sector felt that an investment was uninsurable, whether the concerns were real or perceived. Under the new order, the public insurers are less focused on being "insurers of last resort," but rather tout the argument that their public nature acts as a deterrent. In our experience, however, this deterrent comes at a price, so there is an element of balance.

The differentiation is becoming increasingly relevant as consumers become more sophisticated in their PRI requirements. An understanding of the difference between hard and soft cover is important to this explanation. Hard cover can be described as insurance that is provided on a traditional actuarial valuation basis. In this case, the insurer primarily provides for losses based on actuarial calculations and treats any recoveries as a bonus. Insurers in this case are unlikely to drive the rehabilitation of the borrower, and will go no further than cooperate to the extent necessary. Often these claims are sold to specialists in recovery at a massive discount to face value. This approach to insurance may give comfort to the insured lenders, but it gives little benefit to the investors. Soft cover is insurance provided by insurers whose mandate it is to stimulate development in underdeveloped and often politically fragile countries. The approach here is fundamentally different in that the aim of the insurer is keep the borrower functioning. These insurers will often have parallel relationships with the host government through their shareholders or associated agencies. The host government cannot ignore the overall impact on these relationships, especially where the project is dependent on financial support from the insurer's parent or associates. These insurers will also engage delinquent governments directly in their efforts to undo the mischief that gave rise to the claim. The idea that the insurer becomes an active participant in the process is seen as a clear mitigant to overall political risk of the borrower, rather than a mere protection to the lender. More astute project sponsors are beginning to understand this value; the debate is now the value of this differentiation.

Another influence is that traditional development finance institutions are starting to offer guarantee products that for all intents and purposes are purely political risk mitigation structures. The process that has led to these products being developed will be discussed in more detail when we discuss the demand side trends; however, this introduces another significant competitor in the public sector space.

The last factor to mention in relation to the public sector space is the growth in significance of ECAs from developing countries. These agencies are grappling with the adaptation to a competitive market. While they remain less competitive because they tend to be less flexible, they often offer submarket pricing.

All these factors point to larger capacity for political risk and pressure on pricing in the medium term. We have already seen the private market respond and start to price the preferred emerging market relatively aggressively. In addition, the tenors on offer often pierce the sovereign ceiling of the host country.

As the public sector becomes more efficient and the private sector becomes more aggressive, the differentiation between the two will become less obvious. This will be exacerbated by the development of products that span both sectors. I will discuss these trends in more detail later.

While the space has become more market-driven, and competition is generally for the benefit of the consumer, one cannot help but think about the countries that will inevitably be left behind. At what point will there need to be a review of the mandate of the public sector insurers, in order to allow them back into the lower echelons of the development space to play a more active role in stimulating economic development?

Demand Side Drivers

In this section, two key macroeconomic drivers will be examined: (i) a regulatory driver, and (ii) market conditions in the financial sector that will have significant influence on demand for political risk cover. They are not the only drivers, but they will each in their own way have a fundamental impact on the direction that the market takes.

We are all aware of the Chinese economic miracle and the approaching energy crisis. While these two topics seem to dominate the press, just beneath the surface, there is a more complex set of relationships that will drive the political climate.

Until recently, the concept of a single global market seemed to be attractive; the main demand for commodities came from the traditional developed markets in North America and Western Europe; the United States seemed to have a self-sustaining domestic market, and the Asian and Latin American crises of the late 1990s had driven appetite away from emerging markets. So what happened?

With the United States becoming the single superpower, a number of political conflicts died down and we saw a period of relative political stability. Some even had hope for a settlement in the Middle East. Growth in developed countries was stable if uninspiring. Emerging markets were economically precarious and thus unattractive for investors. In this context, we saw relatively conservative FDI into emerging markets. Yet in the past three years, the market seems to have swallowed the bitter medicine of the late 1990s and is eagerly seeking to ride the Chinese dragon.

The market could see the Chinese success coming but investors saw China as a difficult environment where the barriers to entry were very high. Chinese growth was largely funded by the state and the financial sector remains a cause of some concern. What seems to have been underestimated is the sheer size and momentum of this growth. It has consumed the surplus production of a number of major commodities and there is an expectation that this growth may be sustainable in the long term, albeit not quite at current levels. Even if this growth is maintained at levels above 6 percent, the consequences for commodity stocks are enormous. The irony of this is that there probably won't be a proportional explosion in demand for cover against Chinese risk, as most of the large-scale investment will continue to be funded directly from state coffers while the state sits on a surplus of nearly US$90 billion.

Although the statistics seem to point to a burgeoning Chinese economy sucking the world's supplies of raw materials dry, the pressure on commodities is not solely coming from China's growth. This year, the Indian economy will use 70 million tons of steel. As little as seven years ago, this was China's consumption. While it is difficult to predict whether the growth in the Indian economy will eventually rival China in its demand for commodities, all indications show that this growth will significantly increase the demand. The supply of commodities will come from regions that historically have been underdeveloped and which have less stable political environments. In the rush to accommodate increased demand, capital will need to flow into these jurisdictions with a consequent impact on the requirements to mitigate political risk.

If one looks at the supply of steel and, consequently, the demand for iron ore as an example, new projects will be considered for deposits that 10 years ago would never have been seriously considered. It is a fact that iron ore is not of itself a scarce resource, but the cost of getting the commodity to market has meant that many deposits, though geologically well known, have been considered valueless. As demand has grown, prices have escalated to a point that justifies large investments in infrastructure to make the deposits accessible. An example of this is Gabon, where development of the deposits will require the construction of not only a mine but also a power station, a railway line, and a port, all for a "mere" US$3.5 billion. While the expected pricing levels for the commodity may support the commercial operation of a mining and logistics complex, the project will still take more than a decade to pay back its investment. Gabon is still regarded as an unstable political environment, and managing the political risk over such an extended period will create entirely new challenges to the PRI markets.

It is also important to remember that this is not an isolated case. The Democratic Republic of Congo holds key deposits of copper and cobalt, Guinea is a major source of bauxite, and the future supply of oil is dependent on reserves in the Middle East, the former Soviet Union, Nigeria, Equatorial Guinea, Angola, and República Bolivariana de Venezuela, an interesting bagatelle of political risks if ever there was one. Particular consideration must be given to the former Soviet Union, where there is the highest concentration of reserves across the commodity spectrum—a region that is not regarded as the paragon of political stability. The scale of demand for political risk mitigation will be a challenge to the traditional markets for PRI, and added to this will be the complexity of sponsors and offtakers from countries that are barely investment grade themselves. This new paradigm may drive a change in the approach to political risk mitigation.

The U.S. Economy, Globalization, and the Energy Crisis

Historically, the United States was the dominant consumer of commodities; this allowed it some freedom to influence world trade practices. It has often suited the United States and other developed economies to press for trade liberalization in order to gain access to markets for their manufactured goods, as well as making the market for commodities. The issue around the liberalization (or not) of the trade in agricultural products has raised questions about the true commitment to globalization. Often, developing nations have found themselves in the position of having to accept liberalization of trade in sectors where they will struggle to compete without some level of domestic protectionism, but at the same time, prevented from competing on a level playing field in other sectors where they have a natural advantage. This issue is clearly demonstrated in the sugar sector, where the African, Caribbean, and Pacific countries are naturally more competitive, but the world market price is still significantly below domestic prices in producer countries because of protectionism.

The frustrations of developing nations together with the shift in the competition for commodities has seen a weakening of the WTO and surge in new bilateral arrangements. This has put new bargaining power in the hands of many developing nations, which are major suppliers of commodities. In some cases, this rise of bilateralism has been done in a fashion that is likely to have major political consequences, like the raft of bilateral arrangements that China is forging with a number of African states. Similarly, the AGOA program has given African states preferential access on a bilateral basis to the U.S. market. While the Chinese program is characterized by large concessional loans and more robust engagement to secure opportunities for Chinese entities, both approaches can be seen as wooing the Africans.

Understandably though, the temptation of resource-rich developing countries to flex this newfound strength is proving difficult to resist. We have seen major nationalization programs in República Bolivariana de Venezuela and Bolivia, and similar noises in a number of countries that had been historically dependent on the traditional developed countries as customers.

It has been 30 years since similar interventions were seen on any scale, and that was in the context of the Cold War. In some respects, economic interests drove the Cold War, and it is interesting to speculate whether the current shift in economic power will create economic consequences that are similar to those of the Cold War despite the absence of the split in political ideology that characterized it. While it is highly unlikely that it will develop into the low-intensity war characterized by regional conflicts, the impact of a trade war may have similar destabilizing effects with promises of economic ties driving more radical political elements.

Clearly, this shift in economic power has taken the lid off a number of simmering political situations and significantly complicated the political risk for investors. It will be interesting to see how the PRI industry responds.

Nowhere will this dynamic be in starker relief than in the energy sector, where the United States is faced with increasing its dependence on importation as its reserves of oil and gas dwindle over the next 30 years. Unlike other commodities, access to energy is vital to all sectors of the economy and a global crisis is looming. A lot of innovation is being tried in the energy sector but it is likely to take decades before sustainable and scalable solutions are found. The net result will be increasing competition for access to these resources, with the stakes in the game rising as time passes and alternatives are not found. As the situation becomes more desperate, more bizarre political situations are likely to arise. While the general view has been that the threat of nationalization is becoming less probable as the global economy becomes more integrated, the speed with which the international oil companies have agreed to terms with República Bolivariana de Venezuela indicates that this view is rather a wish than a reality.

This tension has also given a platform to fundamentalists in the Muslim world. Arguably the current level of conflict is unlikely to result in a stable political solution in the short- to medium-term. While one cannot justify nor condone the attacks on civilians in Nairobi, New York, Baghdad, or Bali, the large-scale military interventions in Afghanistan and Iraq seem as unlikely to improve the political situation as the conflicts in Israel-Palestine and the negotiations relating to the Islamic Republic of Iran's nuclear program continue to destabilize the region. In the absence of competition for oil, it is questionable whether this region, which has been politically unstable since even before the coming of the Prophet Muhammad, would have such a significant influence on global political priorities, and consequently, on the political risk market. China, with its quest to secure access to oil, and Russia, with its own oil supplies and ambivalence on the Islamic issue, will provide the tension with the West that will continue to give Islamic fundamentalists a platform in the Middle East as long as oil remains a scarce commodity. The Middle East is not alone, and many other oil-producing states could see the rolling back of gains in the development of stable political environments as the competition for oil becomes more desperate.

If one watches the media, the danger of further fundamentalist attacks would seem to be the greatest risk we currently face; this is unlikely, of itself, to significantly influence the market for political risk although a frenzy for cover against terrorism will undoubtedly feed off this perception. The challenge of mitigating political risk in these unstable regions will be of far greater importance in order to secure access to oil.

Basel II and the Impact on Pricing in the Political Risk Market

After the *sturm und drang* of the previous section, it will be difficult to raise any level of excitement around the impact of the new Basel II regulations. Yet the implications of Basel II will have profound technical consequences for the use of PRI by the banking sector.

Historically, the view that the banking sector has taken to pricing political risk has been largely subjective. The rule of thumb that has been applied is that the banking sector will take short-dated risk uncovered but will look to lay off the risk in the medium- to long-dated exposures. Banks felt that, at the short end, their understanding of the dynamics of the environments was sufficient that they could take a subjective view and that the insurance market's pricing (based on statistical modeling) was too high. Conversely, in the longer-dated exposures, banks felt that their subjective approach had limitations and it was prudent to take cover at the best terms available from the market. Banks in more developed countries would attempt more sophisticated modeling, but at the end of the day, even these processes were limited as the individual bank's point of departure was limited by the profile of their own books. This relatively unsophisticated approach meant that the banks were price-takers, and had to rely on competition between providers of cover to regulate price.

The introduction of Basel II has opened up a debate around the value of PRI that may have a fundamental impact on pricing and on the way in which insurers and lenders interact. The initial response from the project finance community was that Basel II would be the death of project finance. On the standard approach, this might be true, but the major project finance banks quickly came to the realization that they would need to follow the advanced approach. The advanced approach, with its statistical modeling elements, means that banks will have a scientific basis on which to assess and price risk. Political risk is one of the factors that will be taken into account in risk-weighting assets for the purposes of capital reserving. While the risk assessment overall is a nonlinear process, it will be possible to assess the risk weighting and, therefore, the bank's cost of self-insuring against political risk. Inevitably, the banks' and the insurance market's calculations will not follow the same methodology. It will be interesting to see how this arbitrage plays out. However, there is little doubt that the banking sector will use this newfound information to become more sophisticated in their approach to political risk. While the more obvious result will be that pricing will become more transparent, one wonders whether this will result in banks taking a portfolio approach to hedging political risk, or whether banks themselves will become active buyers of political risk exposures, signaling a new chapter in the forfaiting industry.

Rising Liquidity and Domestic Liquidity in Producer Countries

One of the positive results of the high levels of growth globally has been the marked improvement in liquidity—except, that is, for the banks. The high levels of liquidity have significantly lowered the demand for lending, resulting in capital surpluses across the financial sector. This has driven margins to record lows and forced banks to look to more exotic markets to access high yield assets. Similarly, corporates are being forced out of their shells to find new uses for the increased liquidity. This has forced the market to be more innovative in structuring deals, especially in the field of political risk.

The increased liquidity has impacted project finance in particular. Project finance has always been costly, not only financially but also in terms of time and flexibility. In the past, corporates had used project finance to ring-fence the balance sheet against riskier new investments. Changes to accounting practices and the approach taken by rating agencies have significantly reduced the effectiveness of this approach. With the higher levels of liquidity, the balance has tipped against project finance. Corporates are reluctant to go through the difficulties of a project financing when they have balance sheet capacity. The use of project finance by corporates with limited capital continues, but increasingly these projects never get to financing as they are bought by larger corporates.

The challenge of political risk mitigation, however, remains a major concern for investments in difficult political environments. This has led to the development of structured corporate facilities where political risk is mitigated. As the market has matured, corporates have become more sophisticated in their understanding of political risk mitigation. Historically, public sector insurers were seen as a special deterrent and this element is being used in a more strategic fashion to minimize the additional cost associated with cover from the public sector. Lenders are also using the participation of a public sector insurer as part of the sales pitch to the private market.

To this mix is added one more twist. As new markets are tested, greenfield projects are often reliant on their domestic market for their revenue. The revenue stream is denominated in local currency and the experience of the late 1990s drove home the danger of mismatching the currency denomination of revenue streams and debt. In developing markets, the depth and tenor of the domestic market is often insufficient to provide the finance required for the investment. This has led to structures being developed between the public and private finance markets. The PRI market has traditionally focused on transferability risks, leaving currency hedging risk to the banks. In the case of exotic currencies, there is insufficient liquidity in the currency for banks to provide hedging products so that the risk often falls between two stools. As the demand from the market grows to address this issue, it is more likely to be an insurance solution. It will be interesting to see how this issue plays out.

Conclusion

From a macroperspective, it appears that the key drivers of the political risk market will be (i) the shift in economic power as China and, potentially, India become influential in stimulating investment globally, and (ii) the looming energy crisis. There is a lot of speculation that the growth in those two countries represents a fundamental shift in the global economy so that the boom in the commodity cycle is sustainable. This will result in the expansion of capacity in a number of developing countries, creating demands for political risk capacity on an unprecedented scale.

The expanded demand for commodities is best reflected in the energy sector. The Middle East will continue to be unstable and Iraq and Afghanistan are unlikely to see a peaceful resolution. Given the uncertainty around the Islamic Republic of Iran, there will be severe pressure on the certainty of the supply of oil. This will increase political risk across the region, as well as in other oil-producing states as power shifts from the consumers to the producers. This is already showing in certain trends, namely the resurgence of threatened nationalization as a negotiating approach by producer nations and bilateral agreements outside of the WTO to ensure security of supply. China has been particularly active in the bilateral space, and it will be interesting to see if this approach stands the test of time. Bilateralism will create new political dynamics and will affect the appetite of political risk insurers.

The combined impacts of Basel II and the increased levels of global liquidity are changing the approach that borrowers and lenders take to PRI. Political risk mitigation has become a priority in structuring new investments into emerging markets, as corporates become less reliant on full project financing for expansion. While political risk is in the spotlight, consumers are becoming better informed and more selective in their use of political risk cover. Pricing will become more transparent and consumers will demand more sophisticated products from insurers that have not traditionally been used in the PRI space. In addition, users will be looking for answers to the local currency issue.

The above view indicates that there will be an increase in the absolute demand for cover as well as the quality of that cover. In the public sector space, we have seen a growing trend of traditional public sector providers focusing on efficiency and commercial practices in order to remain relevant in a space where the private sector had become more aggressive, due to the slowdown in investment in emerging markets at the turn of the century. Going forward, the private market will be stretched so that they will compete less with the public service providers. This would seem to indicate an increase in pricing from the private market, leading to the public and private sector market returning to its correct structure.

As the project finance market is eroded, DFIs have started offering guarantee products that have equivalent features to insured corporate loans in order to maintain their required absolute returns. We are also seeing the likes of Sinosure looking to play a more significant role in support of exporters and, particularly, investors from developing countries. Public sector insurers like Sinosure will form part of a comprehensive approach between the public sector and private sector, which is characteristic of the development state school of economics where it will be difficult to isolate the economics of the cover. Both these factors may cause distortions in the market, but it will be interesting to see if they are big enough to have a major influence.

This scenario is likely to see a higher degree of cooperation between the public sector and private sector in order to use the available capacity most effectively. It is likely that this will result in a review of the traditional coverages and close scrutiny will be given to breach of contract cover, often touted as the "one size fits all" of PRI.

Our last comment relates particularly to the role of public sector insurers. There is a trend among shareholders of public sector insurers to move away from a highly developmental mandate to a more commercial mandate. While few will question the need to bring a level of economic rationale and efficiency into the public sector to make it more relevant, it begs a number of questions about the developmental impact of the public sector insurer. Where does this shift stop? At what point does the public sector become a slightly more bureaucratic, but otherwise indistinguishable competitor of the private sector? What happens to those countries that are dependent on developmental assistance when they fall off the commercial map?

EINSTEIN AND CINDERELLA

Julie Martin
Senior Vice President, Political Risk, Marsh

The PRI industry is a bit like a cross between Albert Einstein and Cinderella—too esoteric for many, and misunderstood and mistreated by others. Since the events that trigger PRI are not likely to make domestic headlines as earthquakes and hurricanes do, the brilliance and beauty of this product tends to be obscured by a veil of misunderstanding of how it works and to what it responds. Those steeped in an actuarial approach to risk assessment find it difficult to relate to political risk assessment—which is more of an art than a science. Companies used to benchmarking against others similarly situated find it difficult to do so in the political risk market because of the variation in appetite for risk and the degree of adverse selection. One way to clear up some of the misunderstanding is to amplify the information currently available with more data about claims made and paid.

Some attempts have been made to make PRI more transparent, but concerns about confidentiality and the perceived potential adverse effects that disclosure of claims may have on insurers have essentially deterred this effort. In the mid-1990s, the Berne Union began collecting information about claims paid for political risk events from its members, but this early endeavor resulted only in an aggregation of anonymously reported information. In its 2006 Yearbook, the Berne Union gave an aggregate dollar amount of claims paid for each of the years 2000–2004, with no other detail as to where, type of cover, or other instructive information.

The Industry's Theory of Relativity

Why is claims information confidential? Apart from the obvious need to protect confidential business relationships, there are several practical reasons why claims information is confidential.

Underwriters desire to protect host government relationships. Public agencies do not want to disrupt their official relationships with other governments, and a claim may only be one small element of their overall foreign policy objectives. Governments that have violated an investor's rights would rather keep public information about the matter to a minimum, but the investor's government may have the opposite interest.[1] Multilateral insurers may very well be under pressure not to make any of their member countries look bad under any circumstances, and so there may be less hope of transparency from them.

The private market has typically limited disclosure of the existence of an insurance policy and any related claims information not only to protect business confidentiality, but also to avoid moral hazard issues. Specifically, insurers fear that if a government knows that a bank loan or a project investment is insured against expropriatory actions, the government may take such actions without fear of reprisal.[2] (This is less of a concern for inconvertibility claims—which are generally economywide—and for political violence claims, which are usually not under the control of the host government.) However, the concern that governments may expropriate investments that are known to be insured ought to be reduced by the knowledge that the insurer will still have subrogation rights, and that many BITs expressly provide that insurance compensation is not a defense to a claim against the government.

There is some fear that readily available analyses would encourage insurers to be more conservative. Above all, the insurers are concerned that publicly disclosed claims analyses may be introduced as evidence in future arbitrations with respect to similar claims; and any decision would apply not only to the current claim but act as a precedent for future cases. Needless to say, insurers are reluctant to give claimants' lawyers a whole array of precedents from which to pick and choose those most favorable to their argument.

Inertial Motion

As mentioned, the Berne Union, the greatest source of PRI claims information, began aggregating claims data a decade ago. Many brokers, investors, and others have unsuccessfully encouraged the Berne Union to make that data available in some format that would not compromise the contributors' business confidentiality issues, but to date all but the most limited data has remained confidential.[3]

More recently, many private market underwriters have been encouraged to provide information about their claims payment history. This push has come both from their customers and from the rating agencies who, in conjunction with providing ratings to capital markets transactions supported by PRI, needed to assess and report on not only the claims-paying ability of underwriters, but their claims-paying *willingness* as well. Most of the large-company markets now include some claim information on their websites.[4]

However, there is some light in this chasm of claims data. OPIC[5] discloses far more information about claims made and paid for PRI than any other underwriter. Not only does OPIC publish an annual report and provide a cumulative update regarding all claims it has paid, arbitrated, and denied, but it also makes its claims Memoranda of Determinations (MOD) available to the public on its website. These memoranda, which have been the basis of many case studies at various universities, reveal an abundance of information: the chain of events that led to a claim under the scope of coverage; whether exclusions, warranties, or duties prevented an insured from perfecting a claim; and how underwriters calculate compensation. If OPIC also provided more information on the ratio of projects subject to claims or near-claims, this data would provide a perspective on how often projects run into trouble (see table 1).

The transparency of OPIC's reporting has a number of benefits and holds OPIC to a certain standard in the industry. On the one hand, OPIC cannot deny claims unless such denial would withstand the scrutiny of the public; and on the other hand, the organization cannot pay claims that are not meritorious. This transparency instills a certain discipline that should benefit OPIC with the business community and with its stakeholders that include the U.S. Congress, NGOs, etc.

While it may be better to have limited information available than to have none at all, we are still far away from the ideal situation—a repository of claims information

TABLE 1 OPIC Claims History

Claims	1966–1970[a]	1971–2005	Percentage of Total Claims Submitted
Submitted	16	310	
Paid	8	284	91.6%
Denied	8	26	8.4%
Arbitration[b]	1	13	
Amount Paid	US$3.5 million	US$967.5 million	

Source: Author and Robert O'Sullivan, 2005, "Learning from OPIC's Experience with Claims and Arbitration." In *International Political Risk Management Volume 3: Looking to the Future,* ed. Theodore H. Moran and Gerald T. West.

[a] Operating as part of USAID, the program operator preceding OPIC.

[b] The arbitrated claims are included in the paid and denied totals, depending on the outcome of the arbitration.

for the entire industry. Even if the Berne Union agreed to disclose the aggregate information in its repository, there would still remain a gap resulting from Lloyds' syndicates' reluctance to fully participate.[6] If all other underwriters contributed to a repository of claims information, one would hope that Lloyds' central claims bureau might be more willing to release their statistics.[7]

The Glass Slipper

Why should PRI claims information be made available? There are at least two important reasons to disclose it.

A primary reason to disclose information about claims made and paid is to reduce the amount of skepticism that potential clients may harbor about PRI. Producers who promote this product are often asked whether claims have been paid in the country and sector of the proposed investment. When producers are unable to answer these questions because of lack of information, investors often assume either that there is no risk, or that this type of insurance does not pay out. This fundamentally hurts the industry. Aggregate claims information would enable market practitioners to dispel both of these notions.

Another reason to release information about claims made and paid is to educate consumers about what is and what is not covered. While most underwriters are uncomfortable with the degree of disclosure that would be necessary to achieve this level of understanding, and choose not to disclose the information, OPIC does publish claims data and its MODs.

Since most PRI policies have adopted "plain English" wording, some of the nuances of meaning for complex concepts are lost, and experience indicates that some provisions can be read and interpreted in many different ways. It is important for all parties to know how policy wording will respond when reviewed by outside counsel or arbitrators, especially those who are not involved in the business negotiations, or have little background in PRI. Underwriters need to be able to represent what it is they are selling and investors need to understand what they are buying. To that end, interpretations by underwriters should not be confidential, as it does a disservice to all parties to the transaction if the underwriter's view as to the interpretation of widely used policy language is not adequately disseminated.

Certainly, there are limitations on what this information can tell us. See, for example, Robert O'Sullivan's article, "Learning from OPIC's Experience with Claims and Arbitration,"[8] where he notes that the U.S. government paid no claims in Cuba, for example, because no investor had coverage. Similarly, there will be no OPIC claim payments for oil and gas investments in certain Latin American countries because the companies have self-insured. Someone who sees no claims paid should not assume that insurers denied claims. In many high-profile cases, there was no insurance.

All things considered, consumers want to know that the product works—that it is a good fit for them. They want to know that if they experience a politically triggered event that the coverage will respond. And, only public disclosure of claims made and paid will convince the wary consumer that PRI is both effective and responsive.

An Invitation to the Ball

What information should be released? As in any consumer education effort, the more factual information released, the better it is for the insured. At the very minimum, data for claims made and paid for political risk events should include:

- Year of the claim, year of payment, or both
- Country of loss
- Type of loss reported: e.g., expropriation, inconvertibility, political violence, contract frustration
- Sector of claimant: e.g., banking, power, manufacturing
- Amount of compensation

Information on the number of claims denied and recoveries would also be useful.

In order for the industry to get to this level of transparency, the Berne Union and Lloyd's, and any underwriters that are not party to either of those groups, should release their aggregate claims information. This should not be a big step for the market.

A potentially more controversial proposal is to release specific case histories that provide insight into policy interpretation or key elements to success or failure of the claim, e.g., where a failure to adequately disclose an event that could have led to a potential claim barred a successful outcome. If the case studies were redacted to remove telltale information as to the specific parties involved, this should not breach confidentiality and would provide a great service to the market.

While the possibility of adverse affects to insurers from disclosure of this information may still exist, the benefits would far outweigh the risks. Transparency would ease the fears of consumers that the policies do not pay out. The potential result would be a broader, deeper market of prospective clients who are better informed and more eager to invest in the product. Transparency would also encourage greater accountability of the underwriters. In short, the result could only be a more robust industry—not one mired in speculation and rumor, but one where, although the product may still be somewhat esoteric, it would not take an Einstein to comprehend its value.

Notes

1. For example, OPIC put the U.S. government's demand for arbitration against India on its website.

2. For expropriation, once a claim has been paid, settled, or denied, disclosure of the details should at least be considered on specific cases based on a variety of legal and business factors.

3. The Investment Insurance Committee of the Berne Union reports members' claims payments of $17 million in 2000, $45 million in 2001, $17 million in 2002, $117 million in 2003, and $168 million in 2004.

4. For example, Zurich reported on its website a $17.8 million claim paid in July 2006 as the result of a claim made from a series of political violence attacks on power lines in Colombia.

5. OPIC was established as an agency of the U.S. government in 1971. OPIC helps U.S. businesses invest overseas, fosters economic development in new and emerging markets, complements the private sector in managing risks associated with foreign direct investment, and supports U.S. foreign policy.

6. Lloyd's has cooperated with brokers in providing some aggregate information in recent years, but the information has been incomplete and it has required significant work to obtain on an individual syndicate basis.

7. Apparently, Lloyd's will now sell aggregate claims information regarding loss ratios, but the statistic combines trade credit, political risk, and contract frustration.

8. O'Sullivan, Robert. 2005. "Learning from OPIC's Experience with Claims and Arbitration." In *International Political Risk Management, Volume 3: Looking to the Future,* ed. Theodore H. Moran and Gerald T. West. See also Zylberglait, Pablo. 1993. "OPIC's Investment Insurance: The Platypus of Governmental Programs and its Jurisprudence." 25 *Law & Policy International Business 359.*

DISCUSSION OF THE INTERNATIONAL POLITICAL RISK INSURANCE INDUSTRY IN 2010

Symposium Panelists and Participants

The principal areas of discussion included risk mitigation and deterrence, devaluation losses and exclusions, and disclosure of claims.

Question: Investors and lenders want risk mitigation rather than claims payments from insurers. Public sector agencies can have a deterrent effect. Can the private sector also play this role?

Ansermino: Public sector agencies can step in and demand an audience from the government. In my experience the ability of the private sector to do the same is more limited. If there is a role, that role would be for the private sector to go in hand-in-hand with public insurers.

Salinger: Since 1978, when we started the Trade and Political Risk business at AIG, we have paid about $1.3 billion in claims. I forget the amount we have recovered, but we have done very, very well in recovery. We have never had, that I can recall, a case where we could not get access to people that we needed to get access to, and I think, if anything, now that we are part of the Berne Union, that access is enhanced.

In Amsterdam at the Berne Union meeting last week, I was talking with the managing director of a major European purely government export credit agency. We were discussing the pros and cons of collaboration. One thing that was clear was that when they look at recovery actions as a representative of a government, if it is known that they are there, they have to take foreign policy considerations of their government into account in terms of what they can do to pursue recovery. So this managing director actually saw some advantages of reinsuring us, and always having the flexibility to cut out and go separately, if that's what they wanted to do, or to ride behind us, if they agreed with what we were doing.

Question: One of the standard exclusions in political risk investment insurance policies is for losses caused by, or resulting from, devaluation. How do insurers interpret what the devaluation exclusion is meant to exclude? What if devaluation is part of a chain of happenings that leads to a covered event, including, for example, a breach of contract on the part of the government—is that also excluded?

Salinger: In our view at AIG, the devaluation exclusion is a critical part of the policy. It is one of the places where one can draw a sharp distinction between a commercial loss and a political loss. The intent of the policy is to cover political events, not commercial events, and that is one of the instances where the issue is addressed in language which, in my view, could not be clearer or simpler.

In our export credit business, devaluation is the single, largest systemic risk in the portfolio that we take. We have looked at the possibility of covering it in our investment insurance business and have decided not to take it. The simple way to think about the exclusion is to trace through the fact-pattern—this happened, then that happened, then something else happened, then the investor suffered a loss. If a devaluation was part of the fact-sequence, the insurer would ask, if there had not been a devaluation, would there have been a loss? If the answer to that question is no, then the exclusion prevails because the devaluation produced the loss. It is very clear in the policy wording.

Westholm-Schröder: For Sovereign, the devaluation exclusion is usually in the limited context of policies for lenders where devaluation results in the inability of the borrowers to make payments. Devaluation leads to insolvency, which leads to the default on scheduled loan payments—which is an excluded loss. That is how we look at it.

One area where there is progress is to try to provide coverage for local currency financings. This would take away some of the need for, and demand for, devaluation coverage, since there would be no currency mismatch between income and revenues. But there are a limited number of markets with credit standards and currencies that would qualify for coverage of local currency-denominated transactions.

Ansermino: Issues about loan currency and devaluation are obviously huge issues for banks. The devaluation exclusion, I think, is a correct exclusion for the banking industry. The solution is not going to lie with the insurance industry, but with the development of local currency markets. We are increasingly seeing development finance markets focusing on developing the local currency markets. That, in turn, will put pressure on covering local currency facilities.

Question: Is there room for progress on making claims payments public?

Westholm-Schröder: At Sovereign, we do make our claims public. Claims data are available in our annual reports. But with regard to the larger issue of transparency and clarity about what is being bought and what is being sold, it is important that any insurance policy be as clear as possible. The buyer may not want to take the time upfront, but it is better to argue with one's insurer about precisely what is covered before signing the policy, and walk away if there is no agreement. Then hopefully if the transaction ends up in a claims situation, the policy language is clear about what was meant to be covered.

APPENDIX I

BIOGRAPHIES OF AUTHORS

Greg Ansermino

Greg Ansermino is a Director in the Corporate & Investment Banking Division of the Standard Bank of South Africa Ltd., the South African head office of the group's international operations. He joined the group in 1996 in Johannesburg, but was immediately seconded to Standard Bank London Project Finance for two years. During that time he was an integral part of the team advising the National Grid Co. and Cinergy Global Power on the purchase of the Power Division of ZCCM in Zambia. On his return to Johannesburg in October 1998, he was appointed head of the South African project finance business, where he focused more on the arranging and lending operations, beginning with the funding for the South African National Lottery. Under his management, the project finance business has expanded from its original power and infrastructure mandate to include natural resources and industrial projects, as well as the bank's international export finance. In 2001, he led the South African portion of the financing for Avgold's Target Mine, which was the first mining project financing closed in the South African market, and in 2004, he led the team on the Sasol Temane Gas project, which was the bank's first major gas deal. He has now moved on from his role as head of project finance into the senior investment banker role, where his knowledge and experience will be applied broadly across the bank's product offerings. Prior to joining the group, he was an associate at Bowman Gilfillan Inc., South Africa's largest law firm, where he concentrated on South African mining companies and inward investment. He holds a Bachelor of Commerce degree from the University of Cape Town, and Bachelor of Laws and Higher Diploma in Taxation from the University of the Witwatersrand.

Charles Berry

Charles Berry is Chairman of BPL Global and has worked as a London-based specialist PRI broker since 1974, when the private PRI market was still in its infancy.

He cofounded Berry Palmer & Lyle Ltd. (BPL Global) in 1983. BPL Global is an insurance consultant and broker specializing in emerging market risk. BPL Global's clients are major multinational corporations and financial institutions. It has offices in London and Paris, and affiliated offices in Boston, Dallas, Los Angeles, Vienna, Milan, Sao Paulo, and Santiago.

Charles Berry is a regular speaker at international conferences on political risk and trade credit insurance, and has lectured and written extensively on the subject. He has a master's degree from Oxford University, an M.B.A. from Harvard Business School, and is a fellow of the Chartered Insurance Institute.

Peter Charles Choharis

Peter Choharis is a principal at Choharis Global Solutions, which provides international dispute resolution, foreign and U.S. government relations, and emerging market strategic consulting services to business and government clients. He has represented two African countries and a U.S.-chartered organization on expropriation disputes, and advised U.S. companies on expropriation matters. He has also represented foreign governments in multiple international arbitrations and disputes.

Mr. Choharis is also a visiting scholar at The George Washington University Law School, where he is writing a series of law review articles on expropriation under international law, and a visiting fellow at the Center for Strategic and International Studies in Washington, DC. The first of these law review articles is entitled, "U.S. Courts and the International Law of Expropriation: Toward a New Model for Breach of Contract," which is in Volume 80 of the *University of Southern California Law Review*, December 2006. His second article on expropriation has the working title, "Constructing a New Model of Regulatory Takings Under International Law."

He served as the Executive Director of the 2004 Democratic Platform Committee, and advised the John Kerry presidential campaign on foreign and legal policy beginning in November 2003. He is currently advising a gubernatorial and U.S. Senate candidate. He has also been an adjunct professor of law at the Washington College of Law, American University, and taught a seminar on international law as a visiting lecturer at Yale College.

His first law review article appeared in the *Yale Journal on Regulation.* In addition, more than a dozen of his articles on foreign affairs and international law have appeared in the *The National Interest*, *The Washington Post Outlook* section (including the lead article), *The Wall Street Journal*, the *Los Angeles Times*, *The Boston Globe*, and *The Christian Science Monitor*, as well as other publications, and have been broadcast on National Public Radio. He has appeared on

CNN, BBC, NPR, MSNBC, REUTERS-TV and other networks to discuss law and foreign policy.

He is a graduate of the Yale Law School and Harvard College.

Kenneth W. Hansen

Kenneth Hansen is a partner in Chadbourne & Parke's project finance group, resident in the Washington, DC, office. He regularly represents developers of, and lenders to, emerging market project financings, particularly those involving support by multilateral development banks, bilateral development agencies, or export credit agencies. His experience includes debt workouts and the settlement of political risk insurance claims and investment disputes, with sectoral experience ranging from power projects to oil and gas, telecommunications, pulp and paper, industrial, commercial, agricultural, and banking projects.

He joined Chadbourne from the U.S. Export-Import Bank, where he was General Counsel. Previously, he spent nine years as an attorney with OPIC. Today, he represents several such agencies, including OPIC, Ex-Im Bank, EBRD, IDB, IFC, IIC, and ADB, in emerging market project financings. He recently represented OPIC in connection with settlement and recovery of political risk insurance claims arising from the Dabhol power project in India. He also represented OPIC with respect to the AES Tiete (Brazil) bond financing, which OPIC supported with a guaranty against devaluation losses, and the ADB in connection with its special risk guaranties of financing for the Phu My 2.2 and Phu My 3 power stations in Vietnam.

He is a 1974 honors graduate of Harvard College and a 1983 honors graduate of the University of Pennsylvania Law School. He also holds master's degrees in international relations from Yale University and public administration from Harvard's Kennedy School of Government.

Frederick (Rick) E. Jenney

Frederick (Rick) E. Jenney is a partner at Morrison & Foerster LLP in Washington, DC, where his practice focuses on political risk insurance, international project finance, and cross-border investment transactions, with particular emphasis on structuring, lending, political risk, and intercreditor issues.

He has represented lenders, developers, and political risk insurers in project financings in Asia, Latin America, the Caribbean, and Central and Eastern Europe, principally in the power, water, hotel, and manufacturing industries. His political risk insurance experience encompasses both insurance and reinsurance of a broad range of equity and debt investments by developers, commercial banks, and capital markets investors. His project finance experience comprises new loans, refinancings, restructurings, and workouts for projects ranging in size from US$2 million to US$2.5 billion, particularly with respect to colending among multilateral and bilateral agencies, commercial bank syndicates, and 144A lenders.

He has served as an adjunct professor at the Georgetown University Law Center, the Washington College of Law, American University, and The George Washington University Law School, where he taught courses covering foreign direct investment, international commercial transactions, and international project finance.

Mark Kantor

Mark Kantor currently serves as an arbitrator and teaches both international business transactions and international arbitration as an adjunct professor at the Georgetown University Law Center. Until he retired at the end of 1999, he was a partner in the Corporate and Project Finance Groups of Milbank, Tweed, Hadley & McCloy and resident in the Washington, DC, office. He is a member of numerous arbitration rosters, including the AAA international and commercial panels, the CPR Panel of Distinguished Neutrals for Banking and Finance, the LCIA list, and the ICC roster of arbitrators. He is also the Chairman of the Washington, DC, Bar International Dispute Resolution Committee, and a member of the Alternative Dispute Resolution Advisory Committee for the International Law Institute. Mr. Kantor's practice combines Wall Street expertise with Washington experience. His principal transactional focus has been in the area of international and domestic investments and financings. He has represented sponsors, financial institutions, and contractors in complex financings and restructurings, and he has considerable experience with the energy, power, air carrier, telecommunications, and financial services industries. In addition, he has represented acquirers, sellers, and financing parties in numerous acquisitions.

Mr. Kantor was the lead partner in Milbank Tweed's involvement in a number of prominent project financings, including several "Deals of the Year," named by trade periodicals over the years. Among his engagements are the Pinamucan/Batangas, Upper Mahiao and Mahanagdong power projects in the Philippines (representing OPIC); the first project financing by U.S. Ex-Im Bank's Project Finance Division; the first private power project in Indonesia (Paiton, representing the Japanese government); the first private power project in the Gulf; the first limited recourse power project in Turkey; the first World Bank partial risk guarantee; the first capital markets offering to finance an international water project and the first Inter-American Development Bank partial risk guarantee; and the U.S. and Japanese government refinancing of Peruvian arrears to the World Bank and IMF (the only private lawyer involved in the matter). He was extensively involved in Milbank Tweed's Asian workouts and restructurings.

In U.S. domestic proceedings, he has acted as bankruptcy counsel in a number of well-known insolvencies, including the Pan Am, Continental Airlines, AmericaWest, Air Wisconsin, AroChem refinery, and Jesup Plastics bankruptcies, as well as numerous negotiated workouts. He is a member of the editorial board of *Global Arbitration Review,* the board of editors of *The Banking Law Journal* and an Associate Editor of both the online Oil, Gas & Energy Law Intelligence Service and the online journal *Transnational Dispute Management*. In 1990, Mr. Kantor served as the first outside General Counsel of the RTC Oversight Board, the U.S. federal agency with policy oversight responsibility for the savings and loan crisis. Additional background on Mr. Kantor, a list of publications, and a list of Mr. Kantor's recent ADR engagements may be found at http://clik.to/kantor.

Julie Martin

Julie Martin is a Senior Vice President in the Political Risk Practice of Marsh, the insurance broker, and is based in Washington, DC.

At Marsh, she has worked on a range of political risk programs both in an advisory and broker capacity. Working with both public and private political risk insurers, these programs include multicountry placements for manufacturing firms, structuring coverage for large infrastructure investments, and capital market securitizations.

She joined Marsh Inc. after 20 years of experience in the political risk business at OPIC. Serving in a variety of positions, including vice president of insurance and chief underwriter, she worked with a wide range of clients in most emerging markets and established relationships with many private and public counterparts. She was responsible for many OPIC initiatives in the political risk area, including developing the programs for institutional lenders and the capital markets.

She has spoken at numerous seminars and conferences on political risk and has authored several articles. She holds an MBA in finance from George Washington University, a master's of science in Foreign Service from Georgetown University, and a bachelor's degree in international relations from Texas Tech University.

Keith Martin

At the time of the preparation of this volume, Keith Martin was the Senior Marketing Specialist at MIGA. He has since moved on to assume the position of General Manager, International Relations at Companhia Vale do Rio Doce (CVRD),

Brazil's largest private sector firm, and the world's second-largest mining company. At CVRD, he has primary responsibility for relations with governments, NGOs, and international organizations, and an additional role with respect to CVRD's political risk analysis and management.

During his seven years at MIGA, Mr. Martin held several positions, including that of advisor to the EVP, and had responsibility for MIGA's outreach to the investor and lender communities, particularly in Turkey, the Middle East, and Africa, as well as for the agency's relations with the Board of Directors, member governments, and other stakeholders. From 1998 to 2000, he worked at OPIC as assistant to the Vice President, Insurance, and as an underwriter. Additionally, he served for four years as an adjunct professor of international business diplomacy at Georgetown University, teaching courses on international political risk analysis and management.

Mr. Martin graduated magna cum laude from Georgetown University, has a master's degree from McGill University, and had additional educational experience in Poland, Turkey, and Tunisia.

Barry Metzger

Barry Metzger is a member of Baker and McKenzie's Global Banking & Finance Practice Group in the New York office. For more than 30 years, Mr. Metzger has represented Asian financial institutions and corporations internationally, and has represented foreign financial institutions and investors with operations in Asia.

From 1995 to 1999, Mr. Metzger served as General Counsel of the Asian Development Bank. There, he was deeply involved in the ADB's emergency assistance to the Republic of Korea, Thailand, and Indonesia during the Asian financial crisis; its project financing of infrastructure; its investment funds activities; and its work on legal reform in the Bank's developing member countries. Such project finance work has included the Khimti Kola hydropower project in Nepal, the Mei Zhou Wan and Changsha power projects in China, and the Fauji Kabirwala power project in Pakistan.

Among the transactions for which Mr. Metzger has been responsible have been the acquisition of a controlling interest in Huffy Corporation by its Chinese suppliers and Chinese government's export credit insurance agency, the ¥90 billion royalty receivables financing of Tokyo Disneyland Park for the Walt Disney Company, the comparable financing relating to the operations of Seven-Eleven Japan, and the recent ¥70 billion coinvestment arrangements in Japan of the Japan Real Estate Recovery Fund.

Mr. Metzger is a recognized authority on Asian legal systems, economic law reform, and corporate governance. He has advised the Republic of Korea and the

Russian Federation on corporate governance reform, and has written extensively on such issues as they affect economic development and foreign investment.

A few samples of his published work include "American Corporate Governance: Scandal, Reform and the Global Capital Markets," *Euromoney International Equity Markets Yearbook 2003;* "Russia's Code of Corporate Conduct: An Innovative Approach to Solving Shareholder Rights Abuses," International Corporate Governance, April–May 2002; and "The Global War on Poverty: An American Foreign Aid Revolution," KWR International, April 2003. He spoke at the "Governance, Law and Development—An Asian Perspective," Annual Meeting of the Board of Governors of the Asian Development Bank, Istanbul, Turkey, May 2005; and "American Corporate Governance and the Global Economy," The Metropolitan Corporate Counsel, September 2004.

He is a graduate of Harvard Law School and Princeton University.

Theodore H. Moran

Theodore H. Moran holds the Marcus Wallenberg Chair at the School of Foreign Service, Georgetown University, where he teaches and conducts research at the intersection of international economics, business, foreign affairs, and public policy. Dr. Moran is founder of the Landegger Program in International Business Diplomacy, and serves as director in providing courses on international business-government relations and negotiations to some 600 undergraduate and graduate students each year.

His most recent books include *Does Foreign Direct Investment Promote Development?,* ed., with Magnus Blomstrom, Stockholm School of Economics and Edward Graham, Institute for International Economics, 2005; *International Political Risk Management: The Brave New World,* ed., MIGA, the World Bank Group, 2004; *Beyond Sweatshops: Foreign Direct Investment, Globalization, and Developing Countries,* Brookings, 2002; *International Political Risk Management: Exploring New Frontiers,* ed., MIGA, the World Bank Group, 2001; and *Foreign Investment and Development,* Institute for International Economics, 1998.

In 1993–94, Dr. Moran served as Senior Advisor for Economics on the Policy Planning Staff of the U.S. Department of State, where he had responsibility for trade, finance, technology, energy, and environmental issues. He returned to Georgetown after the NAFTA and Uruguay Round negotiations.

Dr. Moran is consultant to the United Nations, to diverse governments in Asia and Latin America, and to the international business and financial communities. In 2002, Dr. Moran was named Chairman of the Committee on Monitoring International Labor Standards of the National Academy of Sciences. Professor Moran received his Ph.D. from Harvard in 1971. He is a nonresident fellow at the Institute for International Economics and at the Center for Global Development.

David Neckar

David Neckar is the Practice Leader for the Willis FINEX Political and Trade Credit Risk business. His responsibility includes strategic and technical development, relationships with ECAs, dealing with Basel II issues, and managing certain key clients.

He has more than 25 years of specialist financial risk experience, which includes senior positions in both brokering and underwriting (including reinsurance as well as direct insurance).

Mr. Neckar has a degree from Oxford University and an MBA from INSEAD.

Yukiko Omura

Yukiko Omura, a Japanese national, joined the World Bank Group as Executive Vice President of MIGA in May 2004.

Ms. Omura brings more than 20 years of international professional experience in the financial services sector. She began her career as a project economist with the Inter-American Development Bank, in Washington, DC. She then spent 10 years at J.P. Morgan in Tokyo, New York, and London, among other duties launching the emerging markets operations in the Tokyo office and heading EMSTAR (Emerging Markets Sales, Trading and Research) Marketing for Northern Europe, out of London.

Ms. Omura joined Lehman Brothers as Senior Vice President and Head of Emerging Markets, Asia, and subsequently became Head of Credit Business, Asia. She then went on to be Managing Director and Head of the Global Fixed Income and Derivatives Department of UBS in Japan. Following a merger with SBC and LTCB, Ms. Omura became the new head of the merged bank, but left to join her global partners and become the new Managing Director and Head of Dresdner's Global Markets and Global Debt offices in Japan.

In 2002, Ms. Omura created the AIDS Prevention Fund, a charitable company based in London.

Born in Paris, Ms. Omura was educated in Switzerland and the United Kingdom, and earned a master's degree in development economics and a second master's degree in political economics from Boston University.

Joanne Palmer

Joanne Palmer joined Export Development Canada (EDC), Canada's export credit agency, in 1980. Since that time, she has worked in a variety of positions in financing, political risk insurance, and business strategy. She has been in charge of EDC's rapidly growing Political Risk Insurance (PRI) program since being appointed Director of PRI in June 2002. As well as underwriting, she is responsible at EDC for all new PRI product development, business development support, and portfolio management. As an active representative to the Berne Union, she regularly contributes EDC's perspective on PRI issues in that forum and has appeared at a number of public conferences in the past.

Ms. Palmer holds an MBA from the Schulich School of Business at York University, and is a graduate of McGill University.

Edith (Edie) P. Quintrell

Edie Quintrell was appointed as OPIC Vice President of Insurance in March 2006; she has been with OPIC since 1991. Prior to her appointment as Vice President, she served as Regional Director and Director of Technical Operations in the Insurance Department at OPIC. She also served as Chair of the Berne Union Investment Insurance Committee in 2004 and as Chair of the Berne Union Investment Insurance Technical Panel from 2002–2003.

Prior to joining OPIC, Ms. Quintrell worked at the Pan American Development Foundation, a nongovernmental organization in Washington, DC. She holds a B.A. in Political Science and Latin American Studies from Princeton University, and an M.A. in International Affairs from the Johns Hopkins School of Advanced International Studies. Ms. Quintrell was a Fulbright Scholar at the Universidad de los Andes in Bogota, Colombia, from 1985–86.

Jeffery A. Safford

Jeff Safford joined AES in 1988 as Director of Finance and Administration, with direct responsibility for all facets of accounting and financial reporting, tax reporting and compliance, treasury, benefits administration, and corporate finance. Prior to joining AES, he worked in the audit group of Touche Ross for approximately five years, where he had responsibility for several large publicly held clients.

In February 1994, Mr. Safford was appointed CFO of AES China Generating (AES CHIGEN). AES CHIGEN was formed as a majority-owned, publicly traded subsidiary of AES, to specifically develop, own, and operate power projects in the People's Republic of China. AES CHIGEN successfully developed and funded nine joint ventures raising equity and debt in the capital markets of approximately US$330 million. In 1997, the public float of AES CHIGEN was acquired by AES in a merger transaction valued at over US$115 million. In late 1998, Mr. Safford was appointed CFO of AES Americas.

From his appointment until 2002, Mr. Safford was involved in several transactions, including various refinancings and project financings in Argentina, mergers and acquisitions in República Bolivariana de Venezuela and Chile, and the sale of certain distribution companies in Colombia. In February 2002, Mr. Safford joined AES Gener as a Board member and COO of this 98.5 percent-owned subsidiary of AES, completing a US$330 million prepackaged bankruptcy filing in Colombia and the refinancing of over US$100 million of additional corporate debt.

In September 2002, Mr. Safford joined AES in Brazil and was appointed CFO of the AES group of companies in Brazil for the ensuing year. Mr. Safford was involved in the restructuring of the US$1.3 billion holding company debt with the Brazilian National Economic Development Bank (BNDES), the refinancing of certain of the Brazil group's operating company debt, the restructuring of AES Sul, and the most recent US$625 million sale of the preferred shares of AES Eletropaulo held by AES Transgas.

During his tenure in Brazil, Mr. Safford has held positions as Vice President of Control and Financial Planning and Executive Director AES/BNDES Relationship, and he is currently Vice President of Corporate Governance for AES in Brazil. In addition, Mr. Safford is a member of the Board of Directors of AES Eletropaulo Metropolitana Eletricidade de São Paulo S.A., AES Elpa S.A., AES Sul Distribuidora Gaúcha de Energia S.A., and AES Tietê S.A. He is a graduate of Pennsylvania State University.

John J. Salinger

John J. Salinger is President of AIG Global Trade & Political Risk Insurance Co., a wholly owned subsidiary of American International Group. AIG Global is a leading private sector underwriter of political risk, domestic, and export credit insurance.

Mr. Salinger currently serves as the Chairman of the Short Term Export Credit Committee of the Berne Union and on the U.S. OPIC Advisory Committee. He has previously served on the advisory boards of the Ex-Im Bank of the United States and the Institute for Infrastructure Finance.

Mr. Salinger is a director of several AIG joint ventures, including Uzbekinvest International Insurance Company, Ltd., a London-based political risk insurer that is a partnership with the Government of Uzbekistan, and the Latin American Investment Guarantee Co., a Bermuda-based political risk insurer that is owned by AIG and the Andean Development Fund.

He joined AIG in 1985 after 12 years with The Chase Manhattan Bank, where he had international business assignments in New York, London, Hong Kong, and Nigeria. At Chase, he was the U.S. Trade Finance Division Executive.

Mr. Salinger was educated at Brown University, and holds a master's in international relations from the University of Pennsylvania. He served as a Peace Corps volunteer in Morocco and Senegal.

Gerald T. West

Gerald West is currently an adjunct professor of international business diplomacy at Georgetown University. Retiring after 15 years of service with MIGA in mid-2006, he had held five different positions in four different MIGA departments, including Claims Administrator, Director of Evaluation, and Director of Policy and the Environment. Prior to joining MIGA, he served in a variety of positions at OPIC, including 10 years as the Vice President for Development.

From 1983–95 and again from 2003 to the present, he has served as an adjunct professor of international business diplomacy at Georgetown University, where he teaches courses on international political risk assessment and management and international business. Over the last 30 years, he has lectured, consulted, and published widely on corporate political risk assessment and management. He is the founder of the MIGA-Georgetown Symposium on International Political Risk Management.

Mr. West received his Ph.D. in international politics from the Wharton School of the University of Pennsylvania. For nine years, he was affiliated with the Foreign Policy Research Institute, where he conducted research on a wide range of international political and economic topics.

Christina Westholm-Schröder

Christina Westholm-Schröder is the Chief Underwriting Officer at Sovereign Risk Insurance Ltd. of Bermuda, a private political risk insurer owned by ACE Bermuda Insurance Ltd., and one of the world's leading providers of long-term political risk insurance (PRI) and reinsurance.

Ms. Westholm-Schröder was previously with MIGA for 11 years, which she joined as one of its first employees in 1988. At MIGA, she worked in several capacities, including Regional Manager for Asia and Latin America, and more recently as Manager for Syndications and Business Development, which also included responsibility for the agency's reinsurance activities.

Prior to joining MIGA, Ms. Westholm-Schröder worked as a political risk insurance broker at Bank of America's Global Trade Finance Department in New York and at AB Max Matthiessen in Stockholm, Sweden. She has an MBA in international business from the Stockholm School of Economics and Business Administration, as well as an MBA in finance from New York University.

Erik J. Woodhouse

Since November 2006, Erik Woodhouse has been an associate with the law firm of Latham & Watkins in its Washington, DC, office. Prior to joining Latham,

Mr. Woodhouse served as a law clerk to the Honorable M. Margaret McKeown on the United States Court of Appeals for the Ninth Circuit, and as a postdoctoral scholar with the Program on Energy & Sustainable Development (PESD) at Stanford University. While at PESD, Mr. Woodhouse was responsible for a study examining the experience of independent power projects in 13 developing countries. The findings of the IPP study were presented for discussion and critique in a series of conferences at Stanford University, and are posted at PESD's website (http://pesd.stanford.edu/ipps). The final product of the study is an article in Volume 38:3 of the *New York University Journal of International Law & Politics.* Prior to working on the IPP study, Mr. Woodhouse published a study on the failed privatization of water services in Cochabamba, Bolivia, in Volume 39:2 of the *Stanford Journal of International Law.* Mr. Woodhouse is a graduate of Stanford Law School (J.D., 2004) and Emory University (B.A., 2000).

Appendix II

PREVIOUS VOLUMES IN THIS SERIES

Previous volumes in this series can be ordered from the World Bank:

P.O. Box 960
Herndon, VA 20172-0960, USA
Tel. 703-661-1580, 800-645-7247
Fax 703-661-1501

or accessed online at http://publications.worldbank.org/

International Political Risk Management: Looking to the Future

Published by the World Bank from the Fourth MIGA-Georgetown Symposium, 2004

International Political Risk Management: The Brave New World

Published by the World Bank from the Third MIGA-Georgetown Symposium, 2002

Appendix III

MORE ABOUT MIGA

1. **MIGA Member Countries**
2. **MIGA Contact Information**
3. **MIGA Publications**
4. **MIGA Websites**

1. MIGA Member Countries (as of July 31, 2007)

Industrialized Countries (23)

Australia, Austria, Belgium, Canada, Denmark, Finland, France, Germany, Greece, Iceland, Ireland, Italy, Japan, Luxembourg, Netherlands, Norway, Portugal, Slovenia, Spain, Sweden, Switzerland, United Kingdom, United States

Developing Countries (148)

Africa

Angola, Benin, Botswana, Burkina Faso, Burundi, Cameroon, Cape Verde, Central African Republic, Chad, Congo (Democratic Republic of), Congo (Republic of), Côte d'Ivoire, Djibouti, Equatorial Guinea, Ethiopia, Eritrea, Gabon, The Gambia, Ghana, Guinea, Guinea-Bissau, Kenya, Lesotho, Liberia, Madagascar, Malawi, Mali, Mauritania, Mauritius, Mozambique, Namibia, Nigeria, Rwanda, Senegal, Sierra Leone, Seychelles, South Africa, Sudan, Swaziland, Tanzania, Togo, Uganda, Zambia, Zimbabwe

Asia and the Pacific

Afghanistan, Bangladesh, Cambodia, China, East Timor, Fiji, India, Indonesia, Republic of Korea, Lao People's Democratic Republic, Malaysia, Maldives, Federated States of Micronesia, Mongolia, Nepal, Pakistan, Palau, Papua New Guinea, Philippines, Samoa, Singapore, Solomon Islands, Sri Lanka, Thailand, Vanuatu, Vietnam

Middle East and North Africa

Algeria, Bahrain, Egypt, Islamic Republic of Iran, Israel, Jordan, Kuwait, Lebanon, Libya, Morocco, Oman, Qatar, Saudi Arabia, Syrian Arab Republic, Tunisia, the United Arab Emirates, Republic of Yemen

Europe and Central Asia

Albania, Armenia, Azerbaijan, Belarus, Bulgaria, Bosnia-Herzegovina, Croatia, Cyprus, the Czech Republic, Estonia, Georgia, Hungary, Kazakhstan, Kyrgyz Republic, Latvia, Lithuania, Macedonia, Malta, Moldova, Montenegro, Poland, Romania, Russian Federation, Serbia, Slovak Republic, Tajikistan, Turkey, Turkmenistan, Ukraine, Uzbekistan

Latin America and Caribbean

Antigua and Barbuda, Argentina, Bahamas, Barbados, Belize, Bolivia, Brazil, Chile, Colombia, Costa Rica, Dominica, Dominican Republic, Ecuador, El Salvador, Grenada, Guatemala, Guyana, Haiti, Honduras, Jamaica, Nicaragua, Paraguay, Panama, Peru, St. Kitts & Nevis, St. Lucia, St. Vincent, Suriname, Trinidad & Tobago, Uruguay, República Bolivariana de Venezuela

Countries in the Process of Fulfilling Membership Requirements (2)

Africa: Niger
Asia and the Pacific: New Zealand

2. MIGA Contact Information

Multilateral Investment Guarantee Agency
World Bank Group
1818 H Street, NW
Washington, DC 20433 USA
tel: +1-202-458-4798
fax: +1-202-522-0316
e: migainquiry@worldbank.org

3. MIGA Publications

All publications can be accessed or ordered through MIGA's website, www.miga.org.

- MIGA Annual Report 2007
- Investment Guarantee Guide
- Small Investment Program
- Corporate Brochure
- *Sector/theme:* MIGA in Conflict-Affected Countries; Mitigating Risks in Oil, Gas, and Mining
- *Case Studies:* Hydropower in Asia: The Nam Theun 2 Project; MIGA: Improving Project Profiles to Get Investments Going—The Case of the Dominican Toll Road; Power Case Study: Maritza East 1, Bulgaria
- *Trust Funds:* Afghanistan Investment Guarantee Facility; European Union Investment Guarantee Trust Fund for Bosnia and Herzegovina; MIGA: Environmental and Social Fund for Africa; West Bank and Gaza Investment Guarantee Trust Fund
- *Factsheets* (by regions): MIGA in Africa; MIGA in the Middle East and North Africa
- *Factsheets* (by sectors): Agribusiness; Telecommunications; Oil and Gas; Mining; Financials; Infrastructure; Manufacturing; Services and Tourism
- *Brokers/Insurance:* Insurance Broker's Program Syndications: Facultative Reinsurance and Cooperation Underwriting Program
- *Advisory Services:* EIOP: The Western Balkans—Europe's Next High-Value Location for Manufacturers; European Investor Outreach Program (EIOP): Grow Your Business in the Western Balkans

4. MIGA Websites

www.miga.org—MIGA's general external website

www.fdi.net—offers prospective foreign investors information on investment opportunities in 26 sectors across 175 countries, including specific investment opportunities, key industry news, and many other documents on investment laws, BITs, etc.

www.pri-center.com—a one-stop portal that provides in-depth information, including ratings, research, tools, interactive directories, etc., on political risk analysis and management issues affecting 160 countries.

www.fdipromotion.com—an online knowledge-sharing and learning portal for investment promotion professionals in developing countries, providing access to knowledge and learning resources that help them attract and retain foreign direct investment.

Eco-Audit

Environmental Benefits Statement

The World Bank is committed to preserving Endangered Forests and natural resources. The Office of the Publisher has chosen to print ***International Political Risk Management*** on recycled paper with 30 percent postconsummer fiber. The World Bank has formally agreed to follow the recommended standards for paper usage set by Green Press Initiative—a nonprofit program supporting publishers in using fiber that is not sourced from Endangered Forests. For more information, visit www.greenpressinitiative.org.

The printing of this book on recycled paper saved the following:

Trees*	Solid Waste	Water	Net Greenhouse Gases	Total Energy
7	318	2,477	597	5
*40' in height and 6-8" in diameter	Pounds	Gallons	Pounds	million BTUs

green press INITIATIVE